THE MAGIC OF THE

Other books by this author:

JOEY DUNLOP
King of the Roads

THE MAGIC OF THE

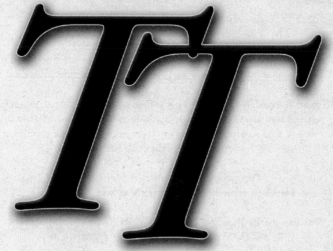

Centenary Edition

MAC McDIARMID
FOREWORD BY JOHN McGUINNESS

Haynes Publishing

First published in hardback in May 2004, as
The Magic of the TT: A century of racing over The Mountain

This paperback edition, published with additional text in April 2007, as
The Magic of the TT: Centenary Edition

A catalogue record for this book is available from the British Library

ISBN 978 1 84425 431 6

Library of Congress catalog card no. 2007921997

Published by Haynes Publishing, Sparkford,
Yeovil, Somerset, BA22 7JJ, UK
Tel: 01963 442030 Fax: 01963 440001
Int. tel: +44 1963 442030 Int. fax: +44 1963 440001
E-mail: sales@haynes.co.uk
Website: www.haynes.co.uk

Haynes North America, Inc.,
861 Lawrence Drive, Newbury Park,
California 91320, USA

Printed and bound in England by J. H. Haynes & Co. Ltd, Sparkford

CONTENTS

FOREWORD
by John McGuinness

Winner of 11 TTs,
including a Junior/Senior/Superbike hat-trick in 2006
and holder of the outright lap record of 129.451mph

Picking up the Senior trophy for the first time in 2005, one of the things that came to mind – apart from just how huge and heavy it is – was the number of truly great men who had picked it up before. I bet that big pot could tell some stories.

I'm probably quite an anorak compared to most of the modern racers. I like all that – the tales, the exploits, the thought of the thousands of people who've been involved in one way or another for so many years. And the characters you meet, like Lucy and her husband who've been stood at Windy Corner at every TT for the last 49 years. The races must be unique in arousing that sort of devotion.

I first went to the races, just for a couple of days, aged ten in 1982. My dad had raced at Jurby Roads the week before, and we stayed on to watch a couple of days of TT practice, including once at Bray Hill. It frightened me to death – the speed, the noise – wow! I don't think anything in racing captures the imagination like that place.

From then on I went to the TT every year, first with my parents, then on my own. Luckily we lived only ten minutes from the ferry, so I just packed a little tent and pedalled there on my BMX bike (and once sneaked it down the boarding ramp for nowt). Obviously, I was hooked, and had the dream of actually racing there one day.

In 1986, after watching Joey Dunlop fly down Bray Hill on that gorgeous RVF750 Honda, I managed to get his autograph. As he was signing it I told him that one day I'd stand on the podium with him – not arrogantly, but the sort of daft thing a bike-mad kid would say. He laughed. But 11 years later, there I was, third on the Aprilia.

That probably sounds like a bit of a fairytale, but racing the TT teaches you so many things – about racing itself but also about yourself. Like in 2000, when Joey was 48, I was British Champion, the 'daddy', and I thought I'd blow him into the weeds on the 250. He started at number three, I was ten seconds behind at number four. And I never saw him once after Glen Vine on the first lap. He was gone. After that I thought maybe I'd best keep my gob shut in future.

That taught me – apart from the TT being a great place for humility – that there's no substitute for experience. You never know what's going to happen on the day. That race with Joey was a touch damp here and there, but I had a great bike with a superb engine – much better than Joey's. But I was too arrogant, and nowhere finds that out better than the Mountain Circuit. From then on I thought much more critically about what it really takes to win over there.

Some people say that my style suits the Isle of Man. It probably does. I like to keep my wheels in line, and I don't hang off a lot, even on short circuits. On the Island, smoothness counts more than anything. Joey and Steve Hislop were both masters at letting it flow, and I consciously tried to take that on board. I used to enjoy watching riders like Brian Reid and Ian Lougher on their 250s – like silk, but so fast. And like everyone else I used to love watching DJ, who looked a wild boy but always had it under control.

Soon there will be a century of TT heroes like that. I never saw Hailwood race, and obviously the likes of McIntyre and Woods were way before my time. But, yes, when you pick up the Senior trophy, it puts you in mind of great men like them. Now that really is humbling. And that's why I bought this book when it first came out, and why I'm proud to recommend it to you now.

ACKNOWLEDGEMENTS

I have been a fan of the TT ever since I first visited the Isle of Man in 1976 and, like so many who witnessed that year's races, have an abiding memory of John Williams' heroic push-in during the Senior TT. It was clear then that racing on the Island possessed some unique quality. Since that time riders almost without number have allowed me to admire their exploits on the TT course, and almost as many have given me their time to explain what it was that they did out there on the ragged edge, and why the Mountain Circuit was so special in their scheme of things.

The TT races are rarely conducted without profound emotions, but prima donnas are surprisingly few. Other than through my own insensitivity, I have rarely encountered any rider who was not prepared to explain or – in the days when I raced over the Mountain myself – freely to help and advise. To all of them, I give thanks, for this is their book.

Many of those riders are no longer with us, and some of them I counted as friends. The pain of losing Steve Hislop and Dave Jefferies, in particular, is still fresh. I would not presume to characterise this volume as any sort of memorial to them, but if it helps us remember their skill and bravery, and the joy they gave us, then so be it.

Influential and much missed, too, is Peter Kneale, 'the voice of the TT', who began broadcasting from the races in the mid-Sixties and was chief TT press officer until his death in 2002. As gentle and authoritative as his soft Manx brogue, yet passionate about the races, Peter did much to inform the work of this journalist, and scores of others.

I must thank, too, the staff at the library in Peel, and at the Manx Museum, Douglas, for their contributions with research, and to the many authors and journalists to whose work I have referred.

I am deeply indebted to John McGuinness for his generous contribution of a foreword. Unquestionably the TT's brightest current star, he is not only the fastest rider ever around the Mountain Course, but has a sense of the history of the event, and a respect and affection for the deeds of years gone by, which is rare in modern riders. This, and his sheer enthusiasm for the TT's century of adventure, shines out in his words.

At the publishers, Haynes Publishing, I must thank the Editorial Director, Mark Hughes, for his constant support, Flora Myer for her customary efficient but kindly encouragement and Ian Heath and Peter Nicholson for the care with which they sifted through the copy. Not least, I should thank all those who contacted me after the publication of the first edition with suggestions and corrections, many of which have been incorporated into these pages. What errors remain are entirely down to me.

I should also like to thank the British Government of 1904, without whose timidity motor racing might never have found a home on the Isle of Man. Let us not forget, too, Julian Orde of the Automobile Club and Lord Raglan, the Island's Lt Governor, whose enthusiasm underpinned the first Manx motor race. And finally, to the thousands of officials, marshals, medics and others who have laboured in often difficult circumstances to make 'the last of the great road races' happen – 100 years of thanks.

All illustrations are by FoTTofinders unless indicated otherwise.

Mac McDiarmid
Peel, Isle of Man
Spring 2007

INTRODUCTION

They are known as 'the last of the great road races' and, whilst plenty of Irishmen might take issue with this, the Isle of Man TT and its sister event, the Manx Grand Prix, stand at the pinnacle of this most venerable of motorcycle sports.

This is not merely by dint of history, although the TT remains the oldest race on the international calendar. They do so, most of all, because the circuit on which they are held, the Mountain Course, remains the most demanding on Earth. At 37.73 miles it far exceeds any other race track in length. Only the purpose-built German Nürburgring, at 14 miles, can be compared. Into those 37-odd miles the TT course packs in something like 250 bends and kinks, each with its own particular problems, and all are potential killers. All this needs to be learned so thoroughly that, even at speeds in excess of 200mph, navigating the route becomes second nature.

Cars first competed across the Mountain in 1904 in qualifying trials for the International Cup over a course far longer even than today's. The first TT, also a car race, was staged one year later. The first motorcycle TT was held in 1907 over a course linking Peel, Kirk Michael and St John's, and four years later, two-wheelers first challenged the Mountain on a predecessor of the present circuit and known as the 'Four Inch' Course, as explained in Chapter One. Minor revisions during the early 1920s left the course essentially as it is today.

Those early competitions were 'reliability trials' designed to test the durability of these new-fangled velocipedes, hence the expression 'Tourist Trophy'. In those days the upland section of the course was nothing more than a rutted track, and the first and last men through had to open and close livestock gates as they went. Even Bray Hill, now a sensational 160mph dive through suburban Douglas, was just a hedge-lined dirt road. The first motorcycle TT was won by Charlie Collier with a fastest lap at just over 41mph. Today, the outright lap record stands at over 129mph.

In those early days almost all competition was conducted on closed public roads, but as racing developed, purpose-built circuits began to appear. These now host the predominant form of motorcycle speed sport. Only in a few countries does public roads racing cling on, partly for reasons of tradition, partly because of the lack of funds to build closed road circuits. Other than the TT, the Formula One car grand prix at Monaco is perhaps the best-known example.

Some of the dangers of racing on roads and streets normally used by ordinary traffic are obvious. No amount of straw bales can make houses, walls, trees, banks, lamp-posts and other street furniture safe when motorcycles roar past them at almost 300 feet per second. Unlike modern short circuits with their generous areas of 'run-off', crashing is something riders can rarely afford to do on the roads. Since its inception, the Mountain Course alone has claimed something over 200 racers' lives.

There are more subtle hazards, too. On short circuits bends will usually be positively cambered across their full width. Road circuits, on the other hand, are cambered both ways from a crown in the middle – so each bend will form a three-dimensional puzzle of positive and negative camber, with associated changes in grip and handling. The surface, too, will vary in terms of composition and grip. Overhanging trees and variable surface texture cause different sections to dry out at different rates after rain. Because of its sheer length, part of the circuit may be wet while others are bone dry. A street circuit will have far more dust, gravel and general muck than any short circuit. Above all, it will have far more humps, ridges, lumps, bumps, leaps, dips and potholes.

The speed at which the top racers tackle these hazards is awe-inspiring. Complex sequences of interlocking bends are knitted together at quite breathtaking speeds, wheels skirting within inches of dry stone walls, ditches and drains. There is nothing more spectacular, or more demanding, in all of motorsport.

In the Seventies the safety of road racing, both at the TT and elsewhere, came under serious scrutiny. First the Ulster Grand Prix, and later other 'classic' circuits found themselves removed from the World Championship calendar. Following the death of Gilberto Parlotti in the 1972 TT, a group of leading riders, notably Giacomo Agostini, Phil Read and Rod Gould, boycotted the event. In a few short years, the TT – the British Grand Prix – was no longer a contest between the world's very best.

Finally, in 1976, the FIM, the governing body of world motorcycle sport, stripped the TT races of their grand prix status and the British GP moved from the Isle of Man to Silverstone in the English Midlands. Certainly the FIM did the racing teams a favour. Most were already of the view that any circuit which took two weeks to contest, three years to learn, and stood a fair chance of wiping out the odd star rider had no place on a modern racing calendar. But many observers – fans and foes alike – saw this as the death knell for TT racing.

Yet the races have not only survived the following 31 years, but remain in reasonable shape. There are fewer star riders, for sure, and the races enjoy far less industry support than they did, but the festival that the TT has become, the very thing which sets it apart, continues in rude good health. If you're a motorcyclist and don't like the TT, then there must be something seriously wrong with you. If you have never been there, your two-wheeled education is incomplete. Whether going across for the racing or just the craic, any biker will tell you that there is nothing else on Earth quite like 'Bikers' Island'.

Chapter 1

BEGINNINGS

It is well known that racing began on the Isle of Man because of the refusal of the British Parliament to sanction the closure of roads for racing. Yet, that is far from the whole story – in fact, it is not even strictly true – but is just part of the jumble of circumstances that first led to racing across 'The Mountain'.

'Don't matter if they're mules or motorsickles, if we got two of anything,' a whiskery old Sacramento race fan once told me, 'we're gonna race 'em.' And so it was with the earliest cars. Motor vehicles first began racing between French cities as early as 1894, and by the turn of the century it was hotly debated which country's vehicles were best. But debate doesn't sell newspapers half so well as events. That was where James Gordon Bennett stepped in.

Owner of the *New York Herald* and a founder of Associated Press, Bennett was a noted playboy and philanthropist who had, amongst other things, funded Stanley's 1869 trip to Africa in search of Dr Livingstone. Having already established competitions for yacht, aeroplane and balloon racing, Bennett proposed a car contest between national teams driving vehicles made in their respective home countries. Known officially as the Coupe International, but popularly as the Gordon Bennett Cup, the event was first held in 1900, and by 1901 tackled a 352-mile course between Paris and Lyons.

British motorsport had been hampered first by the notorious 'Red Flag' Act and, since its repeal in 1896, by a blanket 20mph speed limit. Indeed, not a single British car or driver contested the Cup in that first year, but in 1902 Selwyn Edge drove a 4hp Napier to victory. Although this was to the palpable benefit of both British morale and Napier sales, it posed a serious problem. Much as the winner of the Eurovision Song Contest now gets lumbered with hosting the following year's event, so it was with the Gordon Bennett Cup.

At the time, motor racing's image was far from good. After a series of accidents in 1901, the French government had imposed a total ban on motor racing in the very country in which it began. With the 20mph limit still the rule on British roads, only an Act of Parliament could permit racing in the UK. Yet Westminster, full of 'motor phobist cranks', as the *Isle of Man Examiner* would describe them some time later, had no stomach for inflicting such reckless activity upon its own citizens. But about Irish sensibilities they were far less squeamish, and so the Light Locomotives (Ireland) Bill was passed on 27 March 1903 to permit the 1903 Coupe International to take place on roads south of Dublin. The whole of Ireland was then still under British government rule.

When Germany won that event, and thus the obligation to stage the 1904 Cup, the problem of racing in Britain might have gone away, had it not been for the British Automobile Club's policy of selecting team members on the basis of an eliminating trial (always assuming that breeding and social standing were also up to scratch). In 1903, this had been conducted, highly illegally, on Dashwood Hill on the Oxford to London main road. A year later even this was not possible (not least because the UK police had just begun using electrical speed traps), yet reaction to the Irish race had made a new road closure order equally improbable.

At first – and not for the last time – Britain's racing authorities turned to Belgium. The authorities there were willing, but the price – £200 per car – was exorbitant. Then, Julian Orde, organising secretary of the Automobile Club, had his brainwave. Why not use the Isle of Man? Orde knew that Lord Raglan, the Island's Lt Governor, was himself a motorsport fan, since he happened to be cousin to His Grace.

Raglan, it soon became clear, was keen. After all, his ancestor the first Baron Raglan had given the order that led to the charge of the Light Brigade, so this was a piece of cake. Despite initial opposition from farmers, most Manx interests seemed equally in favour of a notion that soon became known locally as 'Manx Motor Week'. A committee was established, and a few basic rules drawn up. Cars would be silenced, while practice would be on open roads, but only between dawn and 7am. And, above all, on this Methodist redoubt in the Irish Sea, there would be no racing on Sundays.

The proposed 51⅛-mile course began on the outskirts of Douglas, heading south to Castletown, then north via Foxdale to join the present route at Ballacraine. At Ballaugh it deviated towards Sandygate, before rejoining more-or-less the present course at Ramsey, from where it zigzagged over the wind-swept shoulder of Snaefell.

On Tuesday, 15 March 1904, an 'Act to provide the authorisation of Races with Light Locomotives' was passed by Tynwald, the Manx Parliament, by 11 votes to eight. So hurried were Raglan's efforts on behalf of his cousin that none of those voting had actually laid eyes on the legislation before that day. Amongst other provisions, the Act prohibited 'any person, dog, ox or other animal' from wandering on to the course, on pain of a £20 fine.

It may have been cosy and on the nod, but the haste was real – and, despite appearances, the Manx authorities can sometimes move swiftly. With the Coupe International scheduled for 17 June, they had well under three months to organise the event from scratch. Then there were small matters like getting the bill's Royal Assent and the 'promulgation' of the legislation by Tynwald. This ancient process normally required a public reading on Tynwald Day in July. Since this would be far too late to be of use, a special public sitting of the Manx legislature was uniquely arranged for 5 May, a mere five days before the trials were due to take place.

Other measures were less lofty. With the races in mind, George Drinkwater stationed his steam car on the road at Kirby Braddan at specific advertised times in order that people might bring along their horses to become accustomed to the unholy clatter of motor vehicles.

By this time several racing cars had already arrived and were thrashing around the course, disturbing the locals but on the whole, failing to overcome their goodwill, much as the bikers do today. Officially, however, this was not a race. Although the Manx Highway Board's own order referred to roads staying closed until 'termination of the race', the Autoclub was much more coy. Their reasoning, which has echoed down every decade since, was fear of being seen to encourage reckless and possibly deadly speed. As *The Motor* put it: 'If there were a horrible accident, it would be the end for motorsport events.'

So instead, it was to be a 'high-speed reliability trial', with checkpoints and special tests, much like a modern enduro race. That it was 'high speed' can be gleaned from the fact that the 'standard time' allowed from Ramsey to Douglas – a distance of 13 miles – was 13 minutes. If 60mph in a 7-litre monster, over a 1,800ft mountain, on soggy, rutted roads, was not an invitation to speed, then nothing was.

Five hundred marshals, known as 'road stewards', were recruited and equipped with signal flags. Although waving a red flag in front of a ton of car, with its primitive brakes even more enfeebled by the dive down to Douglas, must have been an exercise in raw faith, it was at least rewarded with a fee of a shilling, precisely 5p more than today. The approach of a racing – sorry, trialling – car was announced by bugles.

Some road resurfacing was done, but most of the course, if it was improved at all, saw only a hand-drawn two-man 'scraper' used for levelling ruts. The start line, a white chalk mark on the road, ran from the old Quarter Bridge Hotel's western gable end. That's where the pandemonium began.

Chiefly responsible were the Weir-Darracqs. Unable to meet the 1,000kg weight limit, their drivers had thrown away extraneous heavy items such as their exhausts, the silencing rule evidently being less well policed. As a result, the cars belched flame and smoke. 'A terrifying sight,' choked one eye-witness, 'that smote the eardrums painfully.' Horses bolted, children screamed, stewards leaped for their lives.

For the car crews it was even worse. In practice, Mark Mayhew's Napier suffered 'side-slip' and hit a tree, while 'Mr Earp ran into a house … and Mr Hemery hit a cow.' The first away in the first ever motorised Manx race, held in 'magnificent weather', was Mr Hargreaves in his Darracq at 9.05am on Tuesday, 10 May (another Darracq was due to start at 9am but turned up late). From then on it was pandemonium. Cars crashed and exploded, gearboxes self-destructed, wheels collapsed or fell off. Over those rough, coarse roads, and particularly at 'nail-strewn' Ramsey, almost every car suffered several punctures. Various drivers were lashed by flailing rubber, and at least one tyre landed high in a tree.

Toby Rawlinson, whom startled spectators dubbed 'Brimfire Jack' on account of his fiery antics, complained that 'when I pull out the clutch I get an electric shock and covered in oil.' Meanwhile, Charles Jarrott (who had come to under a sheet, after having been declared dead when he pranged his Wolseley in Ireland the year before), reported what was perhaps the first recorded case of adrenalin rush. 'You do feel it in the nervous system afterwards,' he confided with Edwardian understatement, 'not exactly the sort of thing for an invalid.'

Sadly, the *Isle of Man Examiner* begged to differ, likening spectator excitement to that at a ploughing match. 'The Autoclub,' it thundered on, 'took particular care to eliminate all the elements of racing.' For their part the Island's population had turned out en masse, spurning the grandstands erected near the start for vantage points around the course. Why pay, when you can watch almost anywhere else for free?

The winner of this particular 'ploughing match' was W. T. Clifford Earp, partnered by bother Walter. Driving a 7,708cc Napier, they had covered five laps, a total of over 255 miles, in 7 hours 26½ minutes, an average speed of 34mph. Just six cars finished, with Sidney Girling second and Selwyn Edge third. Although this car now resides in the National Motor Museum at Beaulieu, it had more tasks to complete first. As if the main event weren't trial enough, on the days that followed the cars had to undertake special tests. The first was a half-mile hill-climb from Port-e-Vullen to Ballaterson up Maughold Head, then a 1km sprint along Douglas Promenade, for which 'the tram lines were specially scraped'.

At the hill-climb, won by Stocks's Napier, 'enterprising farmers' were already on the case, charging 6d (2.5p) per spectator. A day later, on 12 May, the sprint was clouded with incident when Clifford Earp lost control when 'travelling much too fast' returning from his second run, and careered into the wall of the Villa Marina, scattering spectators as he went. Both Clifford and Walter were seriously injured – in fact, they were initially feared dead – but quickly recovered. For being 'a little reckless' Earp was disqualified, leaving the overall result as a Wolseley 1–2 through Jarrott and Girling, with Edge's Napier third. This trio was selected to represent Britain in the International Cup although in the event a series of disputes left Girling the sole British representative. Nonetheless, the publicity gained for the Isle of Man was invaluable.

1905: and bikes too

The first year in which the International Cup included a class for motorcycles – or auto-cycles as they were then known – was 1904, although no British selection trials took place. Held in France, it was won by a Frenchman, M Demster, with the British way down the field. For the 1905 Cup, an eliminating event for the British team was planned for 31 May, the day after similar trials for four-wheelers (won by Earp, with rather less drama than in 1904: on a 'glorious morning' after a 'breakfast feast'). It was intended that the trial, run by the Auto-Cycle Club, later to become the Auto-Cycle Union (ACU), would be held over three laps of the same 51-mile course as the cars, 'an ideal proving ground' for British machines.

Sadly, it was not to be. In testing, many machines struggled to get up the mountain at all, even with riders dismounted and pushing. Riders were particularly unhappy with the condition of roads made even rougher by the progress of the cars, with Creg Willey's Hill and the Mountain being particularly chewed up. When one of the favourites, J. F. Crundall, broke his arm at Ramsey Hairpin, it was decided to switch to a less demanding 25-mile course. This followed the route of the 1904 car circuit to Castletown and Ballacraine, before turning back towards Douglas.

If the 1905 course thus happened to use the present Quarter Bridge to Ballacraine route, albeit in the opposite direction, it also set another precedent redolent of today's pre-dawn practice sessions: the start was to be at 3am (equivalent to 4am with BST). Spectators were, however, fortified by the Quarter Bridge Hotel's decision to stay open for the duration in this pre-licensing hours age.

Most of the early racers were Edwardian amateurs who thought that a combination of pluck, breeding and a lick of zinc ointment would help them muddle through whatever the races might have in store. In total there were 18 entries, of which 11 actually arrived on the Island to be officially weighed in at Quiggin's Rope Works on Lake Road, Douglas on 29 May. A few had failed to meet the maximum weight limit, in keeping with International Cup regulations of just 50kg, while others fell out due to accident or machine failure in practice. Not for the last time, mist on the Mountain caused the start to be delayed by 30 minutes and just six machines set off at one-minute intervals beginning at 3.30am with W. H. Hodgkinson. A seventh rider, F. W. Barnes, turned up late and, although permitted to proceed, could not start his Zenith in time.

Although the prevailing opinion was that bikes were not so interesting as their four-wheeled counterparts and many spectators drifted home for breakfast, the race was not without incident. Early leader Charlie Collier epitomised the spirit. After crashing at Braddan, the Matchless man pushed to Quarter Bridge, changed his bent front wheel and set off again, only for the engine to seize while he was trying to make up the time lost. Nor did brother Harry have the easiest ride, running out of petrol on the third lap and pedalling in for the final five miles.

Charlie's troubles passed the lead to Charles Franklin, who so nearly became the first Irishman to win on the Isle of Man. Having set the fastest lap (34m 43s) and led almost throughout, his JAP suffered a broken con-rod at Foxdale, halfway through the final lap. Thus J. S. Campbell inherited the lead, despite his Ariel-JAP having caught fire during a pit stop.

At 7.42am, after five laps and 125 miles, Campbell won in a time of 4h 9m 36s, a speed of almost 30mph, with Harry Collier's Matchless-JAP just half a minute behind in second place. With only two riders completing full race distance, Franklin was declared third. Another notable name was Sir Arthur Conan Doyle, creator of Sherlock Holmes, who entered one of the competing machines.

Campbell, Harry Collier and Franklin were chosen to represent Britain in the International Cup held at Dourdon in France. In an event dominated by Austria, Collier lay fifth when he retired with a lap to go. Both Campbell and Franklin retired after one lap. Campbell never returned to compete in the TT, but both Collier and Franklin, who also went on to become Indian's chief engineer, were to record TT victories later in the decade.

The first TT

Yet even by this time, interest in the Gordon Bennett Cup car races was waning and in 1906 both the British and French withdrew. With the success of the International Cup trials, both the ACC and the Manx authorities were keen to build on their successful formula. It was decided to use the 1905 Highways (Motor Car) Act one more time (in fact, it is still in force today), for a race for road-going touring cars, to be known as the Tourist Trophy. Owing to the harvest and a desire to extend the holiday season, the first TT would begin at 9am on Thursday, 14 September 1905. To the winner would go a prize made from 18-carat gold. Designed by Giovanni da Balogna it depicted the figure of Hermes, the Greek messenger of the gods, flanked by two figures representing industry and invention. This magnificent pot – now in the RAC building in Pall Mall – would later inspire what is now the Senior TT trophy.

Cars would compete over four laps of the same route used for the Gordon Bennett Eliminating Trials, now known as the Highroad Course, a total distance of 203.5 miles. The start line was moved to the junction of Quarterbridge Road and Alexander Drive (about where the bikes now brake for Quarter Bridge), and the first Grandstand was erected. The finish was also on Quarterbridge Road, near the junction with Selbourne Drive. For the record, John Napier's Arrol-Johnston won, with a Rolls-Royce in second place. Twelve months later, over a new 40-mile course, Charles Rolls turned the tables, winning with his own vehicle.

Meanwhile, the 1906 International Cup Motorcycle races did indeed turn out to be as big a farce as the French and British car boys had feared. Held over a 155-mile course near Patzau in Austria, the event was racked with disputes reminiscent of later ISDTs. The results show that Puch twins ridden by Austria's Ed Nikodem and Louis Obrubra finished first and second, with Harry Collier's Matchless in third place. But the home team had enjoyed special facilities, for Puch mechanics motored along the course with sidecars full of spares, fixing Austria's bikes whenever they broke down. Despite loud complaints, no protest was heard and the International series was abandoned amidst controversy. However, it was from these nationalistic ashes that the motorcycle TT emerged.

On the journey back from the Austrian debacle the Collier brothers, the magnificently monickered Marquis de Mouzilly de St Mars (who would later donate the Senior trophy) and Freddie Straight, secretary of the ACC, had begun to formulate the idea of an independent race along the lines of the existing car TT. Surely, with no reason for Manx qualifying trials to be held in 1907, the Isle of Man government would be in favour?

Word got around, and found much favour. Then, in January 1907 during the annual dinner of the ACC, the editor of *The Motor Cycle* formally proposed a competition for motorcycles, to be run on similar lines to the car TT. The Isle of Man authorities were delighted. The bike TT was on.

The first motorcycle TT

But before there could be a race, they had first to find themselves a course. Instead of the 1905 route, a new 15.81-mile circuit, the St John's Course, was contrived with just one demanding climb. Riders would compete over ten laps, and to the winner would go a princely £25.

As originally proposed, the bikes would be limited to a cylinder bore and stroke of no more than 80mm (402cc for a single), and 130lb in machine weight, although by the time of the race the only stipulation was for fuel consumption. Singles were required to average 90mpg or better, twins 75mpg, and a ten-minute mid-race fuel stop was compulsory for all machines. The entry fee was five guineas (£5.25), or three guineas (£3.15) for private entries. 'Official' petrol cost 6p per gallon. Practice, of course, was on open roads, with the Peel Commissioners (the local council) moved to threaten with prosecution any rider practising 'at racing speeds' after 8am. Before that time, presumably, anything went.

To run that first TT, the ACC paid the Manx authorities £250 – ten times the winner's prize money – for the use of the roads. The date was 28 May 1907 and for the record, it didn't rain, but it was cloudy and chilly. There were 25 starters, of whom 18 rode single-cylinder machines. Amongst the makes represented were singles from Triumph, Matchless and Rex, with twins from Vindec, BAT, Kerry, Norton and Rex, once again. Of these marques, only Triumph survives to the present day.

Riders began in pairs, a feature of the TT for most of its history. The first bikes away, at 10am, were the Triumphs of Frank Hulbert and Jack Marshall. Coincidentally, the two winners, Charlie Collier and H. Rembrant 'Rem' Fowler, also began side-by-side.

That first two-wheeled TT may not have been spectacularly fast, but it was tough. The roads, of course, were little more than cart tracks. Brakes, tyres, transmissions and everything else about the bikes were equally primitive. Practically every rider suffered punctures, crashes, plug changes, broken drive belts and near-misses with livestock. Oliver Godfrey's bike burnt out at the refuelling stop, while another bike burst into flames at Devil's Elbow on the Kirk Michael to Peel coast road, Rem Fowler ignoring a boy scout's frantic flagging, to roar through the flames. Rembrandt certainly had an eventful race. His Peugeot-engined Norton also endured two crashes, a puncture and several other mechanical malaises.

According to Marshall, 'those that had pedals pedalled fit to bust themselves', while those without often jumped off and ran alongside, particularly up the sharp climb of Creg Willeys Hill. Although Fowler was shown a sign reminding him to hand-pump oil into his engine, riders had no pit signals, since there were strictly no pits. At half distance the bikes simply pulled into the pub yard at St John's for refreshments for rider and machine. Nor was there much need for elaborate signal boards out on the course. 'As I came up Creg Willeys,' Marshall explained, 'my chap ran alongside and just shouted.'

Charlie Collier, veteran of the 1905 eliminating trial, led from start to finish on his 431cc single, winning by 11m 39s – almost as much time as second-placed Jack Marshall lost fixing a puncture. His winning Matchless used a JAP ohv engine, pedal assisted, to average 38.23mph and recording a staggering 94.5mpg during the race. Marshall's Triumph ran even more frugally: 114mpg. A dozen of the 25 starters made it to the finish.

In the twin-cylinder class, and despite his adventures, Rem Fowler won by over 31 minutes, with the fastest lap of the day, 42.91mph. However, since his overall time was over 13 minutes slower than Collier's, it was the Matchless rider who qualified as the overall victor. Thus the Marquis de Mouzilly de St Mars was able to present the outright winner's trophy, which he had donated, to one of the very men with whom he had hatched the plot to create the motorcycle TT. A silver statuette standing almost three feet tall, it represents Mercury, the Roman equivalent of the Greek Hermes, on a winged wheel, and was clearly inspired by the earlier car TT trophy. To Fowler went a pot presented by Dr Hele-Shaw.

In late September 1908, the bikes returned under much the same standard production formula, except that the fuel allowance was further reduced. This time, there were 36 starters, of which the majority (21) were 'twins' – including two four-cylinder Belgian FNs. Jack Marshall turned the tables on Collier to win by just over two minutes. Third, and splendidly idiomatic of this easy-going Edwardian age, was Captain Sir R. K. Arbuthnot, Bt, RN, on another Triumph.

In 1909, it was Harry Collier's turn to win, with Charlie taking his second victory in 1910, the year before the bikes first went up the Mountain. Between them the brothers had logged three wins and three second places in the TT's first four years, making them the masters of the St John's Course.

Twelve months later, Britain's motorcycle manufacturers were up in arms (partly, it must be said, because they had just been soundly thrashed by an upstart American company, Indian). 'The course is too tough', they cried, 'something must be done.' Nothing much was, but they came back in 1912, just the same. Indeed, 1913 brought a new record entry of 147 machines.

In the same year the TT was besieged on its own doorstep. The novelist Hall Caine led an influential group taking exception to the annual motorcycle invasion which made them prisoners in their own homes (or, in his case, stately pile: Caine lived in Greeba Castle). Again, this was one of those periodic blips on the TT seismograph that came to nothing, but demonstrates that in a history of 100 years, very little is new.

End of the car TT

From 1907, the car and motorcycle TTs continued in tandem, usually with the bikes in June and the cars, much to local farmers' disgust, in September. But in marked contrast to the success of the bike TT, its four-wheeled equivalent went steadily downhill.

Partly because they abandoned the old fuel consumption targets in favour of an almost open formula, plans for the 1908 races were met with violent opposition from the UK parliament and media, accompanied by sensational headlines such as: 'Isle of Manslaughter'. *The Times* condemned the Island's 'audacious flouting of public opinion ... the race is likely to cost several lives', urging legislators to do something to stop it. For its part the *Isle of Man Independent* countered that any such interference would be 'impertinent'.

The Times, it turned out, was correct. In practice, Cyril Roberts's Arrol-Johnston killed two calves being driven across the course. A pet dog was also killed, and the official car of Lord Raglan and Julian Orde knocked over a motorcyclist at Creg Willeys, luckily without serious injury. (Three years earlier an official car being driven along Douglas's Selbourne Road towards the course had run over three children, again without grave results.)

However, the race almost ended in tragedy, although to many of the estimated 20,000 spectators the Hillberry refreshment tent's running out of beer was of more immediate concern. When the steering failed on Beeston's Humber at Kirk Michael, it struck a garden wall, throwing two women and several children into the air. Miraculously, none was seriously hurt, although the car's mechanic, Mr Guttridge, almost died from pneumonia contracted in Douglas Hospital.

A more enduring problem followed Henry Robinson's crash at the bottom of Bray Hill. When his Calthorpe inflicted severe cuts and bruises to a spectator, Mrs Lena Lace, it set in motion a protracted legal wrangle which was only settled four years later, out of court.

In the aftermath of 1908 the car TT was not held again until 1914 and then, due to the Great War, not until 1922, when it was greeted with widespread disinterest from manufacturers and spectators alike. This last event held in 'wet and dreary' weather was 'a miserable TT' all round. The race, run over the New Mountain Course, and headlined 'Nightmare in a Sea of Mud', was won by a Wolverhampton-based Parisian, Jean Chaussagne in an eight-cylinder Sunbeam. The Frenchman's signals were so bad that he didn't realise he had won until flagged down, still 'driving furiously', at Ballacraine on lap nine of the eight-lap race. The winner of the 1,500cc class was Sir Algernon Guinness, who had taken part in the very first car TT, but retired when he crashed his Talbot-Darracq into the steps of Kate's Cottage. One of the rookies in the event was the great Henry Seagrave.

After 1922, the car race moved to Northern Ireland before disappearing altogether. However, Manx car racing was revived from 1933 to '37 with the Douglas 'Round the Houses' race. After the Second World War, the British Empire Trophy Races, known locally as 'Motor Car Race Week' were staged on the outskirts of Douglas from 1947 to '53. In recent times the Manx Rally has been the Island's best-known car event.

TT Formulae

In the earliest years of the motorcycle races, there were no capacity limits at all, just a simple limitation of the amount of fuel which could be used. In 1907, single-cylinder machines were required to average 90mpg or better, with 75mpg permitted for twins. When the winners managed this comfortably, the rule was made tighter the following year: 100mpg and 80mpg respectively. The winning Triumph actually managed 117.6mpg.

For 1909, the fuel rule was dropped altogether, replaced by capacity limits of 500cc for singles, 750cc for twins. As it became clear that this was inequitable, and the authorities were anyway concerned that the lap record had reached a giddy 52mph, for the final St John's Course TT twins were limited to 670cc and then 585cc over the following two years. Undeterred, H. H. Bowen took his BAT to over 53mph in 1910. When bikes first took to the Mountain in 1911, a new Junior class was introduced, for 300cc singles and 340cc twins.

The 'classic' limits of 350cc and 500cc were introduced across the board in 1912 for the two classes, and would stand largely unchanged for over 70 years (although alarm at increasing speeds almost caused the 500cc class to be dropped in 1920, and as late as 1954, the FIM was seriously considering dropping the 500cc and 350cc classes). During that period the two most significant changes were the banning of 'dope' – alcohol fuel – from 1926; and the post-war outlawing of forced induction. Not until 1951 was the Senior class limited to machines of 351–500cc, barring Junior machines. Today, the Senior division is open to all three classes – Superbike, Superstock and Junior – the last now being contested exclusively by roadster-based Supersport 600cc machines.

Chapter 2

THE CIRCUITS

Although the Mountain Course now seems as profoundly Manx as kippers and tail-less cats, it would take 18 years from the time of the first motor race on the Island in 1904 until the present circuit was introduced. The route first suggested by the Automobile Club's Julian Orde ran anticlockwise along the coast from Douglas to Ramsey, then via Ballaugh to Ballacraine, Ballasalla and back to Douglas. It was rejected as being too disruptive to shopping in Ramsey, and to silver mining in Laxey. It did not include what would become known as 'The Mountain'. At the time, there was also a curious theory that cars turned right better than they turned left, so a clockwise route would be safer.

Highroad Course

Orde's second proposal was likened to 'a corkscrew with 72 turns', yet was adopted almost at once. It ran for 51 miles and 1 furlong (220 yards) from Douglas, out to the fringes of Castletown, then via the long Ballamhoda Straight (often used for 'unofficial' testing for many years to come) and Foxdale, to join the present course at Ballacraine. At Ballaugh it deviated towards Jurby and Sandygate, before rejoining more-or-less the present route at Ramsey from where it lurched over the barren moorland of Snaefell. Orde initially thought the present Ballaugh to Ramsey section ideal, only adding the Sandygate detour (which takes in part of the modern Jurby road circuit) to add extra mileage to this motoring ordeal.

In order to help the cars complete such a long lap, a depot was established at Ramsey for fuel, oil and repairs. Local children were paid one old penny apiece to douse overheated brakes and tyres with buckets of water.

The start was also moved, from Quarterbridge Road to the Quarter Bridge Hotel, out of fears that drivers hurtling down to the bridge before becoming warmed to their task might not be fully in control around the 'S' bend which followed. As it turned out, brakes overheated by the decent from the Mountain were far more significant. In the first car race flag man Major Lindsay Boyd was almost pinned to the pub wall by one runaway car.

Alfred 'Toby' Rawlinson, one of the first competitors to see the proposed course, was impressed. 'I fancy it would be impossible to obtain a course more suited to test car and driver,' he boomed in April 1904. By 1905 the route was being referred to as the Highroad Course.

Motorcycle International Cup Trials Course

Although it was initially intended that motorcycles contesting the 1905 International Cup Trials would compete over the same Highroad Course as the cars, after a few practice runs, it was found that the route was far too demanding for the single-geared bikes. Following consultations with the competitors, an abbreviated 25-mile version of the course was preferred, using just its southern loop. Instead of continuing north via Glen Helen, competitors turned right at Ballacraine and returned to Quarter Bridge, following the current TT course, but in the reverse direction.

'Short' Highroad Course

In 1906, largely because of disruption caused to the Island's railway network, the southern section was omitted from the car TT course, making a 40 mile 3 furlong lap. Prior to this, cars and trains had been expected to find their way around each other as best they could. On the one hand level crossing keepers were told to give priority to cars, while on the other, car drivers had on their dashboards a railway timetable and list of crossings which they were expected to take into account. The best that can be said about this arrangement is that no-one was actually killed.

From its start near the junction of Quarterbridge Road with Alexander Drive, the new course headed directly to Ballacraine, before breaking more new ground and continuing west through St John's. From Peel it followed the coast road to Kirk Michael, where it joined the present course at Douglas Corner. The Sandygate section was abandoned in favour of the present Sulby/Glentramman route, and from Ramsey the cars used the same Mountain road as before. Again, cars turned right at Cronk-ny-Mona then raced via Willaston Crossroads to St Ninian's at the top of Bray Hill.

St John's Course

With memories of the Mountain still painful from two years before, the existing Highroad Course was out of the question for the first motorcycle TT in 1907. At the time, practically all two-wheelers were single-speed, often pedal-assisted, with puny leather belts transmitting such power as there was to the back wheel. These devices simply could not manage severe climbs. Where cars could realistically install huge, heavy engines to overcome their inefficiency, this was not a practical option for motorcycles.

The course chosen ran anticlockwise from St John's to Ballacraine and Glen Helen, then via Kirk Michael before turning south on the coast road, including the notorious Devil's Elbow. After a nasty chicane between Church Street and Albany Road in Peel, riders headed west again to St John's via Ballaleece Bridge – still a treacherous spot for the unwary. Particular concern was expressed for the tricky left-hander at Ballacraine, with a deep and inviting ditch on the outside. This was resolved in 1910, by the laying of wooden banking. H. H. Bowen, who led after setting a new lap record on his BAT, duly crashed out on this makeshift 'wall of death'.

Race HQ was alongside Tynwald Hill, with the paddock across the road in what is now the Tynwald Inn car park. The scoreboard, a blackboard from the village school, reportedly worked well enough. Less successful was the organisers' bright idea of spraying

moother, it was also making it more dangerous. The
as that the bumps which characterised the old surface,
do here and there, were in effect 'vertical chicanes'
owed riders down. George was referring at the time to
ng of sections such as the Cronk-y-Voddy Straight, a
rough section which the fastest sidecar boys reputedly
three big leaps'. Resurfacing of other notorious sections
Sulby Straight and Quarry Bends was some years ahead.
particular, was terrifying to ride fast, 'so bad',
rs Rob McElnea, that 'you just aimed down the middle
ad, with your feet hooked *under* the footrests to stop you
f the seat. I did a parade lap in '92 [at 113mph, cruising]
dn't believe how smooth it had become.' Before that, the
simply a jarring grey blur between fuzzy green
vs, brutal enough to give riders double vision. Slowing
Sulby Bridge was the most blessed relief.

almost nobody bemoaned the smoothing of Sulby
ections like the Quarries were quite a different matter.
first left-hander was straightened in the mid-Eighties,
e by at least a full gear. It was physically less punishing,
ut the run-off, negligible at the best of times, hadn't
ne inch. Part of what George was suggesting was
at it was also less testing: anyone with balls big enough
t quickly.

s been much speculation since about what these
ts' mean in terms of lap times. While it is impossible
the circuit has undoubtedly become significantly
very passing decade. Today's fastest lap times would
ately impossible 30 years ago. But 129mph, in
ney, is startlingly fast.

ourse

Course hosted the smaller solo classes, plus the
ng the period 1954 to '59. Previously used for

the circuit with dilute acid to reduce the problem of dust. Within
a few days, much of the riders' clothing was reduced to shreds.

The roads, of course, were little more than cart tracks – rutted,
bumpy, and dusty or slimy depending upon the prevailing
weather. At corners, loose gravel was always a problem and hills
could be a nightmare. Creg Willeys Hill often required several
attempts, riders waiting for a break in the traffic to freewheel to
the bottom before each fresh attempt.

'Four Inch' Course

The car course was further altered in 1908 when the circuit
turned right at Ballacraine, thence all the way to Ramsey along the
current route. The route differed from the modern circuit
through the streets of Ramsey, and in turning right at Cronk-ny-
Mona, before rejoining at St Ninian's Crossroads, just before the
top of Bray Hill. A new start was established at Hillberry, where
the original iron grandstand survives.

Because the racing regulations were amended at the same time to
limit car engines to a four-inch (102mm) bore, this became known
as the 'Four Inch' Course. Since cars no longer had to meet fuel
consumption targets, speeds were expected to soar (and did, to over
50mph), and the organisers were under some pressure to make the
racing safer. Consequently, a few obvious dangers were removed,
such as a derelict cottage at Cronk-ny-Mona. The approach to Sulby
Bridge, a notorious accident spot, was also metalled, and compulsory
eyesight tests for drivers were introduced.

Two wheelers first ventured on to the 'Four Inch' Course in
1911, the same year that the organisation of the TT was handed
over to the ACU. The new route may have swept through
cosmopolitan Douglas, but it was no modern race track. Even
Bray Hill was just a hedge-lined dirt track, and the loop from
Cronk-ny-Mona was even worse. The Mountain road, rutted and
potholed in places, was more like motocross than road racing. In
wet weather, riders slithered on mud, or choked on dust when it

was dry. During practice, the first rider through had to open gates, and livestock was a constant hazard. As if that wasn't enough, in 1913 Suffragette demonstrators littered the course with broken glass. Ironically, Manx women had no such axe to grind as the Isle of Man was the first country in the world to give females the vote.

Initially, the start line for bikes was on the flat section above Quarter Bridge, but in 1914 this moved to the top of Bray Hill. If the steep climb out of Ramsey made chain drive and multi-speed transmissions essential you might think the same was true of brake technology on the plunge down to Douglas, but even in 1914, front brakes were a rarity on TT machines.

The 'New' Mountain Circuit

In 1920, for the first TT after the Great War, the present section from Cronk-ny-Mona via Signpost Corner and Governors' Bridge was first used, and the start moved to its present position on the Glencrutchery Road.

Two years later the races adopted what was essentially the present circuit. Previously, bikes had detoured out of Parliament Square via Albert Road and Tower Road, since one Hugo Teare, who owned the Cruikshanks section, would not allow racing on his land. Eventually, he relented, and the revised circuit left Ramsey by way of May Hill, Cruikshanks and Stella Maris, as it does today. This 'New' Mountain Circuit was first used for the Junior race on 30 May 1922, won by Manxman T. M. Sheard on an AJS at an average speed of 54.75mph. Almost at once questions were asked as to whether it was too tough, or too fast. Paradoxically, the same year brought a major spat between the Manx authorities and the ACU, which led to preparations to hold the races elsewhere. Yorkshire and even Belgium were seriously considered.

The Mountain Circuit may have been 'New' but it was by no means state of the art. Almost all of it was simply rolled gravel, bound by tar only here and there, so that it was dusty when dry, and a glutinous mulch when wet, prone to potholes and ruts. The

Mountain was still the worst of all, r
joke that you picked your rut in Ram
Douglas, whilst cornering was more a
modern road racing. All riders carried t
punctures caused by nails shed from h
1950s, many riders could be seen wit
down one of their boots.

In the 1920s, Sulby Bridge was a ste
was soon levelled. Until it was flattene
1934 TT, another humpback bridge, at
far superior spectacle to its much slowe
George Formby film *No Limit* has
footage of riders leaping flat-out on rigid-fr
was further 'improved' in about 1960.

The Mountain section, however, rema
little more than a car's width. One ne
the Mountain road's east gate was finall
that 'the grass verge had to be used fo
a broken yellow line was first paint
Mountain road, a measure which fai
from postponement due to rain and
contemporary report suggested tha
an International event to be postp
course is such that postponeme
course must be altered.' Alte
suggested, and in 1936 an AC
subject, recommending that 'the
1937' should be explored. Need
The Mountain Circuit has chal
to suit the needs of Manx t
motorcycles. Much of it is now
from Ginger Hall to Milntown

In 1979, the year he beat
Alex George commented on

circuit s
notion w
and still
which sl
resurfaci
wickedly
took 'in
including
Sulby,
rememb
of the ro
flying of
and cou
road w
ugero
down fo
While
Straight,
When th
speeds ro
certainly,
increased
probably t
could take
There h
'improvem
to quantify
faster with
have been
anybody's m

Clypse C

The Clypse
sidecars, dur

bicycle racing, the circuit began in front of the grandstand, just like the full course, before turning right at St Ninian's Crossroads then, via Willaston Corner and Hillberry, to Creg-ny-Baa (the exact reverse of the old 'Four Inch' Course). From the Creg it turned east to Ballacoar Hairpin (still an evil place) and on to Cronk-ny-Garroo and the main Laxey to Onchan road. In Onchan, the circuit turned right at the Manx Arms, reaching Signpost Corner and the Mountain Course by way of Nursery Bends. In total, the Clypse Course was 10.79 miles long, rising to about 900ft at Creg-ny-Baa, roughly two-thirds the maximum elevation of the Mountain Course. The first race over the Clypse was the 1954 Lightweight 125cc event, won by Rupert Hollaus on an NSU at an average speed of 69.57mph. Later the same day, Eric Oliver's Norton won the first Sidecar TT since 1925, at 68.87mph.

Although the Clypse is perhaps the least glamorous of all the circuits used for the TT, much of it remains as rough and narrow as it was 50 years ago, and any modern rider who has scratched along it will empathise with the men and women who raced on it then. The character of the less trafficked sections of the Clypse is, indeed, probably rather better than much of the Mountain Course would have been in the years either side of the Second World War. Imagine lapping that at over 90mph on a rigid-framed Norton, as Harold Daniell did in 1938.

The Mountain Circuit

Although its precise length has sometimes been questioned, since the 1920s, the Mountain Circuit has been regarded as covering precisely 37.733 miles (60.732km). As such, it is comfortably the longest racing circuit in the world, and the one with the longest continuous history. According to the *Guinness Book of Records* it boasts 264 bends, although many of these are barely distinguishable kinks.

While sometimes compared with Germany's Nürburgring (the

building of which it actually inspired), the two circuits are completely different in character. The Nürburgring is essentially a very long short circuit, with chamfered kerbs, helpful cambers, (comparatively) generous run-off and an altogether more sinuous nature.

The Mountain Circuit, on the other hand, is a true road course. Kerbs, run-off, bumps, surface changes and cambers are all exactly what you would expect of busy main roads. Predominantly, these are rural, ranging from wooded valleys and lush farmland to high windswept moors. But the track also includes two fair-sized towns, Douglas and Ramsey, and the narrow main street of Kirk Michael village. Along the way, it takes in three sets of traffic lights, the same number of mini-roundabouts (ignored by the racers) and a number of pubs which varies with the Manx economy.

The TT course is also very much a three-dimensional affair. As well as climbing almost from sea level to 1,400ft at Brandywell, the track is littered with smaller climbs and dips, many of which give the bikes spectacular air time. The line through many corners, too, is influenced by subtleties of gradient, bump and camber – one of the reasons it takes so long to learn. There is simply nothing else like it in motorsport.

Circuit highlights

St Ninian's

The crossroads just a few hundred yards after the start are named after St Ninian – also known as Trinian – who first brought Christianity to the Isle of Man. Prior to the First World War riders turned right here on to Bray Hill, having left the current circuit at Cronk-ny-Mona on the 37½-mile 'Four Inch' Course.

Bray Hill

In the early days, Bray Hill was known locally as 'Siberia' and was just a rutted, hedge-lined track, but it has since become one of the most fearsome sections of the course. The hill has claimed its share of TT greats, notably Geordie sidecar ace Mac Hobson and passenger Kenny Birch in 1978.

Ago's Leap

Named after Giacomo Agostini who won 11 TTs for MV Agusta and was captured on spectacular contemporary photographs wheeling over this crest. When bikes first raced over the Mountain in 1911, the start was located nearby.

Quarter Bridge

The 'Quarter' simply refers to the junction of two local land divisions, or 'quarterlands'. The start line for the very first Manx motor race in 1904 was a chalk mark on the road adjacent to the Quarter Bridge Hotel, once a famous TT landmark but recently demolished to make way for a new ambulance station.

Crosby Corner

Usually regarded as the most innocuous of bends (although it once claimed a sidecar passenger), Crosby Corner leapt to prominence in 2003 when David Jefferies was killed here.

The Highlander

Once the site of the TT's regular speed trap, the Highlander was named after the pub (now a restaurant) of the same name.

Greeba Castle and Bridge

'Greeba' derives from the Norse 'gnipa', meaning peak. Greeba Mountain is therefore the tautological Peak Mountain.

Ballacraine

Also once a pub, famously entered at speed by George Formby in the film *No Limit*. Originally this was Balley-ny-bogie, 'farm of the graves'. It is the one place where both Highroad courses, the

1905–6 motorcycle circuit, the 'Four Inch', St John's and the Mountain circuits coincide.

Doran's Bend
This rapid blind left-hander is named after lantern-jawed Bill Doran who broke his leg in crashing the works AJS Porcupine here in practice for the 1950 Senior.

Glen Helen
The area around the hotel of the same name was originally called Glen Rhenass until renamed after his daughter by Mr Marsden, the Liverpudlian proprietor of the pub. It is also the scene of the first TT fatality, Victor Surridge, in 1911.

Creg Willey's Hill
This steep winding hill was the toughest section on the original TT course. Riders had to dismount and jog alongside their primitive bikes.

Drinkwater's Bends (11th Milestone)
This awesome right-left flick is named after Ben Drinkwater (founder of Robinson's of Rochdale), killed here when he crashed his 250cc Guzzi in 1949. The milestone, incidentally, marks distances from Castletown and Ramsey, not from the start in Douglas, which is 11½ miles away.

Handley's Bend
Once known as Ballameanagh, the fearsome left-right chicane between mountainous stone walls is named after Wal Handley, who broke his leg here in 1933.

Barregarrow
Don't worry if you spell this wrongly – everyone does. According to the Ordnance Survey, it is called Barregarrow (or Barrowgarroo

in the 1873 edition), while the TT course description has it as Barregarroo, but a signpost on the coast road gives it the Gaelic Bayr Garroo, as it is in the title of the Wesleyan Methodist chapel (where John Wesley himself preached in 1871), at the crossroads. Other signs have it variously as Baaregarroo and Bay-R-Garroo. Whichever way, it means 'rough road'.

Birkin's Bends (Rhencullen)
Practice was conducted on open roads until after 1927 when Archie Birkin fatally collided with a delivery cart at this most spectacular of sections.

Bishopscourt
This stately pile is the historic residence of the Bishops of Sodor (the Hebrides) and Mann, whose Archdiocese once included Trondheim in Norway. Mostly built by Bishop Wilson in the 18th century, it was stormed during the 1825 Manx potato riots.

Ballaugh Bridge
Scene of the famous hump-backed bridge, in Gaelic this is Balley-ny-Laghey, 'place of the mires'.

Quarry Bends
The Quarries is smoother and faster than ever, which just makes the run-off more inadequate, yet it is the scene of an astonishing number of survivable get-offs: Phil McCallen, Steve Hislop and Jamie Whitham have all lost it here. Steve Henshaw, sadly, wasn't so lucky.

Sulby Bridge
A sharp right-hander after the long Sulby Straight, this was once a hump-back bridge and the scene of many early accidents. The hedge on the outside was originally planted to give riders a 'sighter' that the bend lay ahead.

Milntown Cottage
The family of Fletcher Christian, leader of the Bounty's mutineers, lived here for 400 years. The bend is brutally unforgiving, particularly when early morning sun shines right into riders' eyes. The death of Mick Lofthouse in 1996 was attributed to this. Ironically, the first TT rider to be saved by the rescue helicopter was Tony Godfrey, who also crashed at Milntown, in 1963.

Ramsey
Ramsey means 'river of garlic' in Norse. Parliament Square is perhaps named because Colonel Dukinfield and the English Parliamentary forces landed in Ramsey in 1651, freeing the Island from Scottish control.

Cruikshank's
Cruikshank wasn't a noted racer, but the local High Bailiff (magistrate), who died in 1916. Due to a land dispute, the bend was not part of the original Mountain Course.

Stella Maris
Named after the nearby house, the name means 'star of the sea'.

Ramsey Hairpin
It is near Ramsey and it is a hairpin. In 1999, a pair of Kiwis almost torpedoed Fred Clarke's commentary box here, causing it to be moved out of the firing line for the next TT.

Tower Bends
Named after the nearby Albert Tower, erected to commemorate the visit to Ramsey of Queen Victoria and Prince Albert in 1847.

Joey's Bend
Formerly the 26th Milestone, renamed to commemorate the great man after his death in 2000.

Guthries

Probably the most scenic corner in racing, this was formerly called The Cutting. The nearby Guthrie Memorial was erected at the site of Jimmy Guthrie's retirement in the 1937 Senior TT, following his death at the Sachsenring in August that year.

East Mountain Gate (Mountain Box)

In the early years, the first rider over the Mountain had to open livestock gates, pick his rut, and stick in it until almost Creg-ny-Baa. East Mountain Gate, at the end of the Mountain Mile (which isn't actually a mile) was really the north gate. The gate itself was removed in 1934.

Les Graham Memorial (Bungalow Bridge)

The bend takes its name from the nearby memorial to the very first 500cc World Champion, from 1949. Graham was killed near Selborne Drive on Quarterbridge Road when he crashed his factory MV in the 1953 Senior TT.

Bungalow

Originally built as a hotel on the new mountain railway in 1896, the bungalow was later demolished and replaced by a rather less prosaic stone toilet block.

Hailwood Rise

Named after the great Mike.

Brandywell

The highest point of the TT course is named after a well below Injebreck Hill where shepherds gathered to brand their sheep.

Duke's 32nd Milestone

Renamed from the simple 32nd Milestone in 2003, this was one of Geoff Duke's favourite sections.

Windy Corner

This windswept downhill right-hander was widened and re-cambered early in 2006, significantly increasing speed both through the corner and on the run to the fast double left-hander of the 33rd Milestone.

Keppel Gate

Keppel Gate wasn't a gate at all. The name comes from Kapel Gata – 'the road to the summit' in Norse, but there was a gate just down the road, next to Kate's Cottage.

Kate's Cottage

Another misnomer. The property was named after its occupants, a Rhodes and Gladys Tate, but was corrupted when misheard by a BBC commentator.

Creg-ny-Baa

The name means 'rock of the cows' in old Manx.

Brandish

The right-hander after the Creg is named after Walter Brandish who broke his leg when he slid off a four-valve Ricardo Triumph here in 1923. The following rider, Geoff Davison (winner of the 1922 Lightweight on a Levis), chivalrously stopped and 'borrowed' a spectator's red blouse to use as a warning flag. The corner was substantially 'improved' before the 2007 races, which is bound to increase speeds and make the first 130mph lap a genuine possibility.

Hillberry

One version has it that Berry was a local witch, and this was her hill. True or not, it is a wizard place to watch. The iron grandstand here was built for the car TT in 1908, at the then start of the 'Four Inch' Course.

Bedstead

This used to be called 'Bedpost', since the adjacent fence really was constructed of old beds.

Governor's Bridge

Named, naturally enough, after the nearby residence of the Island's Governor. The bridge spans the Crutchery Glen, from which the road past the grandstand gets its name. It has become less tricky since a lorry demolished the stone pier at its apex in the mid-1990s.

Women and the TT

The first woman to enter a TT was Dorothy Levitt, for the car race of 1906. Although her gender barred her from competing at Brooklands, this doughty lady had many successes to her name, including setting a women's world speed record of 96mph, also in 1906. In the same year she published a book, *The Woman and the Car* in which, amongst other things, she appears to have invented the rear-view mirror. A contemporary picture shows her in long dress and elegant hat, secured by chiffon scarf, behind the wheel of a 12hp Mors. In the event she did not compete in the TT.

Motorcycle TT regulations originally required that riders shall be 'male persons between 18 and 55 years of age', although the gender qualification was omitted for sidecar passengers. So it was inevitable that when the sidecar class resumed in 1954, a female passenger entered. Inge Stoll-Laforge was highly experienced in Continental grands prix, yet even so the ACU committee accepted her entry by only a single vote. 'Manufacturers Appalled'…'Tynwald Refuses to Ban Fraulein' screamed the headlines. Nonetheless, she and driver Jaques Drion placed a highly creditable fifth. Three years later she returned to the TT, retiring after four laps, but was killed during a Continental meeting shortly after. The first woman to die at the TT was sidecar passenger Mrs Claude Lambert, following a crash on the descent to Brandish in 1961.

In 1958, former World Champion Eric Oliver competed on a

bog-standard Watsonian Monaco sidecar bolted to an equally stock Norton Dominator. The idea was to demonstrate the sporting capabilities of a normal road outfit, to which end his passenger, Mrs Pat Wise, remained normally seated throughout the 10 lap race. Reports suggested that, but for the bumps, Mrs Wise was comfortable enough to do a little knitting. The duo earned a bronze replica for tenth place. The first all-female sidecar crew was the Americans Wendy Epstein and Dawna Holloway as recently as 2000, although the duo failed to make the race.

The first lady to compete in the solo classes was Beryl Swain in the new 50cc division in 1962, by which time FIM rules allowed female competitors, so the ACU had little choice and Swain finished in 22nd place on her Itom. At their next annual congress, the FIM relented and barred women from road racing, although this, in turn, was later reversed. Female riders were not permitted in the Manx Grand Prix until 1989.

In 1997 Evesham's Sandra Barnett lapped at an impressive 114.63mph, and Kate Parkinson has also performed well in recent years. Maria Costello claimed the 'fastest woman' mantle in 2004 when, on the eve of her 27th birthday, she lapped at 114.73mph from a standing start on a GSX-R750 Suzuki.

Clubman's TT

Prior to the Second World War, the TT programme had comprised just the three 'classic' classes: Senior (500cc), Junior (350cc) and Lightweight (250cc). When racing resumed in 1947 the Clubman's race was added for the same three classes, except that 'Senior' included 1,000cc machines. Bikes were required to be in 'showroom' trim – what we'd call production today – complete with lights and kickstarts. Unlike the Manx Grand Prix, there was no attempt at amateurism, since prize money was to be awarded, with any rider finishing within 120 per cent of the winner's time being granted free entry to the Manx Grand Prix. Riders competing in full TT events were ineligible.

There were misgivings, since many thought – despite two

decades of Manx Grand Prix racing – that allowing club riders into the TT would cause carnage. However, TT and Clubman's classes practised separately, although the latter were granted only four sessions in which to familiarise themselves with the course. In total, there were 64 entries for the first Clubman's TT: 33 for the Senior (including two 1,000cc machines, neither of which started the race), 23 Junior, and just eight 250s.

The event proved to be rather less of a nursery for new talent than the Manx Grand Prix. Although Geoff Duke's winning ways began in the 1949 Senior Clubman's, no other winner went on to great things (although five-times MGP winner Denis Parkinson, in one of his rare TT outings, won the inaugural Junior Clubman's race). Other than to pad out the TT programme, and appeal to manufacturers (notably BSA), it is not clear what purpose it was intended to serve which the Grand Prix did not already meet. Unlike more recent times, star riders were not inclined to put a leg over 'production' machines, so the event lacked the glamour which top riders bring to its modern equivalent.

By 1949 the Clubman's programme had extended to four classes: 1,000cc, 500cc (Senior), 350cc (Junior) and 250cc (Lightweight). These lasted only two years, so that by 1951 only the Senior and Junior classes remained. The 1,000s made a one-off reappearance in 1953, when the two-class formula returned. The Clubman's TT was last run in 1956, by which time both surviving classes had become something of a benefit for the ubiquitous BSA Gold Star.

Boy scouts

Boy scouts have been serving the TT since its earliest days, latterly running the scoreboard opposite the main grandstand. Initially, they were given a whistle and a flag and posted at 300-yard intervals to signal in Morse code. Duties later included removing wreckage and livestock away from the course, first aid, and anything else the authorities could think a woggle might accomplish. Helluva job for a bob.

Chapter 3

GREAT MACHINES

Although on the face of it, any consideration of great TT motorcycles ought to be more straightforward than a similar examination of riders, the task is not so simple as it might appear. Bikes such as Yamaha's TZ, the Norton Manx and any number of Hondas, practically select themselves. Yet others, less successful in terms of wins, also beg to be included. Ducati's 864cc Vee-twin won only one race – but what an occasion that was! The AJS Vee-four of the 1930s was even less successful, but merits consideration through its sheer extravagance. BSA never won a 'proper' TT, yet how could the legendary Gold Star be omitted? Even the 500cc Gilera four won only two Seniors, but was such a seminal device that no TT review could possibly omit it.

The review of marque history below is ranked by the number of TT wins, Honda and Yamaha being the most successful. That, again, is not the whole picture. Triumph and BSA, for instance, rank ahead of both Velocette and Moto Guzzi in terms of wins, yet it is the latter two who regularly contested the premier classes, and who contributed most to the history of the races.

You may also notice that the numbers of wins may differ from those published elsewhere – even on the TT's official website. While other compilers may consider results in the modern pre-TT Classic races as warranting the same status as actual TTs, I do not. These, therefore, have been excluded.

YAMAHA
130 wins (plus others as Yamsel, Spondon, Maxton, and various sidecar hybrids)
First win: 1965 125cc Lightweight, Phil Read

Although no company in modern times has been more devoted to the TT than Honda, until 2006 Yamaha held the edge as the marque with the most wins. Much of this success was down to the remarkable – and ubiquitous – series of TZ twins, which during the Seventies and Eighties contributed the bulk of the field from 250cc to 500cc, and to their dominance of the sidecar classes.

Yamaha's TT debut came as recently as 1961 when the factory fielded 125cc RA41 and 250cc RD48 twins. (An American, Sonny Angel, practised but did not race on a private Yamaha the year before.) Their best finisher, Fumio Ito, placed sixth on the 250. The parent company was founded to make reed organs way back in 1887 (hence their logo of three crossed tuning forks, which later became an apt metaphor for two-stroke tuning). In the 1920s they branched out into aircraft components, yet it was not until 1954 that Yamaha – then known as Nippon Gakki – produced their first motorcycle. In July 1955, the Yamaha Motor Co. was founded as a separate entity from the parent company. Within a mere nine years they had claimed their first world grand prix title.

From the outset Yamaha placed great store by competition, winning the prestigious Mount Fuji hill-climb with the YA1 in 1954; a year later the new 175cc YC1 won the same event. Both machines were distinctly European in appearance, but in 1958 Yamaha produced their first 'real' bike, the 250cc YDS1 twin. Three years later this led to Yamaha's first venture into factory-built production racers, the TD1. Slow and hopelessly unreliable as the TD1 was, Yamaha learned quickly, and from this machine sprang a racing dynasty which was to rule for over 20 years.

The Sixties, however, was a decade of full-on factory machines rather than privateer mounts. After their failure in 1961, Yamaha returned in '63 with the RA55 and RD56 parallel twins on which Ito and Hasegawa placed second and fourth.

Although Phil Read and Mike Duff both retired their air-cooled 250s in 1965, Read gave the factory its first TT win in the

Lightweight 125cc race on the 14,000rpm liquid-cooled twin, a feat Read and team-mate Bill Ivy were to repeat for the following three seasons. Part way through the '66 season the first of the liquid-cooled, multi-speed 250cc Vee-fours arrived. Although blindingly quick, they were also brittle, their only TT success being Bill Ivy's win in 1968. In the same year, Ivy lapped at over 100mph on the 17,000rpm Vee-four RA31A 125, an astonishing performance.

When Yamaha pulled out of grands prix later in 1968 (preceded by Honda and Suzuki), it was the turn of their 'production racers' to take centre stage. Both the 250cc TD2 and 350cc TR2 were introduced for the following season. Far from diluting Yamaha's competitiveness, this led to greater things. Although Kel Carruthers' Benelli would win the 250cc TT in '69, the next 11 wins would go to Yamaha twins.

In the Junior division it was initially not so easy, although Tony Jefferies's heroic Yamsel (Yamaha engine, Seeley chassis) win in appalling conditions in 1971 stands out. But following Agostini's retirement from TT racing after '72, 350cc TZ twins ruled supreme, winning all but two 350cc Juniors from 1973 to '93. Only Eddie Laycock's EMC win in '87, and Joey Dunlop's Honda 12 months later, bucked the trend. (Phil Mellor's 1983 win was on a Spondon-framed TZ.)

Most of these wins fell to the TZ twin which had replaced the air-cooled TD3 and TR3 engines in 1973. In 1974 alone, Yamahas took the first 39 places in the Junior TT, and were almost as dominant in other classes, where they claimed the first four places in the Ultra-Lightweight TT, the first 12 in the Lightweight, the first eight in the Senior and the first three in the F750 event.

Although the four-cylinder TZ500 achieved occasional TT success, it was never present in the same numbers as the ubiquitous RG500 Suzuki, nor was it quite so suited to Island conditions. Above all, riders feared its fragile cassette-type gearbox. Charlie Williams recalls with alarm leading the 1981

Senior TT on an ex-Kenny Roberts OW48R when a gear shaft broke flat out in top at Ballacrye. Luckily, it didn't lock up.

If the 500-4 was a marginal TT machine, its TZ750 stablemate was, too, but in a slightly different way. As well as giving Joey Dunlop his first two TT wins, in 1977 and '80, the big TZ earned a reputation for wild handling. Tom Herron reported being half spat off one on Creg Willeys Hill, and 'running alongside' at over 100mph until he could get back on.

It was, however, a fine sidecar powerplant. Yamaha's first such win came in 1976, when Mac Hobson lapped at a tantalising 99.96mph. Having got the taste, Yamaha would win the event for the next decade, an unprecedented 20 victories in succession. And inevitably, when the Sidecar F2 class was introduced in 1984, it was Yamaha twins which began more winning ways.

With the introduction of the liquid-cooled RD250LC and RD35LC roadsters in 1980, Yamaha also had a potent tool for TT Formula racing. Tuners needed no encouraging to slip a TZ bottom end and porting job into the new LC. Between them these loosely street-based projectiles won no fewer than eight F2 and F3 races.

With the factory's concentration on four-stroke products over the past two decades, its TT successes have come predominantly from production-based machines. It is also true that during most of those years, they have put far less store by TT success than has Honda. Even so, their record is remarkable, with numerous wins in all production and Supersport classes – first through FZ machines, and later the R1 and R6 series. In 1992, Carl Fogarty lapped a roadster-based 750 at 123.61mph, a record which would stand until 1999. In the Senior TT one year later, David Jefferies recorded the first 125mph lap on a tweaked R1, the same model on which he had already won successive F1 events.

Yamaha TZ350

Introduced in 1973, the TZ350, along with its 250cc stablemate, won more races during the Seventies and early Eighties – at the

TT and elsewhere – than any other motorcycle in history. Although the first TZ had similar layout and porting to its air-cooled predecessor and produced little more power, liquid cooling stopped it overheating and losing its edge during a race. The first version, the 350A, produced 60bhp at 9,500rpm and, as shown by its success at Daytona, was a match for almost anything on the track. By the time development ceased almost a decade later, this had risen to 72bhp at 11,000rpm.

Although the TZ was a winner from the outset, the introduction of the 'C' model in 1976 took the series into new territory. For the first time the chassis featured an adjustable 'mono-shock' rear end, while hydraulic disc brakes replaced the previous drums, front and rear. And, at around £1,500, it was affordable. Three years later the 350F brought new six-port cylinders, 38mm Mikuni Powerjet carbs and improved tractability (although the lightweight frame was prone to failure around the headstock, so that aftermarket chassis from the likes of Spondon, Maxton and Bakker were much in demand). The final TZs, the G and H, were introduced with minor improvements in the early 1980s. When the FIM dropped the 350cc World Championship class in 1982, development ceased, although the fabulous twin would continue to win TT races for some time.

Yamaha RD05A

Although Yamaha's TT assault began with air-cooled engines good enough to win 250cc world titles in 1964 and '65, it was not until the introduction of liquid-cooling that they enjoyed the reliability to win over the Mountain Course. Even so, the RD05A won only once – but what a performance that was, for Ivy re-wrote the record books with a lap at 105.51mph, from a standing start.

Like the 125cc RA31A, the 250 featured disc-valve induction with two carburettors poking out of each side of the engine. All four cylinders and heads were separate and arranged in pairs in a

60-degree Vee. Peak power was around 70bhp at a screaming 15,000rpm – not much less than grands prix 500s were developing at the time. Initially, the 250 was plagued by appalling handling, which allowed Hailwood's Honda to lead Read home by well over a minute in the 1967 TT. By 1968, however, intensive development had shed a lot of the machine's bulk and weight. Sadly we can only speculate what this fabulous device might have been capable of had Yamaha not shelved their race team at the end of the season.

Yamaha R1

In 1999, Yamaha's svelte, sleek R1 ended Honda's 17-year Formula One dominance when David Jefferies grabbed not only his first TT win, but a sensational F1/Senior/Production treble. Tuned and run by V&M Racing, already hugely successful in 600cc Supersports competition, the 1,000cc dohc four set new standards for power and handling in the street-based F1 class; and, with Jefferies aboard, it proved almost unbeatable, taking a Senior/Production double in 2000 (but losing out in F1 when its clutch basket exploded).

In 2002, Jefferies transferred his dominance to TAS Suzuki, but 2004 brought a new R1 which, partnered with John McGuinness, proved every bit as mercurial as it had with Jefferies. McGuinness dominated F1, winning with a new outright lap record of 127.68mph. Only a broken clutch stopped him adding the Senior crown, while he and the R1 narrowly lost out to Bruce Anstey's Suzuki in the Production 1000 race. Twelve months later the pairing wrapped up a Senior/Superbike double, before McGuinness was lured to ride Hondas for TT '06. Although not the most powerful machine in its class, in McGuinness's hands the R1 proved the best, most usable package. It must be said, however, that its wins owe much to two truly exceptional riders, whereas its chief rival, Suzuki's GSX-R1000, enjoyed a broader success base.

HONDA

130 wins

First win: 1961 125cc Lightweight, Mike Hailwood

Of all the world's motorcycle factories, the company founded in 1948 by Soichiro Honda is the one most obviously devoted to the TT – and the one with the greatest number of solo wins. The eldest son of a blacksmith, Soichiro was born in Komyo, near Hamamatsu in 1906. Trained as a metallurgist, his first business venture was a piston ring factory, but it was his creation of the Honda Technical Research Institute in 1946 which really set the ball rolling. Yet the name was far more lavish than the operation, based in a wooden hut from which he supplied surplus Mikuni two-stroke generator engines, bolted into bicycle frames. The Honda Motor Co. was formed in 1948.

A brilliant yet practical dreamer, Soichiro saw from the outset that there was a clear link between racing and sales success. In 1954, he visited the Isle of Man races, coming away vowing to 'pour all my energy and creative powers into winning the TT.'

Five years later, when Honda finally turned up with their funny dohc RC142 machines, loosely based on the ohc 125cc Benly roadster, many onlookers laughed. Yet within two years Honda were TT winners and World Champions, with riders of the calibre of Redman, Taveri and Hailwood. In 1966, a mere 18 years after the company's foundation, and in the face of the fiercest competition, Honda won manufacturers' titles in all five solo classes – a performance as staggering as it is unique.

Nonetheless, Honda's TT career, in the Ultra-Lightweight 125cc class, began badly, with one of the racing machines crashing on the drive of the Nursery Hotel even before it was warmed up. Under team manager Michihiko Aika, the 1959 squad comprised four Japanese riders – none of whom had previously set foot outside Japan – plus Bill Hunt, an American racer who worked for Honda in the USA.

Come race day, Naomi Taniguchi led the Honda team away, finishing sixth for a silver replica. Although Hunt crashed on lap two, all four Japanese riders finished, with Giichi Suzuki and Teisuke Tanaka earning bronze replicas in seventh and eight places respectively, bringing Honda the manufacturers' award. The fourth rider, Junzo Suzuki, placed 11th.

Two years later, Honda's Ultra-Lightweight TT line-up was as glittering as their '59 effort had been modest. Mounted on a new generation of 125cc twins that day were Jim Redman, Tom Phillis, Luigi Taveri, and Mike Hailwood, along with Taniguchi and Sadao Shimizaki. Riding number 7, Hailwood set a new lap record over the full Mountain Course from a standing start, ahead of Taveri, Phillis and Redman. Although Taveri later lapped faster, Hailwood hung on to win by 7.4 seconds at a new race-record average speed of 88.23mph. Honda emphatically took the team prize through Hailwood, Taveri and Phillis, with Redman and Shimazaki in the next two places.

In the 250cc race the result was just as categorical, a clean sweep of the first five places through Hailwood, Phillis, Redman, Takahashi and Taniguchi. The fastest lap went to McIntyre at 99.58mph before his four-cylinder RC162 Honda gave up the ghost. In the same year, Hailwood and Phillis would go on to present Honda with their first World Championships, at 250cc and 125cc respectively.

Although Honda repeated the same TT double in 1962, in grands prix they later came under an increasing threat from the two-strokes of Suzuki and Yamaha (if less so on the Island, where their fragility was often punished). Cylinders, gears and horsepower proliferated. 'I just lifted my leg and they stuck another bike under me,' recalls Jim Redman, who won the marque's first Junior in 1963. 'Most times I hardly knew how many cylinders or gears it had. It seems incredibly exotic now, but once you got over the jump from Manx Nortons to fours, it seemed normal. The 125-four was a superb bike, fantastic. When we first got on that we thought it was a tricky thing to ride, not knowing a 125-five was coming along which was an absolute bitch. If the revs dropped below 10,000, it just stopped.' One of his favourite bikes, surprisingly, was the RC180 500-4 which Hailwood hated so much. Between 1961 and '67, Hondas won no fewer than 18 TTs.

Unlike Yamaha, Honda had no over-the-counter racers to fly their corporate flag after pulling out of grands prix. Other than Production victories, they scored not a single TT win until the introduction of the Formula classes in 1977, but when they did, they did it in style, winning all three classes in their inaugural year through Read, Jackson and Kidman. Although Hailwood and Ducati snatched the F1 crown in 1978, there is no doubt that this early success contributed to their commitment to the races for the next 25 years. Formula One, in particular, was an event Honda made their own, with an unbroken sequence of wins from 1982 to '98.

No less than seven of those wins went to Joey Dunlop, but it was George, Grant and a young Ron Haslam who posted Honda's early victories, principally on the 998cc twin-cam RCB four. Joey took his first Honda TT win, and his second world F1 title in 1983 on the RS850 Vee-four after a furious tussle with team-mate Reg Marshall, but it was the machine with which he took the 1984 World Championship that went down in history. The bike was the exquisite RVF750 which, more than any other bike, signalled Honda's return to winning ways.

In 1985, Joey took their first Senior win since Hailwood in '67, and it would be 1999 before any other manufacturer got a look in at the premier class. Although far less dominant, Honda's RS250 twin clocked up regular wins in the Junior and 250cc classes, while their 125 has been unbeatable since the reintroduction of the class in 1989.

If the RVF was a factory special built without regard to cost, its successor was, according to Joey, nothing more than a 'glorified production bike'. Yet the machine in question, the lovely RC30, went on to become the definitive TT tool from its winning debut in 1988 – when, uniquely, it won in three classes: Senior, F1 and 750cc Production. From then until the introduction of the far less successful RC45 in '94, the RC30 won almost every TT for which it was eligible.

Yet these successes might never have occurred. In October 1986, Honda Britain dropped a bombshell: with immediate effect, they were withdrawing from F1 racing. Fortunately for the TT, their decision didn't last long. As team manager Barry Symmons later recalled, 'Honda made it very clear to Honda Britain that if they didn't run a Formula One team, there would be no grand prix team, either.' In Japan, head office still adhered to Soichiro Honda's absolute commitment to the TT. In 1987, despite operating with a relatively makeshift team, F1 victory put Joey alongside Agostini and Hailwood as the only men to win the same TT race in five successive years.

Even the emergence of the Supersport classes (and now the Junior) can be credited to Honda. When the first CBR600 appeared in 1987, it hogged every one of the first 18 Production leaderboard places. Sadly for Honda, bad weather meant that the race was never run, but CBR600-based machines went on to dominate at the TT and elsewhere.

Honda's 50th anniversary was marked in 1998. It was fitting that they should choose the Isle of Man as the venue for their celebrations, and equally fitting that they should record their 100th TT win in the process – Jim Moodie's Production victory on the remarkable CBR900RR FireBlade. Indeed, during the late Nineties Honda was the only factory to put a serious effort into the TT, reaping the inevitable rewards. Although in recent times, the lack of a model to rival Yamaha's R1 and Suzuki's GSX-R1000 has led to a relatively lean period on the Isle of Man, their sentimental decision to provide Joey with a factory SP-1 in 2000 culminated in one of the most memorable, and tearful, F1 wins of all time. The association between Honda and Joey Dunlop – instrument of no less than 24 of the marque's TT wins – is almost unique in modern professional sport.

In 2002, Honda UK's general manager Mark Davies said that 'for us the Island is part of our heritage and ... we have no intention of stopping yet. As long as there's an annual Isle of Man Tourist Trophy festival Honda will be there.'

Honda RC174

Surely the most unforgettable result of the 1960s horsepower war was the fabulous Honda six. In 1964, the first 250-six was taken by 23-year-old Soichiro Irimajiri's design team from drawing board to prototype in just two months. The rationale for the six was that if a four-stroke was to compete with the strokers, it had to compensate for having only half as many firing strokes by breathing better and spinning faster. This meant small, short stroke cylinders and, inevitably, lots of them. The 250's cylinders were just 39mm across, with a stroke of 34.8mm. It meant four valves per cylinder – 24 in all – and double overhead camshafts. It required no fewer than six 17mm flat-slide Keihin carburettors. Most of all, it meant revs: the seven-speed engine eventually produced its peak power of 60bhp at over 17,000rpm.

Taken to Italy as carry-on aircraft luggage by two Honda mechanics, the bike was debuted by Jim Redman at Monza in 1964 in a desperate attempt to stem the two-stroke challenge, but could finish only third. In 1965, it was still temperamental, and Read again took the title for Yamaha. But in '66, Hailwood won no fewer than ten of the 12 250cc grands prix.

By 1967, the 250 had a partner, the fabulous RC174 297cc six, the machine Hailwood described as the finest racing motorcycle he had ever ridden. Despite giving away 50cc to the MV Agusta, Hailwood comfortably took the 350cc world title, in addition to the 250cc crown. On the Island, he claimed a 250–350–500 triple, including an astounding record lap of 107.73mph on the

Junior Honda. With nothing left to prove, Honda pulled out of grands prix at the end of the season.

RVF750

If the 250-6 was the machine of the Sixties, Honda's RVF750 was undoubtedly the perfect racing four-stroke from its winning TT debut in 1984 and for the remainder of the Eighties. Until the current grand prix Vee-five proves otherwise in the long term, the RVF of the mid-1980s is arguably the finest four-stroke racer ever built. It instantly became Joey's favourite race machine. Indeed, outside of Japan only Dunlop himself, and the French World Endurance squad, were deemed worthy to ride it.

A diminutive jewel in magnesium and titanium, in 1985 it brought Joey Dunlop the F1 World Championship with victory in every round, and from then on nothing else came close. It was impressively reliable, too, winning every 24-hour race it ever started, bar one. By 1990 the dohc, 16-valve Vee-four was shoving out around 165bhp, yet weighed a mere 130kg. When brought out of semi-retirement for Hislop and Fogarty's memorable dice during the 1991 TT, its featherlight fairing actually deformed at high speed. During that same TT, Hislop set a practice 'lap record', 124.36mph, which would not be beaten for eight years. Equally, Hizzy's average speed in winning the F1 race wouldn't be beaten until Jefferies won on the 1,000cc Yamaha R1 in 1999.

NORTON
43 wins
First win: 1907 Twin-cylinder class, Rem Fowler

Although never as big a company as their enormous racing reputation suggests, decades of racing successes have given Norton a unique place in British motorcycle history, and nowhere more so than on the Isle of Man. Founded by James Lansdowne 'Pa' Norton in 1898, the Norton Manufacturing Company initially made bicycle components, producing its first powered two-wheeler in 1902. Early models used engines by Moto-Reve and Peugeot, and in 1907 privateer Rem Fowler took one of the latter to victory in the Twin-cylinder class of the inaugural Isle of Man TT. It was to be the first of many famous victories all over the world.

Encouraged by this success, 'Pa' Norton designed the first in-house engine, a 633cc side-valve single called the 'Big Four' (it had a nominal 4hp) which was to remain in production in one form or another for almost 50 years. In 1911 this was joined by a 490cc stablemate, tuned 'BRS' versions of which were good for 70mph and prospered at Brooklands, despite being belt-driven and single speed.

Norton's first overhead valver, the Model 18, appeared in 1922. Within two years it had achieved another notable TT success, now on the gruelling Mountain Circuit, when Alec Bennett took the Senior at an average of 61.64mph and George Tucker the second-ever sidecar race, at 51.31mph.

'Pa' Norton died one year later and so failed to witness the first of a dynasty of overhead-cam racers bearing his name on which Bennett again conquered the TT. This milestone machine, the CS1, was designed by Tucker's passenger from the 1924 TT, Walter Moore, a former Douglas technician. When he left the Bracebridge Street company, Arthur Carrol took over the 'cammy' mantle, replacing Moore's CS1 with a more advanced version which was to become the immortal Manx. Under the shrewd supervision of race boss Joe Craig, factory versions of the cammy Norton went on to win seven Senior TTs in the Thirties, raising the lap record from 76mph to over 90mph in the process. From 1931 to '37 inclusive, 350cc versions of the same engine also won.

Craig's utter dedication to the single contributed both to Norton's success, and their eventual decline. By the mid-Fifties it had been outclassed by the new Italian fours, and its decline was swift. The single was only kept competitive by the peerless handling bestowed by its Featherbed frame, which on its debut in

1950, brought a 1–2–3 in both Senior and Junior TTs, at record speeds. But just four years later the official factory team was abandoned, months after Ray Amm brought them the last win by a true factory Norton single. The Manx's last win, Mike Hailwood's first Senior victory, came in 1961, just days after Phil Read's debut win on a 350cc Manx.

In 1962, Norton was absorbed into the AMC Group, which in turn went bust, but in 1967 a new model, the Commando, emerged from Norton's new Andover base. A 750cc twin based on the earlier AMC Atlas, the Commando accounted for more sales than all other post-war Norton twins combined and was voted *Motor Cycle News*'s 'Machine of the Year' on five consecutive occasions. Despite the high profile of the John Player Norton racing squad, on the Island Commando-based machines won only once, when the estimable Peter Williams took Formula 750 honours in 1973.

In the late Eighties, yet another Norton incarnation appeared on the racing scene. Although the JPS team campaigned their rotary-engined machines valiantly, it was a one-off ride by Steve Hislop which captured the public imagination. His 1992 Senior victory in that furious dice with Fogarty's Yamaha may prove to be the marque's last, but few farewells have been more memorable.

The Norton 'Manx'

The epitome of the British racing single, the Manx was certainly Norton's most successful racing model, although its qualities are often overstated. When the modern World Championships began in 1949 the Manx lost out initially to AJS, Gilera and Velocette until the arrival of the Featherbed frame and the great Geoff Duke. In 1951, Duke took world titles for Norton in both the 350cc and 500cc divisions, retaining the former in 1952. He switched to Gilera in 1953 and the Norton's span of grand prix domination, during which it had collected three solo and four sidecar World Championships, was over.

Yet it was on the Isle of Man that Norton scored their most celebrated victories, 31 of which went to the so-called Manx. The appellation 'Manx' originally derived not from Norton's catalogues, but from the job-cards accompanying engines through the assembly shop. 'Inter' referred to the road-going ohc sportster, while 'Manx' simply meant a racing specification of the same machine. Although it is common now to lump all post-CS1 ohc singles under the same generic name, the true Manx arrived in 1949. The intervening years had seen a gradual evolution into the 'classic', 90 x 78.4mm 499cc dohc Norton (350: 78 x 73mm, 349cc). Such painstaking progress was the Norton way.

In total, the Norton single recorded just 41 grand prix wins, placing it equal tenth, with Morbidelli, in the all-time success league table. For comparison, Yamaha's score is around 400. In the immediate pre-war years 350cc and 500cc Nortons were unceremoniously thrashed by supercharged DKWs, BMWs and Gileras (and sometimes, in the 350 class, by normally aspirated Velocettes).

Mechanically, the Manx was immensely strong, and often oily thanks to its exposed hairpin valve springs and primary drive. From a heavy pressed-up crankshaft, valve drive was by bevel gears, operating the twin camshafts via a chain of five spur gears. Valve actuation was by inverted bucket, the exhaust valve often being sodium-cooled. The engine was non-unit with its four-speed gearbox, an exposed chain taking care of the primary drive. With a compression ratio of around 10.4:1 and a 36mm Amal GP carb (350: 10.8:1; 30mm), peak power of the works engines was around 54bhp at 7,500rpm (350: 38bhp at 8,250rpm). Its robustness earned the Manx a unique place as the privateers' racer, a machine on which you could contest GPs heroically, if rarely win, long after the factory had withdrawn from grands prix. In this respect, they were the four-stroke precursor of Yamaha's TZ.

As much as its engine, it was the celebrated Featherbed frame which distinguished the Manx. The brainchild of Irishmen Rex and Cromie McCandless, this steel double cradle was named by works rider Harold Daniell, who described the handling as 'like a feather bed', and the name stuck. Almost as revered were the telescopic Roadholder forks, first raced in 1938. Thus equipped, Nortons became synonymous with the best in handling and steering, assets which for a while did much to repel the threat from Gilera and Guzzi.

Inevitably, though, the multis triumphed. Norton tried all sorts of things to prolong the Manx's life: desmo valves, outside flywheels, horizontal cylinders, kneeler frames, but all to no avail. (They even tried the one thing they most needed: a new engine. Twins and fours reached the prototype stage, but were never raced.) Other than on British road circuits, Norton won only four GPs after the West German in July 1952. So it is all the more surprising that in 1953 Norton's wily race boss, Joe Craig, turned down a Weslake four-valve design which tests had shown offered a power increase of 10–12 per cent.

The Manx embodied much that was good about British motorcycles. But in the lack of development that relegated it into a supporting role, it also epitomised all that was bad.

SUZUKI

40 wins
First win: 1962 50cc, Ernst Degner

Suzuki was the second of the Japanese 'Big Four' to contest the TT, making their European debut on the Island in 1960. Like much of their racing that year, it was something of a debacle, for their two-stroke machines were way down on power. Nonetheless, all three of their 125cc air-cooled twins finished, with Toshio Matsumoto fastest in 15th place.

The company had been founded in 1909 by Michio Suzuki to produce weaving looms. As with Honda, who had first entered the TT 12 months earlier, it was the post-war shortage of personal transport that set them on the two-wheel path, initially with the 'Power Free', a 36cc two-stroke engine designed to be bolted to a bicycle frame. Two years later, in 1954, the Suzuki Motor Co. was formed.

From the outset, the company was wedded to two-stroke technology but, frankly, they weren't very good at it. However, MZ, led by the genius of Walter Kaaden, certainly were. Then came the bombshell. At the 1961 Kristianstad grand prix Ernst Degner, MZ's development rider, defected to the West, joining Suzuki. Kaaden was convinced that a complete engine, plus other parts, accompanied Degner to Japan. Although the Japanese denied this, a new 50cc disc-valve Suzuki ridden by Degner gave the factory their first TT victory and world title in 1962. During the 1961 TT, both Suzuki and MZ were based at the Castle Mona Hotel, where it is likely that the defection plot was hatched.

By 1963, Suzuki had established themselves as a major force, retaining the 50cc world title, in addition to taking the 125cc crown through Hugh Anderson. On the Island, they again won the 50cc race through Mitsuo Itoh, as well as placing an emphatic 1–2–3 in the 125cc TT through Anderson, Frank Perris and Degner. Until their withdrawal from grands prix in 1968, they would battle for technical supremacy with Honda in this class, much as Yamaha would in the 250cc division.

As the pace hotted up, exotic new machines seemed to appear every year including the RZ64, a liquid-cooled 250cc square four whose fondness for seizing earned it the nickname 'Whispering Death', and the exquisite 125cc RS67. The latter is still an incredible machine which must have been mind-blowing at the time: four tiny cylinders in 90-degree Vee formation, four 24mm carbs, four geared cranks, 12 gears, liquid-cooled, with positive oil lubrication, disc-valve induction and 43bhp. Sadly, Suzuki withdrew before it could truly make its mark, and it was never able to distinguish itself on the Isle of Man.

Like Honda, Suzuki's lack of a competitive production racer

put them in the shade in the early Seventies, Jack Findlay's 1973 Senior win on the liquid-cooled TR500 twin being exceptional. However, by 1976 they were a force again, on two fronts. First were the three-cylinder GT750-based Formula 750 machines, evil brutes but fast enough to give John Williams a record-breaking TT win. Then there was the RG500, both in full factory trim, and later as one of the finest over-the-counter production racers money could buy. The RG would have taken the Senior in '76 but for William's push-in from Governor's Bridge. In the event it had to wait until Phil Read's controversial return 12 months later to record its first TT win.

In 1977, Suzuki produced their first four-stroke road bike, the GS750, and would soon become a force in that arena, too. Graham Crosby took the GSX-1000 based factory racer to double wins in 1981, and although Honda would subsequently dominate affairs, Rex White's Suzuki squad would usually give them a run for their money. In the Production classes, however, the revolutionary GSX-R750 and GSX-R1100 took the TT by storm on their introduction in the mid-Eighties. Suzuki finally returned to winning ways in the Senior and Formula One classes with the awesome GSX-R1000 in 2002.

Suzuki RG500

For almost a decade from 1975 the Suzuki RG500 was not only the most successful 500cc grand prix machine, but also the most sought-after privateer racer. Indeed, it was the first multi-cylinder 500 to be made available 'over-the-counter' to any rider with the ambition and wherewithal to buy one. In factory form, this was also the machine on which Barry Sheene won his two world titles. In all, the RG500 captured the 500cc World Championship four times, as well as winning countless other championships and major races.

During the course of development the square four's power rose from 90bhp to 120bhp. Early versions were something of a handful over the Mountain Course. Up to 1978, conventional twin-shock rear suspension was employed, albeit with the shock absorbers laid down to increase rear wheel travel. This later gave way to a more modern monoshock design.

In this intermediate form – steel frame, monoshock rear end – the Suzuki gained the reputation of being one of the finest racers on the most testing circuit in the world – the TT course. When Rob McElnea won the Senior in 1984, it was the RG500's seventh such success in as many years. The combination of extreme power, light weight, supple suspension and reliability made it the machine to beat on the Isle of Man.

Suzuki GSX-R1000

The big GSX-R is arguably the TT machine of the current decade. Its run of success began with David Jefferies's Senior/Formula One/Production treble in 2002. In the Senior DJ took the big TAS Suzuki around at a sensational 127.49mph, also lapping at an impressive 124.31mph on the Production GSX-R. TAS's run continued with Adrian Archibald's Senior/Formula One double in '03, backed up by Shaun Harris's Production 1000 win on another GSX-R. In 2004 Archibald again took Senior honours, with TAS team-mate Bruce Anstey claiming Production victory.

The 2005 season saw a much-revised GSX-R1000 which should have enjoyed more success but for a run of misfortune in the form of John McGuinness. Nonetheless, Anstey's back-to-back Superstock wins in '05 and '06 established the 'Gixer Thou' once again as the ultimate supersports road machine. Archibald's 126.641mph record lap in the 2005 event was a mere two seconds slower than the fastest lap in the Superbike TT.

In the big classes, the Suzuki has become the yardstick by which other pretenders are judged. Like its principal rivals from Honda, Kawasaki and Yamaha, it's a transverse dohc four. Even untuned, peak power is around 170bhp. More vitally, this is probably the most driveable package of all Superstock machines, hooking up and howling out of corners where lesser devices are searching for drive. Not only the stars but also less talented racers love the GSX-R's easy power, especially over the Island's bumps.

MV AGUSTA
34 wins
First win: 1952 125cc Lightweight, Cecil Sandford

If any manufacturer of two-wheelers emulated the uniquely Italian flair of Ferrari cars, MV, surely, was the one. When Gilera pulled out of grand prix racing at the end of 1957, the 'Gallarate fire engines' went on to claim manufacturers' titles in every class for the next three years. Even more astonishingly, MV captured the 500cc world crown every year from 1958 to 1974, through riders John Surtees, Gary Hocking, Mike Hailwood, Giacomo Agostini and Phil Read. In the same period, they would win no fewer than 12 Senior and nine Junior TTs.

MV was founded as an aircraft manufacturer in 1923, and four years later was inherited by Count Domenico Agusta. After the Second World War, he established the Meccanica Verghera Agusta motorcycle factory at Gallarate, near Milan. The first MV racer, a 125cc two-stroke, was built in 1948 and won the national championship. But Count Agusta had his mind on higher prizes, recruiting Gilera's Pietro Remor to design a squad of MV four-strokes. Cecil Sandford gave the Count his first GP success in winning the 1952 125cc title on the 11,000rpm dohc single, including a maiden victory on the Isle of Man, in the class Carlo Ubbiali was to dominate for MV in the late Fifties.

MV also dabbled with six-cylinder machines. The first, of 500cc, was created to counter the threat from the Guzzi Vee-eight and Gilera fours and was first seen in public when John Hartle rode it at Monza in 1957. Producing 75bhp at 15,000rpm, the transverse engine had MV's familiar dohc layout, driving through a six-speed gearbox. When Gilera and Guzzi pulled out of racing the *raison d'être* for the six had gone, and this exotic project was shelved in favour of the existing 500-Four. In 1969, MV developed another six, this time a 350 producing 70bhp at 16,000rpm. Again, the project was shelved, this time because of the FIM four-cylinder limit imposed in 1970.

When Count Domenico died in February 1971, his brother Count Corrado took over the MV helm. Although MV continued to win grands prix until 1976, Agostini's boycott of the TT after 1972 effectively ended their career on the Island. In total, MV claimed 16 world 500cc titles, nine at 350cc, five 250cc and seven 125cc, notching 34 TT wins along the way. Although one was raced at the 2002 TT, and Martin Finnegan was signed up to ride an MV Superstocker in 2007, the recent MV F4 produced by Cagiva in the old Aermacchi factory at Varese shares only the name with the MVs of old.

MV 500-Four

While MV won at all GP solo classes above 50cc, it is for their big multis that they are chiefly remembered, particularly after Gilera pulled out of grands prix in 1957. In later years it would chiefly be on sweet-sounding three-cylinder machines that Agostini so dominated the grand prix and TT scene, but it was with the earlier fours that the company truly established itself, culminating in world titles for Surtees, Hocking and Hailwood.

In its earliest incarnation in 1950, the dohc engine was already making good power, but its handling was no match for British machines, not least due to its shaft final drive. The suspension, too, was distinctly quaint, with friction-damped parallelogram rear suspension and blade-type forks. Thanks largely to the input of Les Graham, signed at the end of the year, the Four began to make progress. Chain final drive, five-speed transmission, conventional rear shocks and telescopics (although Earles-type forks were also tried for a while) all improved the machine. By

1952 it was truly competitive, Graham being unlucky only to place second at the TT and Ulster GP. Perhaps 1953, when it was timed at 137mph on the Island, would have been the big MV's year, but for Graham's tragic death near Ago's Leap.

In the event, the MV did not win a Senior TT until Surtees claimed one en route to the 1956 world title. From then on, the Gallarate four was almost invincible, winning seven of the next nine Seniors and eight world titles before Honda and Hailwood pipped them in '66. MV responded with a new, lighter 500 based on their Junior machine (reverting to a new generation of fours from 1972/73). Its three cylinder howl probably sounded better than the Four's, but it was the latter which truly set them on their way.

BMW

30 wins
First win: 1939 Senior, Georg Meier

BMW – Bayerische Motoren Werke – are indelibly associated with horizontally opposed 'Boxer' twins, and it is on such machines that they have achieved the bulk of their many TT successes. Founded in 1917 to make aircraft engines – hence the famous spinning propeller logo – post-war treaties forced the company to seek projects elsewhere. First came a motorcycle engine, then, in 1923, the first complete BMW motorcycle. Designed by Max Fritz, the R32 was to become the archetypal 'Beemer': two horizontally opposed cylinders and shaft drive.

BMW's first attempts at supercharging began in 1929, when a 750cc flat-twin took the world flying mile record at 135mph, a figure they would raise to 174ph by the late Thirties. Their first serious assault on the TT came in 1937. Two years later Georg Meier took the twin to victory in the Senior TT, with Jock West in second place. Sadly, that result was marred when their

BMW team-mate, Karl Gall, only recently recovered from injuries sustained on the Mountain the year before, was killed at Ballaugh.

In the post-war years, BMW's racing successes were mainly confined to the sidecar class (their best Senior result being Walter Zeller's fourth place in 1956). From 1955 to '75, BMW won no fewer than 26 sidecar TTs (19 in the 500cc class and seven in the 750cc division introduced in 1968). In fact, the only occasions they did not win during this period were 1962, when Chris Vincent brought home a BSA twin, 1968 when Terry Vinicombe's 750cc BSA won, and when Ralf Steinhausen won in '75. That latter win for Konig was the first by a two-stroke outfit, and heralded almost two decades of 'stinkwheel' dominance in the class. In 1976, BMW's new R90S scored a 1–2–3 class result in the Production TT. BMW's final three wins, from 1997 to '99, came through the late Dave Morris riding F650 roadster-based machines in the single-cylinder class.

BMW supercharged twin

In circuit racing BMW was the first company to fully exploit its experience of supercharging gained in earlier speed record attempts, and the result was one of the most exciting – if short-lived – race bikes of any era. In 1935, their engineers united a Zoller vane-type blower mounted on the front of the crankcases with a new dohc flat-twin engine. With a boost pressure of 15psi – over one atmosphere – power was never in short supply. The twin would eventually develop some 68bhp, at a time when even a factory Norton would struggle to reach 50bhp.

Nor were the bike's credentials confined to its powerplant. It not only wore the first hydraulically damped forks, but BMW's own plunger suspension soon followed at the rear.

Even so, due to a succession of teething troubles the 140mph twin was not an instant TT success. In its debut year, 1937, Jock West could place no better than sixth in the Senior, although an

Ulster GP win two months later showed the true potential of the device. At the 1938 TT West was fifth, but his new team-mate, Georg Meier retired. West again won the Ulster.

In the final TT before the Second World War, what turned out to be its last Isle of Man outing, the supercharged twin finally came good. In only his second race on the Island, Meier won the Senior at a record race speed of 89.38mph, with West in second place. Due to the FIM's post-war ban on forced induction, the supercharged twin would never race again.

TRIUMPH

15 wins
First win: 1908 Single-cylinder class, Jack Marshall

Triumph has the distinction of being the only manufacturer represented at both the first motorcycle TT, and at today's races. So while their total number of wins is relatively modest, its time span is anything but. In 1907, Jack Marshall's Triumph single placed second, winning the following year. Fully 94 years later, in 2003, New Zealand's Bruce Anstey took a 600cc ValMoto Triumph Daytona to victory in the Junior TT, at a race record average speed of 120.36mph. Back in 1908, Marshall's winning speed was just 40.4mph.

Indeed, of literally hundreds of British motorcycle manufacturers, Triumph is the only one producing motorcycles in any numbers today, and even that in a completely different guise from the original company. Founded in Coventry in 1885 by a German, Siegfried Bettmann, to import and later make bicycles, Triumph built their first motorcycle in 1902. Another German, Mauritz Schultz, provided most of the technical input for this, a 1¾hp Minerva, and much of their products for the next 20 years. Other machines with proprietary engines followed, until the first Triumph engine arrived in 1905. From the outset their kit was soundly built, earning Triumph motorcycles a reputation for quality and dependability, as demonstrated by Marshall's performances in early TTs.

But perhaps the most far-reaching event in Triumph's history was Edward Turner's 1937 design for the Triumph Speed Twin, an ohv parallel twin layout so successful that for over 30 years it would be the blueprint for almost every other manufacturer. Yet even then the company was steadfastly opposed to racing, a position it would maintain for many decades. As a result, Triumph's track successes were few, and invariably due to private efforts: Walter Brandish's second in the 1922 Senior, Clubman's wins in 1947 and '52, and successive Production victories in the four years from 1967, through John Hartle, Ray Knight and Malcolm Uphill (twice). Uphill, in the course of winning the 1969 event became the first rider to lap at 100mph on a production machine, a success that led to the renaming of his Dunlop K81 tyres as 'TT 100'.

However, in the early Seventies the BSA Group, then owners of Triumph, began to campaign the new 750cc Trident triple. In full race trim in the new Formula 750 class, the Rob North-framed machines took back-to-back honours in 1971 and '72 through Tony Jefferies and Ray Pickrell. Also in 1971 the Production Trident, Slippery Sam, notched up the first of what would be five successive TT wins.

Triumph Slippery Sam

The celebrated 750cc triple dubbed *Slippery Sam* is the only machine ever to have won five TTs – and consecutive ones at that – in taking the Production crown from 1971 to '75. Along the way *Sam* brought wins for Ray Pickrell (twice), Tony Jefferies (father of David), Mick Grant, and finally the pairing of Dave Croxford and Alex George in the ten-lap Production event. For good measure *Sam* also won other major races at the NW200 and Bol d'Or.

In the Seventies, 'Production' meant something slightly different than it does today. More of a silhouette class, the rules permitted wholesale internal changes. Although essentially a T140 Trident, *Sam* boasted higher compression, 8cc more capacity, gas-flowed heads, racing cams and springs, close-ratio gear clusters, better brakes, and even – bending the rules shamelessly – a lighter frame. Overall, Sam was about 70lb lighter than a stock 470lb Trident and 17bhp more powerful at 75bhp.

Mick Grant recalls that *Sam* was called *Slippery* because it was notoriously oily, but 'it was also as legal as a bent copper: a real factory special full of bits you couldn't buy at any price. It felt a lot lighter and a lot faster than a standard production Triumph.' Grant, who owes his first TT win to *Sam*, remembers the bike (despite riding with a broken wrist) as a 'nice, very well set up machine, which never got into serious bother. The feel of the engine had a raw edge, but with effortless mid-range. It was a top gear bike, which is what gets you round the TT quickly. For a racer, the riding position was good, too.'

In its heyday, *Sam*'s best IoM lap was Alex George's 102.82mph in 1975. Yet in essence this five-times TT winner was little more than 1½ pushrod Triumph Tigers on a common crankcase, introduced in the late Sixties as a stop-gap measure to counter the threat of bikes such as Honda's CB750.

Triumph made little attempt to cash in on *Slippery Sam*'s success. Certainly there was never a factory replica. If there ever was such a plan, it evaporated with the collapse of BSA/Triumph in 1973, after which *Sam* was bought by his creator, Les Williams, but perished in the fire at the National Motorcycle Museum in 2003.

BSA

13 wins

First win: 1949 Junior Clubman's, H. Clark

BSA's TT successes are almost exclusively due to a single model, the 350cc and 500cc Gold Stars which so dominated the Clubman's races in the decade to 1956. This is slight reward for a company which was, during the Fifties, the largest motorcycle manufacturer in the world, which was also owner of Triumph, Sunbeam and other evocative TT names. The company began life in 1862 as Birmingham Small Arms, an association of 14 gunsmiths formed to supply arms for British forces in the Crimean War. For the next 110 years, three stacked rifles remained the Small Heath company's logo.

Although BSA's bread-and-butter was straightforward commuter machines, the post-war years brought not only the glorious Gold Star, but also a succession of highly successful parallel twins, beginning with the A7 Shooting Star. It was derivatives of this engine that brought the marque its two 'proper' TT wins, Chris Vincent in 1962 and Terry Vinicombe in '68, in 500cc and 750cc sidecar classes respectively.

BSA Gold Star

The DBD34 'Goldie' was both the ultimate clubman's production racer and the definitive single-cylinder street racer of the Fifties. The Gold Star name came from the coveted Brooklands prize awarded for 100mph laps at the legendary banked Surrey circuit (where Yamaha's UK base is now located). In 1937, Wal Handley had lapped Brooklands at 107.57mph on a tuned Empire Star BSA. A year later M24 'replicas' were the first to bear the Gold Star name.

Post-war 'Goldies', apart from being some of the most antisocial motorcycles ever produced, were in fact little more than hopped-up ohv B31/32 and B33/34 roadsters. The 350 appeared in 1947, the B34 500 in September 1949. The 500's first success was off road, winning 11 gold medals at the 1949 ISDT. In 1950, it acquired swing-arm rear suspension, and in a few short years had achieved such utter domination of the Clubman's TT that the races themselves were threatened. Of 37 Junior Clubman's entries in 1955, for instance, no less than 33 were Gold Stars.

Although produced in many specifications, the ultimate DBD34 'Goldie' had a huge Amal GP carb, no tickover, no air-cleaner, almost no silencing and fouled plugs like a two-stroke. In road trim it produced around 38bhp at 7,000rpm, perhaps 5bhp more in race trim. Gold Star production ceased in 1962 when BSA declared their highly strung single uneconomic to produce, but by then its favourite stamping ground – the Clubman's TT – had long since been abandoned.

VELOCETTE
11 wins
First win: 1926 Junior, Alec Bennett

On the face of it, Velocette's 11 TT wins ranks them behind the likes of Triumph and BSA, yet the company was not only very much more race orientated, but a dominant force in TT affairs from the late 1920s until 1950. Although a small manufacturer and always family-run, the Hall Green company claimed eight Junior TT wins between 1926 and '49, and the first 350cc World Championship in 1949, through the great Freddie Frith, and then again in 1950 with Bob Foster. Indeed, if Velocette had a commercial handicap, it was their sheer addiction to racing.

Despite occasional adventures since with twins, scooters and oddball two-strokes, Velocette will always be associated with classic four-stroke singles. The first, an ohc 348cc single designed by Percy Goodman, son of the company's founder, arrived in 1925. Three such machines were entered in the 1925 Junior TT race, but all retired. One year later Alec Bennett made ample amends by taking a 'Velo' to victory by the astonishing margin of ten minutes at an average speed of 66.70mph.

Roadster versions of the ohc machine were sold from 1925, leading to the KSS sports roadster and, in 1929, to a production racer, the immortal KTT. A year later, KTTs swept the first eight places at the Manx Grand Prix and it was no surprise that they were to become the ultimate clubman's race tools for a generation, rivalled only by Norton's International and Manx.

Although always associated with the 350cc class, at which they won nine races up to 1949, a rare prototype 495cc 'Velo' was ridden by the great Stanley Woods to second place in the 1937 and '38 Senior TTs. Woods had also taken fastest lap on a 348cc Velocette in the 1936 Senior TT. A prototype for the company's most ambitious project, the supercharged 500cc twin cylinder 'Roarer', debuted during practice for the 1939 TT but was effectively killed off by the post-war ban on supercharging.

In the first TTs of the post-war years, Velocette scored consecutive Junior wins – making five on the trot with Stanley Woods's pre-war victories. During this time, the factory sometimes fielded dohc engines, although riders generally preferred the more tractable sohc layout.

Velocette KTT MkVIII

The ultimate development of the ohc single, which first appeared in 1929, the MkVIII, made its public debut at the 1938 Earls Court Show, and was the nearest thing to a factory racer the privateer could buy. Like the Norton Manx (and later Ducati singles and twins) the overhead camshaft was operated by shaft and bevels. Although factory bikes sometimes sported twin camshafts, the customer MkVIII always had a single cam. The distinctive square cylinder head finning was first seen on factory racers of 1937, and it was on these machines that the 'customer' MkVII (1938) and MkVIII were very much based.

Both the MkVII and MkVIII ran on swinging fork rear suspension, with twin shock absorbers and oil damping. When introduced on the factory bikes in 1926, this was a Velocette first, although the girder-type front forks were more conventional. The MkVIII lacked some of the more esoteric factory parts such as sodium-cooled valves, but this legendary bike was good enough to continue its winning ways long after the Second World War.

MOTO GUZZI

11 wins

First wins: 1935 Lightweight 250cc and Senior, Stanley Woods

Although Moto Guzzi was not the first foreign factory to win a TT, a distinction which went to Indian (USA) in 1911, they were the first to establish a dynasty of winning machines, and when they did first obtain victory they did so in style. In 1935, Stanley Woods brought the Italian marque a 250/500cc double, putting them emphatically up with the big boys of the racing scene. That Senior win was scored on Guzzi's 120-degree Vee-twin – surprisingly, the last time a Vee-twin won the premier TT race.

Originally known as Guzzi & Parodi, the company built its first prototype machine as late as 1920. For its time, the 498cc single was very advanced, with four valves, short-stroke dimensions and bevel gear drive to the camshaft. However, by the time production versions of the 'Tipo Normale' (Standard Model) were announced in December 1920, both the company name had changed – to the familiar Moto Guzzi – and the machine's specification had been downgraded to two valves actuated by push-rod. However, the four-valve design later appeared as a racing machine, winning first time out in the 1924 Circuit del Lario. Thus began a long tradition of track success from the Mandello del Lario factory, mostly based on light, aerodynamic singles.

In 1926, the year of the first real Continental challenge at the TT (as well as a solitary Guzzi, there were a Garelli and three Bianchis), Pietro Ghersi's 250cc Guzzi led for six laps, only to drop to second behind Paddy Johnston's Cotton when the Italian had to refuel. But even this disappointment was nothing compared to what happened next. To the disgust of many, Ghersi was disqualified for the trivial offence of using a different spark plug from the one he had specified. His 63.12mph lap record, however, was allowed to stand. In the Senior, Ghersi retired.

Despite this rebuff, Guzzi competed again in 1927, their 250s placing second and fifth through Archangeli and Varzi. Ghersi, still unlucky, retired. Archangeli also managed a lowly 14th in the Senior. The factory sat out the next three TTs, returning in 1931 when Paddy Johnston placed eighth in the 250cc Lightweight, with Ghersi managing a sixth two years later.

It was in 1934, however, when they played the master card, signing Stanley Woods to ride the 250 (he was contracted to Husqvarna in the 500cc class). The Irish genius placed fourth first time out, before making history in 1935. If Woods's win was technically the first by a foreign rider on a foreign machine, Omobono Tenni's 1937 Lightweight win for Guzzi was the first by an Italian on Italian hardware.

Even from the ruins of post-war Italy, Guzzi remained a potent force. From 1947 until the rise of NSU in 1954, their 250cc single was well-nigh unbeatable. When they turned their attention to the 350cc class, they were no less successful. Yet at the other extreme, there was a supercharged transverse four as early as 1930, the awesome 500cc Vee-eight, numerous other twins and triples and even a fuel-injected four. Most were the brainchild of their brilliant designer, Guilio Carcano. The Eight's one TT outing came in 1957, when Dickie Dale placed fourth on a bike still very much under development. At the end of that season Guzzi pulled out of grands prix. Although roadster-based Guzzi twins have competed in subsequent TTs, there have been no further wins.

Moto Guzzi 500cc Vee-twin

The Guzzi Vee-twin, which won the 1935 TT with new race and lap records, ought to have been the writing on the wall. As the first machine to usurp an unbroken sequence of single-cylinder wins going back to 1914, it showed the way ahead, yet against all reason most British factories continued with thumpers into the post-war era.

The twin was essentially Guzzi's four-valve flat-single, with an additional rear pot grafted on at 120 degrees to the first, somewhat like a modern Ducati. Despite its iron heads and barrels, it was relatively light (375lb), and since the single had so comprehensively trounced the four-valve Rudges in the 1935 Lightweight TT, it was obviously going to be fast. Drive to the single overhead cam was by bevel shaft. At the front, the bike wore conventional girders, with Guzzi's unusual system of triangulated, friction-damped rear fork.

Although the twin returned to the TT in 1949 and '50, with Tenni and Foster respectively setting fastest laps, they retired on both occasions. The twin last competed on the Island in 1951, when Banasedo could finish no better than 31st. In the same year, however, it was still highly competitive, winning the Swiss GP by no less than two minutes. Although the twin recorded only one TT win, in introducing two cylinders and rear suspension to the rostrum, this Guzzi was many years ahead of its time.

Moto Guzzi 350cc Single

Having won every Lightweight TT bar one from 1947 to '53, Guzzi's Giulio Carcarno set about applying the same principles to the more prestigious Junior class. The result was the lightest, lowest, slimmest, most slippery racer of its generation, a machine which amply made up in subtlety what it lacked in outright power.

Carcaro's masterpiece showed the virtue of simplicity and superior aerodynamics, developed in Guzzi's own wind tunnel, in defying the mighty MV and Gilera fours. At its peak, the 350 weighed just 216lb – almost 50lb less than the earlier 250cc flat-single – and was capable of 140mph despite a relatively meagre 38bhp. Blessed with superlative handling from its leading link front forks and swinging-arm rear end, it could maintain higher cornering speeds than its rivals, too. The 350 captured the world title from 1953 to '57, also winning the Junior TT in 1955 and '56. If this was the means to make British singles competitive once more, the lesson was never learned.

AJS

8 wins

First win: 1914 Junior, Eric Williams

AJS is another marque whose relatively modest number of wins belies its special place in TT history. Albert John Stevens, 'AJS' – had the right background to become one of the founders of the British motorcycle industry. The son of a blacksmith, 'Jack' was one of five brothers, raised in the Black Country hotbed of light engineering. He built his first internal combustion engine as early as 1897, although it was not until 1909 that A. J. Stevens & Co. was founded, in Retreat Street, Wolverhampton. Their first complete machine, and first TT entry – indeed their first race of any kind – came in 1911. A 292cc side-valve two-speeder, it placed 14th and 15th, with no retirements.

Absent from the 1912 races, AJS returned in 1913 but could manage no better than ninth through Jack Haslam, with Cyril Williams retiring. But by 1914, with a machine enlarged to a full 350cc and boasting a novel 'two-by-two' four-speed chain drive, they scored a sensational first, second, third, fourth and sixth places, with no retirements. Eric Williams won at record race speed, almost five minutes ahead of Cyril, with the next make, Walker's Enfield, a further seven minutes behind. A consequent surge in orders left AJS wedded to racing as a promotional tool. When racing resumed after the war, AJS claimed three further consecutive Junior wins.

The first ohc AJS, the R7, appeared in 1927, with a chain-driven cam, not unlike the later 7R. Although it was not as successful as the new Nortons and Velocettes, a special 250cc version won the 1930 Lightweight TT through Jimmy Guthrie.

After the Second World War, the factory's main effort was concentrated on the Porcupine, which never won a TT, although a model with more humble pretensions would give the marque its next – and final – TT win. The machine, introduced in 1948, was the 7R Production racer. Although mainly raced by privateers, in 1954 Rod Coleman took a factory triple cam, three-valve 7R 3A to Junior honours. However, perhaps the 'Boy's Racer's' finest achievement came in 1952 when Bob McIntyre took one not only to victory in the Junior Manx GP, but to second place in the Senior, as well. By this time, AJS was part of the AMC empire, which finally went broke in 1967, although some 'AJS' two-stroke scramblers were later built by Andover Norton.

AJS 350cc 'Big Port'

During the Great War, AJS was heavily involved in aero engine work, to the benefit of their post-war racing technology. The resulting race bike, later dubbed the 'Big Port', had an advanced ohv layout with inclined valves, cross-flow hemispherical combustion chambers and aluminium pistons. Producing up to 20bhp at 6,000rpm, during the early 1920s it outclassed every other machine.

Although most of the 'Ajays' blew up racing each other in the 1920 Junior, Cyril Williams brought one home in first place. Despite pushing in for the final three miles, he won by fully nine minutes. A year later, brother Eric Williams won again for AJS, with a third rider, Manxman Tom Sheard, making it a unique four in a row in 1922. But perhaps the Big Port's most remarkable performance came in 1921 when Howard Davies rode one in the Senior, beating all the 500s at race record speed.

AJS Porcupine

The Porcupine, so named because of its spiky cylinder head finning, was another AJS might-have-been. Like the Vee-four, the 500cc parallel twin was another ambitious AJS project thwarted by the ban on supercharging. The engine featured gear-driven twin overhead cams, but AJS never fully redesigned it to suit normal induction, and power was a disappointing 40bhp. Although the later E93 version, with inclined cylinders, made around 55bhp at 7,600rpm, this was still substantially less than the Gilera four.

In total, the Porcupine contested 22 TTs from 1947 to '54, Bill Doran scoring its best result, second place, in 1951. But the 500 came agonisingly close to winning in 1949 when Les Graham led by two minutes from Harold Daniell's Norton, only to stop at Hillberry and push in to tenth place.

AJS 500cc Vee-four
Although it never won a TT, the Vee-four must go down as one of British racing's most audacious and exciting failures. Originally launched as a roadster at the 1935 London Motorcycle Show, the Bert Collier-designed 495cc AJS mercifully never found its way on to public roads. With four cylinders arranged in a 60-degree Vee, chain-driven single overhead camshafts in each pair of cylinders and a further chain driving a front-mounted Zoller supercharger, when first raced in 1936 it was air-cooled, slow, unreliable and only just about rideable. By 1939, it was liquid-cooled, more reliable, and more than a match in speed for the supercharged Gilera fours, recording the first 100mph lap at the Ulster GP. Unfortunately, it handled and stopped like a Douglas horse tram, and could manage no better than 11th and 13th at the TT through Walter Rusk and Bob Foster. AJS engineer Matt Wright was quoted as saying that this 130mph, 405lb monster 'frightened me just to look at it.'

DUCATI
8 wins
First win: 1969, 250cc Production, A. M. Rogers

For all their present high profile, Ducati's TT pedigree is surprisingly slight. Founded as a manufacturer of electronic components in 1926, they moved into motorcycle production after the Second World War, and in 1954 were joined by a brilliant young engineer, Fabio Taglioni, who would oversee their racing hardware for the next 25 years. Their first rostrum positions came in the 1958 TT when Taglioni's new desmodromic single took second, third and fourth places in the 125cc race. One year later, Mike Hailwood brought a similar machine into third place. However, it would be another decade before they scored their first win. This came in the 250cc Production class in 1968, a feat repeated 12 months later. However, the one everyone remembers is Mike Hailwood's comeback triumph in the 1978 Formula One event. The Bologna marque's most recent win was as long ago as 1995, when the late Robert Holden took the pretty Supermono to victory in the short-lived Singles TT.

In between those wins, one man and more-or-less one bike accounted for fully half of Ducati's total of eight wins. Of the five Formula Two races from 1981 to '85, Tony Rutter won four, only missing out when 'Macca' McGregor won for Yamaha in '84. His bikes, based on the street-going 600cc Pantah desmo Vee-twin, introduced the lattice-type steel frame, as still employed by the factory Superbike machines.

Ducati NCR 900SS

Although there had been full-on factory Ducati Vee-twins – Paul Smart took one to an historic win at the Imola 200-miler of 1972 – the bike Hailwood rode to win the 1978 Formula One event was created in the Manchester workshop of Steve Wynne's Sports Motorcycles. Initially prepared by NCR, a Bologna tuning house with a special relationship with the factory, it was little more than a stripped down 900SS road bike with just a sprinkling of race-ready bits – plus that gloriously swoopy bodywork.

However, after some inspired fettling from Wynne, and with the peerless talent of Hailwood on board, it turned into a TT winner. The lightweight frame was visually almost identical to the 900SS roadster's, itself based on a Colin Seeley design for Ducati's unsuccessful 500cc grand prix Vee-twin. Its long wheelbase and conservative geometry suited the TT course, allowing Hailwood not only to see off Phil Read's Honda four, but to set a new lap record of 110.62mph, with little more than 80bhp on tap.

And yet that memorable win so nearly did not come about. Literally, as it crossed the line at the end of the six-lap race, the big Ducati's bevel drive sheared, terminally wrecking the engine. It couldn't have raced another yard.

NEW IMPERIAL

5 wins
First wins: 1924 Lightweight 250cc, Eddie Twemlow; 1924 Junior, Kenneth Twemlow

Scarcely a household name now, 'New Imp', as it was colloquially known, was one of the more technically adventurous companies during the early years of the TT. In the 36 years of their existence, from 1903 to '39, they built some of the prettiest and most technically interesting machines. Their first competition success came in 1922 when a 348cc JAP New Imperial set the fastest lap in the Lightweight TT at 56.46mph. The rider that day was the great Bert le Vack, responsible for designing both the Junior engine and its 248cc Lightweight counterpart. Although fast, neither proved very reliable.

Two years later, however, Kenneth and Eddie Twemlow made amends with a spectacular double in the Junior and Lightweight races respectively, with Eddie also taking the 250cc race in 1925. In 1926, New Imperial began manufacturing their own engines at their Birmingham factory and in 1932, the year Leo Davenport brought them their fourth TT win, they embarked on a wholesale programme of unit-construction engines under designer Matt Wright. By 1938 their entire range of roadsters was built in-unit, with primary drive by helical gears.

Following Bob Foster's Lightweight TT win in 1936, it was hoped that roadster sales would improve, but sadly, it was not to be. The following year brought the death of New Imperial's driving force, Norman Downs, and Wright soon moved to AJS.

The company continued to slide until swallowed by Jack Sangster's Ariel/Triumph in 1939.

New Imperial in-unit 250

Designed around the Unit Super 250 by Matt Wright, the machine raced by the factory in 1935 and '36 was superficially unremarkable, and yet it was a development of the bike which, in 1932, had become the first 250cc to exceed 100mph. The unit 250 made a last-minute debut at the 1935 TT where, in dire conditions, Bob Foster emerged from the mountain mist only to crash at Signpost. Although a spectator – the recently retired Wal Handley, of all people – helped him on his way, Foster retired at the pits. Later in the race Foster's team-mate, Doug Pirie, died after crashing at the 33rd Milestone. Despite these setbacks, Foster brought the Imp into second place at the Ulster GP in August '36, a sure sign that it had the credentials to succeed.

In the 1936 Lightweight TT, however, the little ohv 250 found itself pitted against a pair of blown factory DKWs, one ridden by Stanley Woods. To no-one's surprise Woods led for much of the race before his engine went sick. Foster, a notoriously hard rider, tore the sole off his boot on the wall at Ballacraine making up for lost time, emerging the winner at a record 74.28mph by fully five minutes from Tyrell Smith, with Geiss third on the second DKW. It was to be the last 250cc win by a British four-stroke, and the last by any normally aspirated, rigid-framed, pushrod two-valver. At the Ulster two months later the Imp was so dominant that by prior arrangement Foster and Ginger Wood dead heated for first place.

EXCELSIOR

5 wins
First win: 1929 Lightweight 250cc, S. A. Crabtree

Initially known as Bayliss Thomas & Co., Excelsior was possibly the first British manufacturer of powered two-wheelers, initially using motors from Minerva, Werner and de Dion. Always competition orientated, their first TT win came with S. A. 'Leslie' Crabtree's victory in the 1929 Lightweight TT. A road-going 'replica' of the JAP-engined machine, the B14, was quickly created for an eager public, becoming Excelsior's premier model.

In 1931, the factory almost captured the world speed record when their supercharged 1,000cc JAP-engined Silver Comet clocked 163mph but was unable to complete the return run. At the opposite capacity extreme, 1933 brought the legendary 'Mechanical Marvel', a 250 of sensational complexity, on which Syd Gleave again won on the Island. This time, however, the Marvel's intricacy ensured that there would be no replicas, for the company immediately set about creating a new range of overhead cam machines.

The resulting Manxman series used a bevel-driven overhead cam and ultimately comprised 248cc, 348cc and 498cc models. It was four-valve versions of the 250 which took Tyrell Smith and Ginger Wood to second places in 1936 and '37 respectively. Even in two-valve form after the war, the 250 remained competitive, claiming the company's final three TT wins in the Lightweight Clubman's TT in 1948–50. Excelsior folded in 1965.

Excelsior 'Mechanical Marvel'

By the 1930s, four-valve cylinder heads were 'in', and Excelsior wanted part of the action. The resulting 'Mechanical Marvel', designed by Ike Hatch and built by Burney & Blackburne, employed a unique twin-cam pushrod system with intricate rockers and bearings, which allowed the valves to be radially disposed in the centre-plug cylinder head. Although far more complex than the arrangement favoured by Rudge, it was also more efficient. For better breathing, each of the inlet ports had its own downdraught carburettor.

The Marvel was a success right off the drawing board, winning the 1933 Lightweight at record race speed. Yet an 'improved' version lost out to a Rudge 1–2–3 the following year.

RUDGE

5 wins

First win: 1914 Senior, Cyril Pullin

Rudge-Whitworth, named after Dan Rudge, a Wolverhampton innkeeper who also built bicycles, had a colourful early history but did not make their first motorcycle until as late as 1911. From that year they immediately did well in competition, setting records over one hour (first machine over 60mph) and at Brooklands circuit, but their 1911 Isle of Man ambitions ended tragically when Victor Surridge became the first TT fatality.

Two years later Ray Abbot might well have won them the Senior had he not overshot at St Ninian's, the very last corner of the race, losing by five seconds to Tim Wood's Scott. However, 12 months later Cyril Pullin set the record straight, winning at a record average of 49.49mph on a Rudge Multi which, using a variable belt-drive system similar to that seen 60 years later on Daf cars, offered a notional 20 speeds.

When racing resumed after the war, Rudge suffered a barren period, often not competing at all. It was not until the late Twenties that the glory years returned with a new range of four-valve singles designed by Fred Anstey. In 1928, Graham Walker (father of Murray) took one to victory in the 500cc Ulster GP, the first race ever to be won at over 80mph. The 'Ulster' name was to grace sporting Rudges for the next decade.

Under the shrewd direction of race boss George Hack, 1930 was the factory's best TT year. In their debut Junior race, Tyrell Smith led home a Rudge 1–2–3, whilst Wal Handley took the Senior on a private Rudge. Yet within a year the company was taken over, racing only under semi-factory colours such as those of the Graham Walker Syndicate. This clearly suited Murray's dad as he won the following year's Lightweight TT. The marque's last win was claimed by Jimmy Simpson, also riding for the Walker Syndicate, in the same event in 1934. For all this success,

Rudge suffered badly during the Depression. The race shop closed after 1933 and, following a succession of abortive rescue plans, motorcycle production ceased in 1939.

Rudge Ulster

Named after Graham Walker's 1928 Ulster victory, the immortal 500cc four-valve Rudge was designed by George Hack. In early examples, the valves were in parallel pairs in a pent-roof head, but later adopted a fully radial (1932) or part-radial layout inspired by the successful Junior Rudges of 1930. In Rudge's case the radial layout – used recently on some advanced Honda singles – required a novel arrangement of 'see-saw' rockers by which pushrods actuated all four valves.

Although both Norton and Velocette had overhead camshaft racers, the volumetric efficiency of Hack's four-valve design kept the pushrod Rudge more than competitive well into the Thirties. There were other novelties, too, such as linked front and rear brakes operated by the same foot pedal. As an over-the-counter racer or fast street machine, the Ulster was also way ahead of its time. Its finest moment surely came in the 1930 Senior TT when Wal Handley, having switched at the last moment to a private Rudge, blew away the field in the Senior race, winning at record speed – in the wet! Despite rarely using more than three-quarter throttle (or so he claimed) Handley's record lap at 29m 41s (76.28mph) was the first under the half-hour mark.

KAWASAKI

8 wins
First win: 1969 Lightweight 125cc, Dave Simmonds

It may be a surprise to find one of the Japanese 'Big Four' way down amongst the TT minnows, but Kawasaki's Island history has been a case of more promise than real success. Nor was their introduction any more auspicious than Rudge's. The factory first entered the races in 1966 with a 125cc machine ridden by Toshio Fujii, who crashed fatally at Ramsey during the final practice session.

The giant industrial conglomerate that is Kawasaki dates back to 1878 and the creation of the Shozo Kawasaki dockyard in Tokyo. Most of their focus since has been on heavy engineering, but 1949 saw the first in a series of forgettable four-stroke motorcycles produced at Akashi. In 1960, a new plant was established at Kobe, from which a stream of increasingly potent two-strokes emerged.

Their first Island success came through Dave Simmonds in 1969, the year he took the 125cc world title with no less than eight GP wins on the disc-valved twin. Simmonds had debuted for Kawasaki in 1967, placing fourth in the 125cc Lightweight TT. Tragically, the Londoner, whose last GP win came on board a 500cc 'Kwacker' at Jarama in 1971, was killed in a caravan explosion near Paris the following year.

During the Seventies, Kawasaki briefly emerged as a major player, with back-to-back victories in the prestigious Classic 1,000cc TT in 1977–78. The rider on both occasions was Mick Grant, the machine the potent KR750 two-stroke, and together they marked a dramatic sequence of new records. Before he retired in the 1975 Classic TT, Grant finally broke Mike Hailwood's 1967 lap record. In 1976 he became the first man to average over 110mph, with new lap record of 112.77mph. Twelve months later he again set new outright race and lap records.

Kawasaki's relative lack of success since – just Geoff Johnson's win on the GPZ900 in the 1985 Production race and two recent wins for Ryan Farquhar – is less to do with the quality of their hardware than the want of any sustained commitment to the TT.

Kawasaki KR750

If the Sixties was the decade of the screaming tiddlers, the Seventies was the 'Animal Decade', the years of Formula 750, of

brutal horsepower, skinny tyres and flexi-frames. From 1972 to
'78, Kawasaki's roadster-based triples, and the even grosser
Suzuki GT750s, were the quintessential racing superbikes.

Loosely based on the H2 roadster and earlier H2R racer, the
KR was a liquid-cooled two-stroke triple producing up to 120bhp,
depending on the state of tune. In winning in 1978 Grant was
speed-trapped at over 190mph. The figure has been questioned,
even by Grant himself, yet KRs regularly clocked 180mph at
Daytona, without the downhill advantage of the TT speed trap.
Only in the last 15 years have grand prix machines come to
exceed those figures. For events such as the TT the KR's biggest
handicap was its over-stressed crankshaft, which accounts for its
lack of success before 1976.

SUNBEAM

4 wins
First win: 1920 Senior, Tommy de la Hay

The 'Gentleman's Motor Bicycle', as it was marketed, was not an
obvious choice for TT success, but during the Twenties
Wolverhampton-based Sunbeam produced some remarkable
results. In 1913, a new 500cc single and 770cc JAP-engined Vee-
twin, both with three-speed transmissions, did well in reliability
trials. The following year a 500 ridden by Howard Davies placed
second to H. O. 'Tim' Wood's Scott in the Senior TT.

When racing resumed after the war, Sunbeam immediately
captured TT honours. In 1920, Tommy de la Hay took the win,
the record lap going to team-mate George Dance. One year later
it was Alec Bennett's turn to win. Those first two wins were
recorded on simple side-valve machines, but when Sunbeam next
came to the party it was on a new overhead valve machine, the
Model 90.

Alec Bennett's 1929 TT win was Sunbeam's last, for ICI,
Sunbeam's owners, set about making the marque more cost-

conscious. Their last sporting model, the Model 90, was dropped in 1934, the same year they contested their last TT. Eventually, Sunbeam became part of the BSA Group, but disappeared completely after BSA and Triumph merged in 1956.

Sunbeam Model 90

Sunbeam developed their first ohv machines around 1923, but two years later developed an ohc cam engine on which to base their future racing plans. However, when they were unable to get it to work satisfactorily, they reverted to ohv for 1926, and immediately found success at the Ulster and in European grands prix. Known as the Model 90, it was essentially an over-the-counter Model 9 specially breathed on by the Sunbeam race shop. In 1928, in filthy conditions and despite sliding off at Keppel Gate, Charlie Dodson took a 90 to Senior victory by a mammoth eight minutes. Twelve months later, now with foot gear change for the first time, he repeated the feat, this time in the dry at record lap and race speeds, the latter the first at over 70mph. This was the last Senior to be won by an ohv two-valve engine.

MATCHLESS

4 wins

First win: 1907 Single-cylinder class, Charlie Collier

For all their dominance of the contemporary classic racing scene, not least at the Manx Grand Prix, Matchless's Isle of Man record is surprisingly thin. However, as the winner of the very first motorcycle TT, the company has a special place in history. Unique amongst the major manufacturers, the company was founded by two brothers, Charlie and Harry Collier, who as riders were also pillars of the early racing scene. Even before the motorcycle TT, both competed with distinction in the International Cup races, and in the first Manx trials.

In 1907, both brothers rode 432cc ohv singles of their own

manufacture, Charlie emerging the overall winner and thus being the first to receive what is now the Senior trophy. In 1908, Charlie placed second to arch-rival Jack Marshall's Triumph, with Harry turning the tables for Matchless 12 months later. It was Charlie's year again in 1910, with the first 50mph TT lap. The following year, in the first bike TT over the Mountain, Charlie originally placed second before being disqualified for refuelling illegally.

Ironically, considering these heady beginnings, racing soon became a secondary consideration to the Plumstead factory, so that even in the Thirties their racers were essentially stripped-down roadsters such as the 347cc cammy single. In later years they built over-the-counter racers such as the G45 twin (1953–58) and G50 single (1959–63) which did well, if not spectacularly so, in private hands. But, discounting the efforts of AJS, which Matchless acquired in 1931, their next TT victory did not come until the Historic event of 1984, when Dave Roper became the first American winner on a G50, surely the last on a Matchless.

Matchless G50

Designed by Jack Williams, and derived from the AJS 7R, the 496cc G50 was never envisaged as a grand prix winner. It was popular because it was a true privateer's racer, competitive enough straight out of the crate, and far simpler to maintain than Norton's Manx. Like the 7R, with which it shared the same stroke, it used a chain-driven overhead camshaft for its two valves. The aim was simple: a practicable racing machine at an affordable price. It wasn't until Colin Seeley began making special lightweight frames that the 47bhp Matchless regularly began to beat the 500 Manx. Indeed, the G50 has never won a truly competitive grand prix, its three successes – at Finland in 1962, Argentina in 1961 and '62 – coming in the absence of the prevailing Hondas and MVs. Nor did it win a contemporary TT, although Peter Williams's two second places in 1967 and '73 on a Jack Williams-tuned machine, stand out heroically.

DOUGLAS

4 wins

First win: 1912 Junior, W. H. Bashall Senior

While most major British motorcycle manufacturers followed a largely conventional approach, Douglas was one which resolutely set its own style. In this respect, and even more in the choice of engine layout, the Kingswood, Bristol company has often been compared with BMW, who also specialised in horizontally opposed twin-cylinder machines for the classier end of the market. The very first Douglas machine was of this design, although its cylinders lay fore-and-aft rather than transverse.

The company's first competition success came in 1910, just three years after producing their first motorcycle, when they took the coveted team award in the International Six Days Trial. Two years later, in appalling conditions, Bill Bashall brought them their first TT win, the 1912 Junior – a resounding success in which 'Duggies' were also second, fourth and eighth and took the fastest lap through Eddie Kirkham. The immediate pre-war years saw the Douglas side-valve twin dominate in Continental grands prix, and it was no surprise when a year later, Billy Newsome placed second on the Island.

After the Great War it was the turn of a new ohv Douglas, the first British 500cc machine to better 100mph over the flying half-mile, in 1922. A year later Manxman Tom Sheard took the Senior and Freddie Dixon the inaugural Sidecar TT, the latter on a curious banking outfit. Equally strange, considering their name, was the company's choice of TT HQ: they were usually based in Peel. Douglas's final TT win came through Len Parker in the 1925 sidecar event, although Douglas continued to contest the races for another seven years.

By this time, the flat-twins had become so established that even King George VI acquired one. In 1935 they were taken over by BAC, and after the Second World War, by Westinghouse, who seemed more interested in the production of Vespa scooters than the regeneration of their motorcycle range. Bike production ceased in 1957. What was left of the company continued to import and assemble Vespa scooters and later Gilera motorcycles.

Douglas ohv twin

Douglas's first ohv twin appeared in 1920, but after limited success was redesigned with light alloy cylinder heads, twin carbs and four-speed transmission in the nick of time to contest the 1923 TT. As well as more power than before, the new bike was shorter and lower, and equipped with front and rear disc brakes, a development of those pioneered by Douglas in 1920. At just 250lb, it was some 50lb lighter than most of its rivals.

Despite its hectic development the twin completely dominated the 1923 races. Again in sodden conditions, Whalley's Douglas led for three laps before losing a cylinder. This handed the lead to Sheard with, at one stage, other Douglas twins lying in second, third and fourth places.

In the same year, Dixon used a similar machine, this time of 600cc, to win the first Sidecar TT after Harry Langman's Scott crashed out at Braddan on the final lap. The versatile Dixon went on to place third 12 months later with a new lap record, which he smashed once again the following year when losing out to Parker's 'Duggie'.

VINCENT
4 wins
First win: 1948 Senior Clubman's, J. D. Daniels

In one sense Vincent can claim six TT wins, for the company began life as HRD before being purchased by Philip Vincent in 1928. Early Vincents, like HRD before them, originally used proprietary engines from the likes of Blackburne and JAP. Their principal innovation was a novel form of cantilever rear suspension of Vincent's own design. Then, after a duff batch of

JAP engines were foisted on him at the 1934 TT, Vincent resolved never to be dependent on outside engine suppliers again.

The in-house engines which replaced them, largely the work of the ingenious Australian, Phil Irving, have gone down in legend. First, in 1935, came the Meteor, a high-camshaft 499cc single later capable of 90mph in sports Comet form. Then came the engine for which the Stevenage company was famous: a 998cc Vee-twin, essentially two Meteor top-ends arranged in a 47-degree Vee on a common crankcase.

At the TT, Vincent's strength lay in the Clubman's class introduced in 1947. Initially opposed by machines of half the capacity in the Senior Clubman's (won by J. D. Daniels in 1948), the 1,000s were given their own class in 1949, and inevitably triumphed on the three occasions it was contested up to 1953. George Formby, who already owned several bikes including a Norton Inter, bought a Stevenage twin after testing a Rapide during the 1948 races. Sadly, with sales dwindling and costs of the already very expensive machines rising, Vincent production ceased in 1955.

Vincent Black Lightning
Although Vincent's TT successes were all achieved in what was frankly a minor class and against no great opposition, the machine for which they are best remembered was one of the all-time greats. Post-war 'Vinnies', both Series B and, from 1949, the Series C, were arranged in a 50-degree Vee. Both series were built in touring, sports and racing guises as the Rapide, Black Shadow and Black Lightning respectively.

All featured Vincent's unique Girdraulic forks, cantilever suspension and abbreviated frame, but what really set them apart was their sheer speed, for their performance remained unequalled by any production motorcycle until well into the Seventies. With over 60bhp from its 998cc ohv Vee-twin engine, the Black Lightning could better 130mph, although it was a handful over the Mountain Course. In 1955, Russell Wright took such a

Vincent through the timing lights at Christchurch, New Zealand at 185.15mph, a new world record.

REX-ACME

3 wins
First win: 1925 Ultra-Lightweight and Junior, Wal Handley

Rex was one of the jewels of the early British motorcycle scene. Beginning as car manufacturers in Coventry in 1899, the Williamson brothers, Billy and Harold, soon produced their own single and twin-cylinder power units, and in 1906 were responsible for the first telescopic forks. A year later a Rex so equipped took Billy Heaton the third place in the first TT. Shortly after, the founders were ousted, although the irrepressible Billy subsequently created the Williamson, a touring flat-twin.

In 1919, under new boss George Hemingway, Rex took over neighbours Coventry-Acme, adopting the name Rex-Acme two years later. This period was to be their prime, although much of their greatness derived from one special man, Wal Handley. Having impressed for OK at the 1922 and '23 TTs, Handley joined Rex in June 1923, promptly romping to victory in the Belgian and Ulster GPs. Two years later he recorded the first ever TT double in winning the Lightweight and Junior events, adding the Lightweight again in 1927. (Rex was rarely a force in the larger class, although they campaigned a 498cc ohv Vee-twin in 1926.) However, by this time sales were sliding disastrously and in 1932 the company was taken over by a sidecar manufacturer, Mills-Fulford, who dropped motorcycle production the following year.

GILERA

3 wins
First win: 1955 Senior, Geoff Duke

Between the start of the World Championship in 1949, and 1957 when they pulled out of racing, Gilera won a remarkable 33 grands prix, three Manufacturers' Championships and six world titles. Like their Italian competitors MV Agusta, the company had aristocratic beginnings. In 1909 the Arcore company was founded by Count Giuseppe Gilera, rapidly making its mark as a producer of high-quality singles and later Vee-twins.

The basis for their later success was Count Gilera's 1936 acquisition of the Rondine engine, a supercharged, liquid-cooling dohc four. In 1937, a development of this engine brought Gilera a world speed record of 170.373mph (274.181km/h) at the hands of development engineer Piero Taruffi – a success a certain Sr Mussolini was not slow to exploit. Two years later, Dorino Serafini won the 500cc European Championship on a similar machine.

Redesigned to conform with the post-war ban on supercharging, the four soon racked up a succession of world titles. They first entered the TT in 1953, but for a while Isle of Man wins eluded them, until Geoff Duke took the Senior in 1955. Two years on, Bob McIntyre brought them a TT double, with wins in the Senior and Junior.

In 1957, the company pulled out of racing. Gilera was taken over by Piaggio in 1970, concentrating on small capacity commuter and off-road machines. After an abortive return to 250cc grand prix racing in the early Nineties, this once great name died in the name of 'rationalisation' in 1994, but has recently returned with a range of stylish scooters and a successful 125cc grand prix machine.

Gilera 500-Four
Based on the pre-war dohc Rondine, the four was redesigned into air-cooled, normally aspirated form by Pietro Remor and in its first competitive season brought Nello Pagani two grand prix wins and a second place in the inaugural World Championship in 1949. A year later, Umberto Masetti went one

better, but in 1951, Geoff Duke brought Norton's 500 single their first title.

Masetti won again on the four in 1952, with Geoff Duke, now with Gilera, taking the title in each of the next three years. Libero Liberati brought Gilera their last world title in 1957, the year Bob McIntyre made history when his 500 Gilera became the first machine to lap the Mountain Course at 100mph.

In the flesh the 500-Four is a tiny jewel of a machine. Indeed, part of its continued competitiveness lay in its aerodynamics. Although the same Remor was responsible for both engines, the Gilera, just 15in wide at the crankcases, was a considerably more compact engine than the MV four, with more efficient and stable streamlining.

A long-stroke design, less revvy and more driveable than later MV and Benelli fours, the Gilera produced up to 70bhp. With full 'dustbin' fairing, top speed was in excess of 160mph. Most examples had five-speed transmission, although a seven-speed gearbox was later developed.

In 1963, the elderly Gilera fours returned to racing under Duke's Scuderia Duke banner. The venture lasted only one season, but it was a measure of the bike's prowess that John Hartle, Phil Read and Derek Minter brought the six-year-old hardware to second place in the Manufacturers' World Championship. In the TT, Hartle placed second, comfortably beaten by Hailwood's MV, with Read third.

Such an exceptional device really deserved more than its two TT wins (plus one for the 350cc four). As the first of the post-war fours to achieve racing success, the Gilera enjoys a special place in racing history. Its penultimate TT outing came in 1964 when Florian Camathias lay second to Max Deubel's BMW on a Gilera-powered outfit before running out of fuel and pushing into 15th place. Two years later, Derek Minter was loaned one of the old fours, but slid off at Brandish during practice, breaking an arm.

KEY

〰 High Road Course

〰 Motorcycle International Cup Course

〰 1907 Bike TT Course (St John's Course)

〰 Short High Road Course

〰 Four Inch Course (where different from Short High Road Course)

〰 Clypse Course

〰 Mountain Circuit

○ Bride

○ Andreas

○ Jurby

○ St Jude's

The Cronk ○

Milntown Cottage
Sulby ○
Ballaugh ○   Quarry Bends   RAMSEY ○
Ramsey Hairpin
Gooseneck
Bishopscourt   Joey's Bend
Guthrie's   Maughold ○

Birkin's Bend
Kirk Michael ○

East Mountain Gate

Barregarrow

Handley's Bend   Les Graham Memorial
Drinkwater's Bend   The Bungalow ○
Cronk-y-Voddy ○   Brandywell   Hailwood Rise

Cregwillys Hill   Dukes 32nd Milestone
Glen Helen   Laxey ○

PEEL ○

Doran's Bend   33rd Milestone
Kate's Cottage
Ballacraine   Creg-ny-Baa
St John's ○   Greeba ○
Brandish
Hillberry

Glen Maye ○   Lower Foxdale ○
Crosby ○   Glen Vine ○
Foxdale ○   Union Mills   Onchan ○
Governor's Bridge
Braaid ○   Quarter Bridge   Bray Hill
○ DOUGLAS

Closeclark ○

Ballamodha ○

○ Santon

Ballasalla ○

PORT ERIN ○

○ PORT ST MARY   CASTLETOWN ○

Above: *Bikes line up outside the official weighing station at Quiggin's Rope Works, Lake Road, Douglas, prior to the first motorcycle race on the Isle of Man, in May 1905.*

Below: *The start of the first motorcycle TT, adjacent to the Tynwald Inn at St John's. First away at 10am on 28 May 1907 were the Triumphs of Frank Hulbert and Jack Marshall.*

Left: *Rembrandt Fowler and his victorious Norton twin in 1907, with the company's legendary founder, 'Pa' Norton, on the right. Despite two crashes and a puncture, Fowler set fastest lap of the day.*

Above: *Charlie Collier astride his winning Matchless in 1910. The belt final drive and complete absence of front brake can clearly be seen.*

Right: *Ever spectacular, Jimmy Simpson flies over Ballig Bridge in 1930. Inevitably, his Junior Norton broke down, although he managed third place in the Senior event.*

Below right: *Jimmy Guthrie pictured in 1935, the year of his memorable Senior battle with Stanley Woods. A works Norton rider from 1931 to 1937, the Hawick man had scored a Senior/ Junior double the previous year.*

Left: *Woods aboard the 120-degree Guzzi Vee-twin on which he so narrowly beat Jimmy Guthrie to win the 1935 Senior TT.*

Below: *The plunger-framed 'Garden Gate' Norton was far less competitive than the 'Featherbed' version which followed. This example has the Roadholder forks introduced in 1938.* (Author)

Opposite top: *In the 1954 Lightweight race, the NSU Rennmax won the first four places, with Happi Muller, in fourth spot.*

Opposite bottom: *Gilera's seminal 500-Four, successful in its own right and the inspiration for the multis which dominate to the present day.* (Author)

Above: *Bob McIntyre rounds Quarter Bridge on the dustbin-faired Gilera four – he would put in the very first 100mph lap of the Mountain Circuit.*

Left: *Phil Read, in the TT parc fermé in 1966.*

Opposite top: *Mike Hailwood cranks the 500 Honda round Quarter Bridge during his epic dice with Giacomo Agostini's MV in the 1967 Senior TT.*

Opposite bottom: *Ago hustles the MV, determined to get the better of Hailwood.*

Above: Slippery Sam, *winner of five consecutive TTs, took the Production crown from 1971 to 1975. The bike was destroyed in the National Motorcycle Museum fire of 2003.* (Author)

Below: *Peter Williams on the Arter Matchless on which he achieved a dogged second place to Jack Findlay's Suzuki in the 1973 Senior TT.*

BENELLI

3 wins

First win: 1939 Lightweight 250cc, Ted Mellors

By any standards the Benelli story is remarkable. This resilient little company began life in 1911 when the widow Teresa Benelli established a toolshop employing five of her six sons. Based in Pesaro, 'L'Officina Meccanica di Precisione f.lli Benelli' was flattened by an earthquake in 1916, but emerged in new premises to make its first motorcycle engine in 1919, and its first complete bike one year later.

After considerable domestic racing success in the Twenties and Thirties, Benelli first ventured to the Island in 1939, reaping instant dividends when Ted Mellors took a 250cc single to victory. In the same year, the company was working on an outrageous 250cc supercharged, liquid-cooled dohc four, reputedly producing 52bhp at 10,000rpm. Sadly, the Second World War not only finished this project, but saw the Benelli factory bombed flat. The Lightweight TT trophy, incidentally, somehow survived the war in Italy, spending part of it buried for safekeeping.

Undaunted, Benelli came back strongly after the war, winning the Lightweight TT in 1950 and placing second 12 months later through Dario Ambrosini. A superb rider, Ambrosini would surely have gone on to even greater things had he not been killed at Albi the month after being narrowly beaten by Tommy Wood's Guzzi in the 1951 Lightweight TT. The following year the factory pulled out of grands prix.

In 1962, Benelli produced an astonishing 250cc four, which later grew into a 350 and then a 500. Thus equipped, the little Italian factory took on MV and the Japanese, with Renzo Pasolini placing second in both the Lightweight and Junior TTs of 1968. Twelve months later, Kel Carruthers won the 250cc TT on the way to taking the world title.

Off the track, the company is best known for the six-cylinder Sei of the mid-Seventies. These models, and contemporary 350cc and 500cc fours, grew out of the extravagant ambition of Alessandro do Tomaso – an entrepreneur who attempted to rationalise Italian motorcycle production. Ultimately, do Tomaso's dream failed and Benelli practically disappeared until taken over by the Merloni group, owners of Ariston and Indesit, in 1996. Scooter production resumed a year later, followed by development of the three-cylinder Tornado roadster and World Superbike machines.

Since their heyday, Benelli's best position was a brace of fifth places in the F2 TTs of 1978 and '79 through Joey Dunlop and Steve Ward respectively. In the latter year, Joey also raced a 900cc Benelli Sei – one of his more cumbersome TT mounts – for the British Importers, Agrati Sales, but retired on lap two.

Benelli single

Although Benelli's fours get more attention, they came after a host of even more successful multis from Gilera, MV and Honda. In many ways the more remarkable machine was the dohc 250 on which the factory scored its first TT win, and which was technically so far ahead of its rivals.

Development of the single began in 1933, and by 1938, when it romped away with the Italian Grand Prix, the little Benelli was demonstrably faster than even the factory 350cc Velocette. The engine boasted twin, gear-driven overhead camshafts, an external flywheel and, at 30mm, its carburettor was huge for the time. The suspension was a combination of girder front end with a friction-damped pivoted rear fork. Producing 30bhp at 8,400rpm, it was good for around 110mph on TT gearing, even in this pre-streamlining age. On its TT debut in 1939 it won by no less than 3m 45s from the blown DKW of 1938 winner, Ewald Kluge.

Nor did war finish the feisty little single. In 1949, Dario Ambrosini placed second in the inaugural 250cc World

Championship on a development of the pre-war single. In the following year he went one better – including victory in the Lightweight TT by just 0.2 seconds from Maurice Cann's Guzzi.

MONDIAL

3 wins

First win: 1951 Lightweight 125cc, Cromie McCandless

Not to be confused with the Belgian La Mondial which competed in the Thirties, FB (Fratelli Boselli) Mondial began in Milan producing three-wheeled delivery vehicles, but after the Second World War branched out into motorcycle production. They were fortunate to have in their ranks designers such as Lino Tonti and Alfonso Drusiani, and for a while in the early Fifties, Fabio Taglioni, later of Ducati, cut his teeth as Mondial's race director.

Initially, Mondial produced two-stroke roadsters, but soon switched to four-strokes, developing a superb range of 125cc, 175cc and 250cc ohc and dohc racing singles, as well as a 250cc twin, which helped them to three consecutive 125cc Manufacturer's World Titles in 1949–51. And no marque has had quite such an emphatic TT debut, for in 1951 their screaming 11,000rpm 125cc single swept the board, taking the first four places, with Cromie McCandless winning. Amazingly, they did not gain the team award, having omitted to enter for it. DOT took that gong, instead. Twelve months later Mondial did collect the team prize, but narrowly missed out on first place.

For a while, Mondial's fortunes faltered as NSU and MV took 125cc honours, but in 1957 they returned to the rostrum in style, with Cecil Sandford winning the TT on the 250, and Tarquinio Provini on the 125. In the same year, both men took world titles. Along with Guzzi and Gilera, Mondial pulled out of grands prix in 1958, although Hailwood rode their 250 in the 1959 TT, failing to finish. Mondials last competed in 1967 through Derek Chatterton, who also retired.

SCOTT

2 wins

First win: 1912 Senior, Frank Applebee

Alfred Angas Scott was one of the great innovators of motorcycling's early years. In 1904, he patented his first engine, which he fitted on to his Premier bicycle (and occasionally into a small boat, the Petrel). Scott motorcycle production began in 1908, initially in Bradford, later in Saltaire. The first Scotts used a triangulated frame which was to survive substantially unchanged until 1930 and a new 333cc engine with the same two-stroke parallel twin layout with which the Scott name will forever be associated. The engine later grew to 450cc, 498cc and ultimately 596cc.

In 1911, two-strokes were handicapped by a 1:32 capacity penalty (allowing them only 443cc), much as rotary engines would be eight decades later. But by 1912, now on a level playing field, the 'yowling two-strokes' had a string of competition successes behind them, and posted the first of their TT wins. When H. O. 'Tim' Wood repeated Scott's win in 1913, it would be the last Senior win by a two-stroke until Suzuki in 1973. Although the Scott name survived into the Fifties (and even beyond with the Spondon-framed, Scott-engined Silk), the company's innovative tradition died with its founder in 1922.

Scott twin

With their telescopic forks, rotary inlet valves (with variable timing), liquid cooling and all-chain drive, the Scotts which dominated the races prior to the Great War were way ahead of their time. At the 1910 TT an air-cooled version became the first two-stroke to go the full race distance, and 12 months later in the first Senior over the Mountain, Frank Philipp claimed the fastest lap. Also that year, Philipp created almost as big a stir when he rode in outlandish purple leathers to match Scott livery.

During practice for their victorious 1912 TT, the two-stroke twins had shown themselves 'very fast and marvellous on corners', and so it proved in the race. Frank Applebee led from start to finish, with Philipp second on another Scott until his tyre 'blew off' on the final lap. Applebee's winning margin was fully seven minutes from Jack Haswell's Triumph. A year later, by which time the engines wore twin-plug heads, Applebee looked set to repeat his win but retired whilst leading. This allowed Tim Wood, a Scott employee riding in his very first race of any kind, to win by just five seconds, despite a six-minute stop to repair a leaking radiator. Wood also led in 1914 before retiring.

HRD

2 wins

First win: 1925 Senior, Howard Davies

Howard Raymond Davies's brief but glorious adventure could scarcely have enjoyed a better start. After a series of TT breakdowns the former First World War airman resolved to ride a machine he could depend on – his own – and HRD motorcycles was formed. The first 'factory' was a house in Wolverhampton, yet within months its founder had raced to Senior TT victory on one of his own machines, a JAP-engined 500cc single. When Bert le Vack added to that win with a host of 500cc Brooklands records, HRDs became desirable machines. In 1926 a new duplex frame appeared, a new 600cc Model 90 and, for customers who could not afford the very best from these 'Leaders in Design and Speed', a pair of 'cooking' models, the 350cc HD65 and 500cc HD75.

When the great Freddie Dixon added the Junior TT to HRD's list of successes in 1927, it might have looked as though the young company had a bright future. It seems, however, that sport was far dearer than commerce in the heart of Mr H. R. D., for his company went bankrupt shortly after the 1928 motorcycle show. The name and rights passed briefly to OK-Supreme, only to be sold on again to another great innovator, Phil Vincent.

NSU

2 wins

First win: 1954 Lightweight 125cc, Rupert Hollaus and
Lightweight 250cc, Werner Haas

NSU's grand prix adventure was as utterly dominant as it was
brief. Founded in Neckarsulm, Germany in 1901, the company
had the distinction of competing in the very first motorcycle TT
where M. Geiger placed fifth. They were regular entrants during
the Thirties, although their most potent device never reached the
Island. In 1938, NSU began development of a 350cc
supercharged twin which, when expanded to 500cc, clocked
211mph at Bonneville in 1956.

With the blown 350 unable to race after the war, NSU built a racing
500cc four in 1951 which, while fast, proved hugely troublesome. The
four was quickly dropped, but under the brilliant Albert Roder and
Walter Froede, one of its cylinders was developed into the 125cc
Rennfox, and two became the 250cc Rennmax. Both these dohc
machines would set new landmarks in engine power. They debuted on
the Island in 1953 when Werner Haas placed second in both the
250cc and 125cc events. Twelve months later Haas and Hollaus won
the Lightweight 250cc and 125cc races respectively.

After 1954, NSU closed their race department, and three years
later ceased motorcycle production altogether in favour of cars, but
their machines continued to contest the TT until 1963. In 1958,
Mike Hailwood gained his first rostrum position on a 250 Rennmax.

NSU Rennmax

The Rennmax, for all that it won only one TT, had one of the all-
time great engines. In its earliest form it used a square (54 x
54mm) cylinder configuration, and even by early 1952, the bevel-
driven dohc twin was producing 27bhp at 9,000rpm, rising to
31bhp at 10,400rpm by the end of that debut season. For 1953,
NSU replaced the Max's tubular frame with a pressed-steel

beam, added leading link forks, and won practically everything except the TT, where Haas finished second to Anderson's Guzzi.

For its ultimate incarnation in 1954, the Rennmax featured not only more streamlining, but a new short-stroke engine (55.9 x 50.8mm). Developing fully 39bhp at 11,500rpm, it was capable of 135mph with the full bodywork used at some grands prix, but about 10mph less with the Dolphin fairings preferred on the Island. Such extremes of specific power – 156bhp per litre – required an elaborate starting ritual, but once fired up, it was unbeatable. At that year's TT the twin hogged the first four places (and sixth), with Haas adding no less than 6mph to both race and lap records. Little wonder that Haas took the 250cc world title in both 1953 and '54.

OK-SUPREME
1 win
First win: 1928 Lightweight 250cc, Frank Longman

Founded as bicycle makers, Humphries & Dawes in Birmingham in 1882, OK became Supreme only in 1927, and to prove the point, Frank Longman won the Lightweight TT one year later using an OK powered by a proprietary ohv JAP engine with a special cylinder head. By this time the company already had something of a TT pedigree. As plain OK, they had first entered in 1912, when E. V. Pratt finished third from last. But ten years later an 18-year-old prodigy named Wal Handley, whose talent had been spotted by OK's burly and notoriously rude boss, 'Black Ernie' Humphries, set the fastest Lightweight TT lap on a 250cc OK-Blackburne. Two months later Handley won the Ulster GP, then set the fastest TT lap again in 1923 before crashing out and remounting to finish eighth. In 1927, the great Alec Bennett lost out in a colossal tussle with, ironically, Handley's Rex-Acme, when his piston let go late in the race.

After his win, Longman went on to finish third in the 1929 Lightweight, and 12 months later Paddy Johnston placed second on another OK-Supreme. Although OKs would continue to race on the Island until the early Fifties, and during the Thirties had produced some of the prettiest ohc racing machines, usually in sky blue livery, they never again finished higher than seventh and more often than not broke down. The company ceased production after the death of Black Ernie's son, John, in 1946.

INDIAN
1 win
First win: 1911 Senior, Oliver Godfrey

Indian, based in Springfield, Massachusetts, were one of few foreign manufacturers to play a prominent role in the early TTs, first competing in 1909 when G. L. Evans placed second. Spurred on by their British importer, Billy Wells, they fielded a seven-man team the following year, but five bikes retired, with Jimmy Alexander their top finisher in a lowly 14th place.

In 1911, the regulations bizarrely allowed twins of 585cc, while singles were limited to just the half litre, so the factory scaled down their inlet-over-exhaust 1,000cc racers to 585cc (70 x 76mm) specifically for the Island. Striking in bright red livery, the Vee-twins ran all-chain-drive and two-speed transmission, with a hand gearchange and clutch. Their riders that year, in a record entry of 104 machines, were Oliver Godfrey, Charlie Franklin, Arthur Moorhouse, Jimmy Alexander and Jake de Rosier, the American champion.

For a while it looked like going horribly wrong. After three of the four laps Charlie Collier's Matchless led by nearly a minute, with four Indians on his tail, but he punctured and dropped to third. Although he fought back tenaciously to second place, the Matchless man was disqualified after Franklin and Moorhouse protested that he had illegally taken on fuel. The final standings were Godfrey, Franklin and Moorhouse, with Alexander 18th after crashing and gashing a knee. De Rosier was also disqualified for accepting outside assistance. Indian had humbled the British hardware with the first clean sweep of a TT rostrum.

After 1911, the twins' capacity advantage was removed, and although Indians would place third in 1913, and second a year later, they never again attained the same level of dominance. Far more innovative than Harley-Davidson, they later produced ohv racing twins with four-valve heads, and road bikes with rear suspension and even electric starters. In the early Twenties, Indians secured further rostrum places through Freddie Dixon (twice) and Bert le Vack. By the Fifties the now-moribund marque was acquired by AMC – ironically, the descendant of the same Matchless with whom they had battled in 1911. Recent attempts to revive this evocative name have foundered in insolvency.

DKW

1 win
First win: 1938 Lightweight 250cc, Ewald Kluge

Pronounced 'Dekkavay' in its German homeland, the DKW was produced in the same Zschopau factory which, after the Second World War, housed MZ. Although the factory claimed only one TT win, during the Thirties and Fifties (by then in West Germany) they were major international players.

From their first race in 1925 until the ban on supercharging, DKW always ran blown two-strokes, but in a number of novel configurations. In 1931 they developed the split-single layout – a clever way of getting asymmetric port timings, with a separate cylinder, complete with reed valves, performing the supercharging function. At their TT debut in 1935, Arthur Geiss brought a 'Deek' home in seventh place, after his two team-mates retired.

The following year, Geiss placed third, but team-mate Stanley Woods set a record lap of 76.2mph, only to break down, for seven laps and 264 miles was a tough ask for the screaming twin. Ernie Thomas brought another third in 1937 after Ewald Kluge, on his

TT debut, had set the first 80mph lap by a 250. This succession of breakdowns caused DKW to abandon their reeds in favour of a rotary valve which gave not only more reliability, but also a boost in power from 25bhp to 30bhp. One of the noisiest machines ever, it was reputably audible as far away as Lancashire, and guzzled petrol at an alarming 22mpg. Yet, in 1938, Kluge became the first German to win a TT on the 250cc DKW.

After the war, DKW campaigned a succession of normally aspirated strokers, most notably the 350cc 'Singing Saw' designed by Helmut Görg. The triple was ear-splitting to listen to, and complicated to ride. Cecil Sandford had to cope with no less than three air levers, one for each cylinder, on his way to third place in the 1956 Junior race. This was to be DKW's last TT, for they became part of Zweirad-Union (later Audi) the following year.

AERMACCHI
1 win
First win: 1984 Historic 350cc, Steve Cull

Originally an aircraft factory – hence the name – Aeronautica Macchi SpA began motorcycle production in 1948 at the Varese factory which is now home to Cagiva/MV Agusta. Their first models were 123cc singles – two-strokes, but already possessing the horizontal cylinder which was to become so typical. Overhead valve four-stroke singles followed, both road bikes and the potent Ala D'Oro (Golden wing) production racer from which Alfredo Bianchi designed the 'classic' racing 'Macchi'.

By 1960, Aermacchi was part of Harley-Davidson. As well as continuing development of the four-stroke singles, Varese produced the RR-250 and RR-350 twins ridden by Walter Villa to three consecutive 250cc world titles and one 350cc title etween 1974 and '76. In 1978, the company was sold once more, to Cagiva.

Aermacchi 350

Even during the Sixties, a single-cylinder push-rod machine was an anachronism amongst the exotica crowding grands prix grids, yet the 350, in particular, exploited its fine handling, light weight and slim profile to the full. Its best World Championship performance came in 1966 when the late Renzo Pasolini took third place in the 350cc Grand Prix Championship.

However, it was as a privateer mount that the little 'Macchi' achieved its greatest popularity and success, the precursor of Yamaha's TZ. By the time of its one TT win, in the one-off Historic event of 1984, it had a string of notable performances to its credit. Perhaps the most remarkable came in 1970 when Alan Barnett lapped at a stunning 99.32mph on Syd Lawton's 350, recording well over 40mpg in the process.

Over the years the single was produced with many variations, but the 350's typical power output was around 38bhp at 8,400rpm. Bore and stroke were under-square at 74 x 80mm, although short-stroke and ultra-short-stroke examples followed.

Tiddlers

The 50cc class was run from 1962 until 1968, by which time interest was dwindling. The lap record was raised from 75.52mph (Degner, Suzuki, 1962) to 86.49mph (Bryans, Honda, 1966). The Honda twin (on which the 125-five was based) produced almost 12bhp at 21,000rpm, although when it was first introduced Honda technicians believed its safe rev ceiling was a mere 18,000rpm. Even the 50cc two-strokes spun wildly, the 17,000rpm RK67 Suzuki having a power band so narrow that it needed no fewer than 14 gears. At the time they pulled out of grands prix, Suzuki were working on a 50cc Vee-three, the RP68, which reportedly produced 19.8bhp at 19,000rpm – for many years the highest specific output ever recorded by a normally aspirated internal combustion engine. It was so peaky that its 14 gears were insufficient.

Chapter 4

GREAT RIDERS

Any consideration of great TT riders is necessarily subjective, and I make no claim that this choice of TT greats is in any way definitive. Clearly, it is not enough simply to base such a list on the number of TT wins a rider might have recorded. First, it is undoubtedly true that wins were harder to come by in the early TT years. Prior to 1951, there were only three races per year, compared with six now (and many more than that in some years). Also, competition was undoubtedly stiffer – for both men and machines – during the time the TT was also the British GP.

Then there are men such as Jimmy Simpson, a rare talent who trashed machines and lap records with equal facility, yet recorded only one TT win. His status as a master of a circuit on which lap records are prized more than any other must put him firmly on any list of greats. One might say the same of that singularly unlucky Irishman, Reg Armstrong.

To number amongst the select band a rider had to bring something special to the Isle of Man. Of superstars such as Dunlop, Hailwood and Woods there can be no argument. But Jack Marshall, despite scoring 'only' one win, epitomised the tenacity needed in the races' early years. Howard Davies built – and won on – his own motorcycle when established offerings were not up to stuff. And the likes of Artie Bell and Bill Ivy were simply talents too mercurial to overlook.

However, I have included most riders with three wins or more, but quite a few with less. Sometimes riders scored fewer TT wins than they might have done due to outside circumstances. Eric Oliver, for instance, would surely have won a hatful if the sidecar class had been reintroduced before 1954. Interruptions for two world wars also compromised many riders' racing careers. Then there are men such as Ray Amm, who died before they could make their full mark, as well as others who retired in their prime through injury.

From the earliest years, riders such as Frank Applebee and W. H. 'Harry' Bashall helped create TT history, without numbering amongst the all-time greats. Applebee, who won the 1912 Senior for Scott, took part in the first bike TT on a Rex twin, and continued racing until the First World War. Bashall, also a one-time winner, raced for even longer, 1908–23, and is thus the only man to have raced on all four 'full-length' bike TT circuits: St John's, 'Four Inch', Mountain and 'New' Mountain. With one and two wins respectively, Tim Wood and Eric Williams both won every TT they finished, retiring in the rest.

From recent decades my list omits riders of the calibre of Steve Cull, Mark Farmer, Con Law, Sam McClements, Johnny Rea and Norman Brown (all Irish), Ron Haslam, Trevor Nation, Robert Holden, Mez Mellor, Nick and Tony Jefferies, albeit narrowly. From earlier years you can add a comparable roster of TT talent. Tommy de la Hay, Bill Doran and Manliff Barrington, to name but a few, were all TT stars without quite making the grade as 'great'. From the Sixties, the same can be said of John Hartle, Derek Minter, Stuart Graham, Tommy Robb, Barry Smith and a dozen more besides. Even Rem Fowler, winner in the very first TT, isn't in there (he never again finished higher than 16th).

Even a world grand prix title is no guarantee. No less than 16 riders fail to make the cut despite having won both World Championships and TTs. In the solo classes these include names as illustrious as Dario Ambrosini, Fergus and Hugh Anderson, Dieter Braun, Ralph Bryans, Kel Carruthers, Ernst Degner and Cecil Sandford. In the sidecar classes there are almost as many. Max Deubel, Klaus Enders, Helmut Fath, Fritzes Hillebrand and Scheidegger, Walter Schneider and Rolf Steinhausen all won TTs and world titles. All were great racers, certainly, without quite making the mark as TT greats.

JOEY DUNLOP

1976–2000: 26 TT wins; 5 World F1 titles

Although the duels between Hislop and Fogarty provided some of the finest racing the TT has witnessed, for the last two decades of the 20th century William Joseph Dunlop *was* the TT. Not only was he comfortably the most successful TT racer of all time, but the introverted wee fellow from Ballymoney somehow captured the public's affection like no other rider before or since. He was that sort of guy, a throwback to another age who raced because he loved to, not for fame or money. In his own words, this generous, humble man 'never wanted to be a superstar. I just wanted to be myself and hope people remember me that way.'

Joey's TT career began in 1976 when he brought the Rea Yamsel into 16th place in the Junior, earning a bronze replica. 'He liked riding there, right off', remembers one of his helpers from the time, 'but wondered if he'd ever get to learn it and struggled to get the 100mph lap.' In fact, he managed 102.3mph.

Within a year he was a TT winner, beating George Fogarty in the Schweppes Jubilee Classic. Although this was frankly not against a top-class field, there was nothing second-rate about his fastest lap, 110.93mph on a 750cc Spondon Yamaha. More telling was his performance in the Senior, a solid fourth place on John Rea's 350cc Yamsel.

The next two years were anticlimactic, but in 1980 Joey posted the win which would give him the greatest satisfaction, beating all the factory teams and fancied runners in the Classic TT with a record lap at 115.22mph. Undoubtedly now one of the big boys, he was promptly drafted into the Suzuki squad to shepherd Graeme Crosby to the World F1 crown. However, over the next winter Suzuki somehow let him escape from their grasp, and he signed for Honda instead.

Joey's hugely successful relationship with Honda (and, shortly after, with Arai helmets) would become unique in modern sport.

While his lack of a smooth public persona was not a sponsor's dream, his loyalty and popularity were. He enjoyed a fertile relationship with both companies until his death.

Although he took some time to settle into the Honda squad (and attempts to relocate him in England were a disaster), from 1982 when he brought them the first of five consecutive World F1 titles, and 1983 and his first Honda TT win, it was glory almost all the way. In total Joey clocked up over one fifth of all Honda's 118 TT wins up to the time of his death. Had he not been seriously injured in a crash at Brands Hatch early in '89, causing a four-year barren spell, he would surely have won even more.

In all, Joey scored 26 TT wins including three hat-tricks – the last that fairy-tale triumph in 2000. His six consecutive wins in the one event, the Formula One race, is unparalleled. He also logged four Senior wins, two Juniors, six at 250cc and five at 125cc. During the Eighties he raised the lap record from 114.18mph to almost 119mph. He won in all conditions, and on all types of machine.

As a rider he was brave, canny, tough and breathtakingly precise at fearful speeds on even the bumpiest, narrowest roads. But Joey's greatness also lay in his humility, his kindness and compassion, whether ferrying aid to Rumania or helping some struggling novice in the Cookstown paddock. He always won generously, lost graciously and never stopped being the same genuine bloke from Ballymoney. One of the few things to unite the whole of Ireland during the Troubles was admiration for this one man.

Joey had no time for the trappings of stardom and invariably preferred a pint with his mates to a plaudit. In 1986, his racing success earned him an MBE while a decade later, his heroic efforts for charity brought him the OBE. He was flattered, but hated all the fuss.

Dunlop was killed when he crashed racing near Tallin, Estonia on 2 July 2000. He hit a tree and died instantly when he slid off the same 125cc Honda on which he had won his last TT.

MIKE HAILWOOD

1958–79: 14 TT wins; 76 GP wins*, 9 world titles (plus World F1 title, 1978)

Ask almost any post-war racer to nominate their Number One, and 'Mike the Bike' is it. From his first world title in 1961 to that never-to-be-forgotten TT comeback of 1978, he evoked awe and adulation everywhere he raced. Fast and fearless, he seemed to be equally at home on any track on any type of bike. In total, he competed in over 700 races, of which he won over half.

Yet it is a myth that he was the complete natural. In his first race, riding a factory 203cc MV at Oulton Park, he finished 11th. In fact, the 17-year-old was only competing at all because his millionaire father didn't know what to do with his trouble-prone son. But by 18 he stood on his first World Championship rostrum, winning his first grand prix, the 1959 Ulster, aged 19.

Even when he was at the top, Hailwood loved to give the impression of being the easy-going playboy racer. But those close to him knew better. Allied to a blinding talent was a capacity for hard professional effort and an absolute, Foggy-like hatred of defeat. The late Alan Baker, an old flatmate of Mike, recalled: 'It didn't matter if it was go-karts or table-tennis, he just couldn't stand being beaten. A lovely bloke, but a real tough bastard, too.' On the track he would typically put in more practice than anyone else, often deliberately going off-line – in case he needed to in the race – to find where the bumps and grip were.

Born in Oxford in 1940, Mike first raced the TT in 1958, finishing third on a 250 NSU and taking the Westover Trophy for best newcomer. Two more third places followed in the next two years, on a 125 Ducati and 500 Norton respectively, until he hit the headlines in 1961. Entered by Kings of Oxford, he rode all four solo classes, with factory 125 and 250 Hondas, a 7R AJS and a 500 Manx. In the first race of the week, the Lightweight 125,

---

*TT wins in grand prix classes 50cc, 125cc, 250cc, 350cc and 500cc during the period 1949 to '76 were also GP wins.

he led from start to finish to score his (and Honda's) first TT win. Later the same day he won the 250cc race, when Bob McIntyre's Honda and Gary Hocking's MV both retired at Sulby.

In the Senior, Hailwood also had the luck when early leader Hocking pulled out with a sticking throttle. His win made him the first man to win three races in one week, at just 21 years of age, yet it might so easily have been even better. In the Junior, Hailwood had led throughout until retiring at Milntown on the final lap, handing Phil Read his first win on the Norton. It would be 1996 before anyone did win four TTs in the same week, but by then there were no less than six solo classes to choose from.

Hailwood's list of achievements is almost endless: first man to win three TTs in a week; most grand prix wins in a season (19 in 1966; Agostini equalled this in 1970); first man to win titles in three divisions (later equalled by Phil Read). Only two riders – Hailwood and Redman – have won three races at a single grand prix, and Hailwood managed it five times. In 1967 he came within one point of winning world titles at 250cc, 350cc and 500cc in the same year.

When Honda pulled out of grands prix in 1968, they actually paid Mike not to ride for anyone else, as well as providing him with privateer machines to race in non-championship events. But soon he moved over to four wheels. In Formula One car racing, his best result was a second at Monza in 1971 – good, if not quite in the John Surtees league. In 1973 in South Africa he hauled Clay Reggazoni out of a blazing Ferrari as marshals stood impotently by, a feat which earned him the George Medal. Only a few months later his own car racing career was shattered when he crashed his McLaren at the Nürburgring, seriously damaging a leg.

Although he had made a fleeting return to bikes in 1971, news of 38-year-old Hailwood's planned return to the TT in 1978 was greeted with a mixture of joy and disbelief. Yet, despite the doubts, the fairy tale came true, as he romped to Formula One victory on Steve Wynne's unfancied Ducati. Senior victory a year later took his tally to 14 TT wins.

Hailwood died on 23 March 1981 from injuries sustained in a road accident when returning home from a chip shop in Tamworth-in-Arden. His daughter Michelle was killed in the same accident, although his son David survived.

STEVE HISLOP
1984–94: 11 TT wins

Steve Hislop's Isle of Man career began on a grassy bank during a holiday to the 1983 TT. Spectating at the 11th Milestone, he was awe-struck by the dice between Joey Dunlop and Norman Brown in the Senior Classic race. 'I couldn't believe the speeds … I just had to have a go. So I went behind everyone's back [his brother Gary, a Manx Newcomers' winner in 1982, had recently been killed racing at Silloth], bought an old TZ350 and got a racing licence.'

For the next three years his only interest was racing over the Mountain Course. He debuted in the 1983 Manx Newcomers' event, place-splitting Robert Dunlop and Ian Lougher on the 350cc class rostrum, before tackling the TT the following year. In four races in 1985, he had a best position of tenth.

What would truly set Hislop apart was successfully making the transition from being a complete TT specialist to becoming a world-class short-circuit star, a process which began almost by accident. In 1986, he decided that if he was to go any faster around the Isle of Man, he needed 'more energy, more aggression and more technique' in his riding – qualities he thought short-circuit scratching in the then buoyant F2 series could provide.

Not only did his TT performances soar – his fastest lap went up by over 11mph in two years – but he proved himself an absolute natural on short circuits as well. In 1987, he posted the first of 11 TT wins, in the Formula Two TT on a private 350 Yamaha, a result which brought him to the notice of Honda's Bob McMillan. By 1989 he was a Honda Britain rider.

Armed with quality machinery for the first time, he shot to public prominence by winning three TT races in one week in 1989, recording the first 120mph lap along the way. In 1991, the year he repeated the same treble, he set an unofficial TT lap record that wasn't eclipsed for eight years. Although his stunning Senior triumph for Norton in 1992 was perhaps the most celebrated of his TT wins, his two-week duel with Fogarty in '91 was the most revealing. Riding identical RVF750 Hondas, the duo spent practice week balanced between fear and oblivion – not helped by the death of four other racers. In a furious practice week battle of wills, 'Hizzy' emerged narrowly on top, with that lap at 124.36mph. Nobody would go quicker until Moodie in '99.

Although by this time a Manx resident, Hizzy's attitude to the races became increasingly ambivalent. He elected to sit out the 1993 TT but returned the following year to prove himself once again by far the classiest act of the field. Consummate victories in the Formula One and Senior races gave the Scot 11 career TT wins, overhauling Agostini and another Hawick flier, Jimmy Guthrie, to stand third in the all-time rankings.

On short circuits Steve won the British 250cc Championship (1990) and the British Superbikes series (1995 and 2002), a measly reward for his abundant talent. The 'nearly' list is far longer: World Formula One Championship in '89, three World Endurance Championship near-misses, as well as runner-up slots in domestic racing. 'From a career point of view,' he acknowledged later, 'I probably spent too many years concentrating on the TT. The TT was the making of my career, so obviously it means a lot to me, but I concentrated too much on it for too long.'

He nonetheless came close to returning to the TT in 2001 on the Monstermob Ducati, only for the races to be cancelled because of the Foot and Mouth epidemic. The following year, aged 40 yet still riding at world-class pace, he became British Superbike Champion, but in July 2003 was tragically killed while piloting a helicopter near his home town in the Scottish Borders.

PHILLIP McCALLEN

1989–99: 11 TT wins

Ballymena's Phillip McCallen was always destined to become one of the TT greats. On his debut over the Mountain Course in 1988 he became the first man to win a Newcomers' race and Manx GP in the same week, and was already being picked out by Joey Dunlop as the Irishman most likely to succeed his winning ways. Ironically, Joey's career outlasted the younger man's.

In his first TT in 1989, McCallen had no less than six rides, but in a disappointing week could manage no better than seventh in the Ultra-Lightweight race. The following year brought a best of sixth in the Junior, but 12 months later he began to hit consistent form with a second in the Junior, plus a third, two fourths and one fifth place. To no-one's surprise '92 brought the first – and second – of his 11 wins when he began the week with Formula One victory, followed by a Supersport 600 win.

Following further triumphs in the '93 Senior and '95 Formula One, in 1996 McCallen became the first man ever to win four TTs in one week, doubling his all-time tally of wins in the process. His haul of Formula One, Senior, Junior 600cc and Production garlands may never be equalled, and for good measure he led the 250cc race until his engine lost power, dropping him to fourth place. The following year he returned to the Island and scooped a hat-trick of wins. It was an astonishing run of form: although he never truly threatened the outright lap record, at his peak McCallen seemed invincible.

That 1997 Senior win turned out to be his last. He sat out the '98 event after a crash at Thruxton had left him with damaged vertebrae, and a year later competed while struggling with a painful shoulder injury sustained at Donington Park. Although he bravely reached his customary place atop the Production leaderboard (118.27mph), he struggled to last the race distance and scored a best position of third in the Production TT, his 21st rostrum finish. It was to be his last Island outing (and his only one not on Hondas), for he wisely decided that his battered body had had enough. He is now a successful motorcycle dealer.

JOHN McGUINNESS
1996– : 11 TT wins

Winner of the Newcomers Award on his TT debut in 1996, McGuinness has matured to become the outstanding TT star of the current era. Once a supreme short circuit performer on 250s and Supersport machines, the Morecambe man has harnessed this basic speed to a technical mastery of the Mountain Course. Deceptively easy-going off the bike, his calm manner and smooth, flowing style has turned him into a record-breaking machine, almost untouchable from a standing start. In the 2006 Senior he set a new outright lap record of 129.451mph.

McGuinness's first Island successes came with third place in the Lightweight 250 Races of 1997 and 1998, and 12 months later he won the same event in the year that he became British 250cc Champion. In 2000 he took the Singles race. While he also placed third in the Formula One TT that year, in the larger classes he remained very much in the shadow of his friend David Jefferies, winning only the 2003 Lightweight 400cc race over the following three seasons.

In 2004 he exploded to prominence, taking a Senior/Junior/400cc treble, and with a little more luck might even have racked up an unprecedented six solo wins. Twelve months later he scored a Superbike/Senior double, again for Yamaha. Lured to Honda for 2006's races, he notched his second TT treble with victories in the Superbike, Senior and Junior events to put him level with Hislop, McCallen and Molyneux in the all-time standings.

STANLEY WOODS

1922–39: 10 TT wins

With ten wins from 1923 to '39, Dublin's Stanley Woods was surely the greatest TT racer of the inter-war years, and arguably motorcycle racing's first superstar. In his prime during the Thirties, the top factories literally queued up to get him on board their machines. He raced bikes as diverse as Cotton, DKW, Husqvarna, Moto Guzzi, Norton and Velocette, yet managed to excel – and win – on all bar the Swedish machine. A canny rider, he was probably the first to arrange for signal boards out on the course, from a telephone box on Sulby Straight. Nor was he a slouch racing on dirt or even ice.

Woods first competed aged just 18 in 1922 and showed, if nothing else, how resourceful he was prepared to be. When his Cotton caught fire in the pits he shrugged off the attention of marshals to put out the flames and carried on with barely any brakes to finish fifth. (At the time bikes were refuelled with engines running, a practice which was promptly outlawed.) Within a year he had won his first TT, the Junior, also on a Cotton. Even this was fraught with drama, as he overcame a crash at Ramsey, and a two-minute deficit, to win by the same amount.

In 1926, he moved to Norton, whose CS1 overhead camshaft singles were then becoming a major force. He rewarded them with a Senior TT win at the first attempt, at race-record speed, when Jimmy Simpson's AJS gave out. There followed a relatively lean period for both Norton and Woods, until the development of the machine which would become the Manx. In 1932, and again in '33, he posted Senior/Junior doubles (the first 'double double') for the Bracebridge Street factory. He rode for Husqvarna in 1934, which proved a blank, before he switched again to Moto Guzzi in 1935, giving them their first wins, including a thrilling victory over Guthrie's Norton by a mere four seconds. That Senior/Lightweight double was the first recorded by a foreign marque, and included what would prove to be Woods's sole Lightweight win.

Another switch came in 1936, to DKW and Velocette. Although he posted three record laps – including a Senior record on the 'Junior' 348cc Velocette – victory was not to be. A year later he took a prototype 495cc 'Velo' to second place in the Senior, a feat he repeated in '38. His final two wins came, again Velo-mounted, in the 1938 and '39 Junior events.

Although world war effectively ended his racing career, Woods never quite got the Mountain Circuit out of his system. In 1957 he practiced on a 500cc Guzzi under a reserve plate for 'a bit of fun'. During the Eighties, when he himself was much the same age, this genial and popular racing ambassador rode several classic parades, astonishing onlookers by lapping almost as fast as he had in his prime.

Woods started in 37 TT races, of which he finished 21, recording 11 fastest or record laps along the way. In total he scored ten wins – comfortably more than any other rider until Mike Hailwood came along – three second places and one third. He won two races in a week on three occasions – also unprecedented. Had Velocette possessed a competitive 500 during the late Thirties, his record might well have been even better. Woods died of natural causes on 28 July 1993, aged 90.

GIACOMO AGOSTINI
1965–72: 10 TT wins; 122 GP wins*, 15 world titles

Agostini was as precocious as compatriots Rossi and Melandri were more recently. Some observers are quick to dismiss the most successful grand prix racer of all time because, for much of his career, his bikes were so much better than all the rest. They weren't around when the Brescia rider hit the racing scene like a tornado. 'When he took the Italian title from Provini', remarked one eye-witness, 'he was just a kid but smashed records everywhere he went. He was unbelievably, horrendously quick. He looked like an accident waiting to happen but when he stayed on, boy was he fast.'

After taking that 250cc title in 1964, 22-year-old 'Ago' was signed to ride as Hailwood's 'apprentice' in the MV team of 1965. He took four GP wins that year, to the maestro's ten. Then, when Hailwood moved to Honda for '66, spectators were treated to one of the greatest head-to-heads ever, as the pupil beat his former master to take the 500cc world crown, with positions reversed in the 350cc class. The same fabulous Ago v Hailwood duel, and outcome, was repeated in '67.

His Isle of Man career began less auspiciously, with a 75mph first practice lap in the wet in 1965. Later that week he finished third behind Redman and Read in the Junior, when team-mate Hailwood retired. In the same event one year later he scored his first Mountain Course win on the new MV triple when Hailwood, now with Honda, pulled out at Bishopscourt. In all, Ago started in just 16 TT races, all for MV, of which he won ten and retired three times. He posted Senior/Junior doubles four times, in 1968, '69, '70 and '72.

Although many of his 15 world titles were achieved against inferior opposition, Ago showed his true mettle after losing his 500cc title to Phil Read in 1973 and moving to Yamaha. A 350cc title in 1974 and the Japanese factory's first 500cc title in '75 proved all the doubters wrong. By this time Ago had long since abandoned the TT, after the death of his close friend Gilberto Parlotti at the Verandah in atrocious conditions in 1972. His boycott gave impetus to the movement to remove the TT from the grand prix calendar. Although this made him a controversial and an unpopular figure to many in the TT community, when he returned to ride a parade lap in 2002, he was warmly welcomed.

DAVID JEFFERIES
1996–2003, 9 TT wins

In just a few short years 'DJ' soared above all-comers to become indisputably the modern master of the Mountain Course. Yet remarkably, he might never have raced there at all. 'I always said I'd never come here – you had to be a nutter to race at this place. But my dad reckoned my style would suit the place, and after a few good results at the North-West and Scarborough, I decided to give it a try.'

And what a try. After the best part of a decade in which the outright lap record seemed inviolable, it took Jefferies only three TTs before he unleashed a blistering onslaught on almost every statistic in the books. His TT career began with the Newcomers' trophy in 1996, and a brace of fourth places two years later, after he had sat out '97 injured.

Then came the fireworks: 1999, a treble – Formula One, Production and Senior; 2000, another treble – Junior, Production and Senior. In 2002, on the way to recording a unique triple treble, he began by becoming the first rider to dip under 18 minutes and ended with that staggering Senior lap at 127.49mph. As mercurial in its way was a lap at 124.31mph on a proddy bike, in the 2002 1,000cc Production race. Not bad for a man who claimed still to be learning the Mountain Circuit.

As impressive as those records are, the manner of their achievement was equally beguiling. DJ's sheer enthusiasm at riding the TT course was transparent. 'I learn tracks pretty quick', he said during that final treble, 'and really enjoy riding ordinary road bikes on public roads, so this place really suits me. And it's awesome. Like at Bishopscourt, where you hit top gear and it just comes up on the back wheel. You just don't get that feeling at any other circuit.'

Although he raced at the top level in World Championship grands prix and World Superbike events, DJ's size and bulk – he stood 6ft 2in and weighed in at 14 stone – were always against him. Nonetheless, he scored a number of successes in British championships, notably in 1996 when he took both the British Powerbike Production and the Triumph Speed Triple titles. In 2001, he added the British Superstock Championship to his tally.

Invariably breezy and cheerful, to TT fans DJ's appeal was his lack of star ego. He was a down-to-earth bloke who loved riding motorcycles, just like them. His death after crashing at Crosby Corner during practice for the 2003 races cast a pall over all of racing.

PHIL READ

1961–79: 8 TT wins; 52 GP wins; 7 world titles (plus World F1 title, 1977)

'Pilli Riddi', as a Finnish commentator named him at Imatra in 1974, was possibly not TT fans' favourite racer, but a peerless talent, nonetheless. Only five riders have won more grands prix than his 52. His successful defence of the 500cc world title for MV in 1974 – the last by any four-stroke until the GP1 formula – ranks as one of the most heroic feats of any era. Even in '76, with Sheene and the RG500 in the ascendancy, he posted wins at Brno and Spa – two wickedly fast and hairy old-style road circuits. Whatever his critics might allege, Read had no shortage of bottle.

The Luton man's TT career was equally mercurial. After winning the 1960 Senior Manx Grand Prix aged 21, he scored a debut TT win on a 350cc Manx just nine months later, by a margin of no less than 1½ minutes. The following three years were surprisingly lean, with only a second place on a 7R AJS and third on a Gilera brought out of retirement. Then, in 1964 he joined Yamaha. Despite his unfamiliarity with two-strokes, in his first season he won no less than seven 250cc grands prix and one 125cc, the latter being Yamaha's first win on the Island. As a Yamaha factory rider, and later as one of racing's most successful privateers, he scored a further two 125cc Ultra-Lightweight and two 250cc TT wins, before quitting the TT under a cloud of controversy in 1973.

In 1977, Read made an equally controversial return to the races he had declared too dangerous, winning the Senior and Formula

One events – despite being pelted with stones by irate spectators during practice, and crashing at Brandish on open roads while scrubbing in tyres. In his last TT, 1978, he played baddy to Hailwood's good guy, a swansong that did his prodigious talent less than justice. Now in his late-60s, Read is still a regular and stylish rider in classic parades, notably on the glorious MV.

CHARLIE WILLIAMS
1971–84; 8 TT wins; 3 GP wins*

Born almost within earshot of Oulton Park in Tarporley, Cheshire in 1950, and 'obsessed with bikes' from an early age, Charlie Williams finished fifth in the 1970 Junior MGP on his Isle of Man debut, also taking the Newcomers' award. In 1971, his very first TT appearance brought a remarkable second place on a YDS7 Yamaha in the 250cc Production class to fellow Castrian, Bill Smith. Three months later he was back, winning the Lightweight Manx Grand Prix on a TD2B. In the 1972 TT he finished in five races, including two second places. In the Junior he lay third behind Agostini and Phil Read (between them, the reigning World 250cc, 350cc and 500cc Champions). When Read retired at the 33rd, Williams 'got a bit over-exuberant' and slid off at the Creg. But within a year, he had posted his first win, in the 1973 Lightweight 250cc TT. Over the next seven years he recorded further wins at Lightweight 250cc, Junior (2), Junior 250 (2), Production 250 and Formula Two, all on Yamahas, as well as a Production race class win and 19 other rostrum placings.

Williams's lap on a 'not particularly fast' TZ350 at 112.34mph in the 1979 Senior stands out as one of the finest Island laps of all time, for no 350 went quicker for another decade. If there was a major omission in his TT cv, it was in never winning the Senior, largely through the self-imposed handicap of preferring Yamaha twins. On one of the few occasions he had a competitive 500 – an ex-Boet van Dulman factory Yamaha – he was leading by almost two minutes when the mainshaft snapped and locked the rear wheel at Ballacrye. 'CW' last contested the TT in 1984, placing second in the Senior, although he had been semi-retired for a couple of years before.

Away from the Island, Williams was always a force on the 'shorts', no more so than in the World Endurance series. He won at Spa with his Cheshire buddy John Williams in 1973, at Barcelona and Zandvoort with Stan Woods in '76, and at the daunting Nürburgring one year later. He now runs a motorcycle accessory shop, 'Everything but Bikes', as well as working as a TT radio commentator during race fortnight.

JIM MOODIE
1988– : 8 TT wins

Jim Moodie's Island career took a while to get rolling, but he has since established himself as one of the TT's leading lights. He began inauspiciously with 37th place in the 1988 Production 'C' race, faring even worse a year later with a solitary DNF. Although he placed third in the 1991 Supersport 400 event, the organisers evidently had a low opinion of his talent, for in '93 they seeded the fiery Glaswegian to start 24th in the Supersport 600 TT and an absurd 63rd in the Junior. To the relief of most of the riders ahead of him, officials eventually relented, allowing Moodie to start nearer the head of the field and take a unique Supersport 400/600 double.

Twelve months later, Moodie bagged a second double, this time in the Singles and Supersport 400 races (his Singles and 400 lap and race records still stand). After sitting out the races in '95, he returned with another Singles win in '96, second place in the '97 Senior and victory in the Production race of 1998.

In 1999, he rode for Honda Britain and, with a little luck, he could have posted three or even four TT wins. Yet he had to battle heroically to manage even one, in the Junior. In the Formula One his RC45, fastest in practice at over 120mph, expired at Glen Lough with ignition problems. His wretched luck continued when his 250 retired with a faulty slick-shift. Then, in the Senior he beat Fogarty's 1992 mark to set a lap record of 124.45mph from a standing start, only to retire at Ballig on lap 2 with his rear tyre falling apart. Twelve months later, this notoriously gutsy and outspoken rider was controversially sacked by Honda in the middle of race week. His eighth and last win came on a V&M Yamaha in the Junior TT of 2002, at an average speed of 119.22mph.

MICK GRANT
1970–85: 7 TT wins; 3 GP wins*

In 1975, Mick Grant was the man who finally broke Hailwood's 1967 record, with a lap at 109.82mph on the second lap of the final race of the week, the six-lap Classic. Although that race ended in retirement, Grant had already won the Senior earlier in the week. From then on, until Joey Dunlop came into his prime in the early Eighties, Grant would be the man to beat in the larger classes of any TT. Yet the way his Isle of Man career began – flat last in the 1969 Manx Grand Prix on a Velocette – must be an encouragement to all other racers.

Although the Wakefield rider raced private Yamaha twins, factory Honda and Suzuki fours and British kit, and first won in 1974 on Triumph's famous *Slippery Sam* production machine, he is probably best remembered for battling the awesome Kawasaki KR750 two-stroke around the Mountain Course. In '78 the 120bhp triple was speed trapped at 190mph – a reading as sensational as it probably was wrong. After that, the 'gritty Yorkshireman' – actually a former art student – went from strength to strength, winning a total of seven TTs on four different makes of machine. He also won two overseas grands prix, at Assen and Anderstorp in 1977, both on the 250cc tandem twin Kawasaki on which Kork Ballington would win his world titles. His final TT win came in '85 on the new GSX-

R750 Suzuki, in the same class as his first, 750cc Production. He retired the same year and has since been mainly involved in race team management.

IAN LOUGHER
1984– : 7 TT wins

Lougher, from Rhoose in Glamorgan, first raced at Llandow in 1982 and little more than a year later was riding in the Manx Grand Prix. In the 350cc class of the Newcomers' event, he placed third behind Robert Dunlop and Steve Hislop. The following June, riding a G50 Matchless, he finished second to Dave Roper in the 500 Historic Race. The rest of the Eighties saw him struggle with shoestring budgets and poor machinery, bringing a best position of second in the 1989 Ultra-Lightweight TT.

In 1990, on competitive kit at last, 'Lucky' triumphed in one of the closest races ever when he set new lap and race records to win the Lightweight 250 race from Steve Hislop. Yet still support didn't come, leaving Lougher 'struggling for sponsors and racing second rate bikes. The temptation then is always to ride too hard, which always slows you down on the Island where you've really got to flow. I didn't really get good equipment again until 1996 … when I did, the results started to come again.'

That was in 1996 when he won the 750cc class of the Production TT, plus the Ultra-Lightweight race with new lap and race records. Another win came in 1999, again on the 125cc Honda. Riding as Dave Jefferies's team-mate in the TAS Suzuki squad in 2002 brought the Dromore-based rider's best TT to date, with a brace of wins and three second places, including an astounding 120mph lap on the Production GSX-R600. Along the way he once and for all laid the notion that he couldn't hack it on big bikes, lapping at over 125mph on the GSX-R1000. Twice a winner of the prestigious Duke Road Race Rankings title, his last win came in the 2005 Supersport Junior 'A' race, at a then record 120.928mph.

TONY RUTTER

1965–91: 7 TT wins; 2 GP wins*

Impeccably neat and smooth, 'TR', as his helmet design announced, was a master of road circuits, both on the Isle of Man and elsewhere. During a TT career which spanned over 25 years the Brierly Hill rider won seven TTs, with a further 11 rostrum places. His maiden win came in the Junior race of 1973, by which time he was already a veteran of 31. He would win the same event in 1974 and '76, the latter with a fastest lap of 108.69mph, finally removing Hailwood's 1967 mark from the record books.

Those first three wins were all on Yamaha two-strokes, on which he was singularly adept. Yet Rutter is best remembered as the man who kept Ducati on the international racing map, through his exploits in the TT Formula Two World Championship. As well as winning the F2 TT races of 1981, '82, '83 and '85, he wrapped up four World F2 titles for the Italian factory during some of their most difficult years. Sadly, his winning ways were cut short just weeks after that final TT win at a pile-up at Barcelona's Montjuich Park. Although he made a partial recovery from serious head and leg injuries and returned to contest the TT in 1987, he would never regain his previous form. Tony's son, Michael, is one of British racing's present day stars.

CHAS MORTIMER

1968–84: 7 TT wins; 7 GP wins*

Born in London in 1949 and the son of a famous Brooklands racing father, Chas Mortimer, was a tough competitor who belied his well-bred origins. Like his contemporary, Charlie Williams, he was at his best on 250cc and 350cc machines, both on the Isle of Man and in overseas grands prix. Although his first TT success came on a four-stroke Ducati, his career was synonymous with Yamaha TZ twins.

Mortimer contested the MGP from 1966 to '68. His first TT win came on a 250cc Ducati in the 1970 Production race, the same event in which he had placed eighth on debut two years before. In 1971, and again in '72, he took 125cc Lightweight honours, both for Yamaha. A Lightweight 250 win came in 1975, plus three other rostrum finishes. Twelve months later he scored a Junior/Production double on a TZ350 and RD250 respectively. His final TT win, in 1978 was also in the Junior race.

As well as his four Isle of Man GP wins, Mortimer also won at Montjuich Park, Jarama and Opatija, the first of these being in the 500cc class. After retiring he went on to race team management and is now frequently seen riding at classic events.

JIMMY GUTHRIE
1923–37: 6 TT wins

Hailing from Hawick, just a few miles from Steve Hislop's home town, Jimmy Guthrie was a contemporary of Jimmy Simpson who certainly did know how to win. During the Thirties, he became one of the giants of TT racing, close to the great Stanley Woods in commitment and talent. Yet his Isle of Man career began haltingly, with an unremarkable ride on a Matchless in the 1923 event. It would be four years before the Scot would return, finishing second on a New Hudson in the Senior. From then on he was a TT regular, posting his first win on an AJS in the Lightweight race of 1930.

From that point on it was solid Norton, for whom he posted Junior wins in 1934, '35 and '37, and Senior wins in '34 and '36. His 1934 double made him only the third rider to win two races in one week.

Jimmy died at the Sachsenring circuit just a few weeks after that final TT win. While leading the German Grand Prix by some distance, he unaccountably crashed within a mile of the finish, dying of his injuries shortly after. The Mountain Course corner named after him is probably the most scenic anywhere in world racing. Formerly called 'The Cutting', the Guthrie Memorial was erected at the site of his retirement in his final TT race, the 1937 Senior. On a clear day, it is possible to see his native Scotland from this lofty position.

GEOFF DUKE
1949–59: 6 TT wins; 33 GP wins*, 6 World titles

As a rider Geoff Duke was renowned for his immaculate neatness and precision, but his contribution to bike racing's image was at least as pronounced. Long before Barry Sheene came to prominence, Duke was the original pin-up racer, the first man to lift motorcycle sport to national prominence. In the grey days of post-war rationing, national newspapers added colour with tales of his exploits.

Born in St Helens in March 1923, Duke was already a skilled scrambles and trials rider when he made his road racing debut at the 1948 Manx Grand Prix. That year he retired with a split oil tank, but was irrepressible in '49, winning the Senior races in both the Clubman's TT and Manx GP. Within a year he had become a factory Norton rider and won his first TT, the Senior, by fully 2 minutes 40 seconds, to finish runner-up in both the 350cc and 500cc World Championships behind Bob Foster's Velocette and Umberto Masetti's Gilera. Along the way he had discovered that the factory's financial tightness was not restricted to R&D. 'The prize money for winning the 1950 Senior was £200 – which Norton kept because it cost so much to get to the Isle of Man. But eventually I got a better deal out of them.'

Duke more than made up for that disappointment by becoming the first man to take two world titles in a single year, in 1951. He retained the 350 crown in '52, but his Norton single was outpaced in the bigger class and in 1953, after dabbling with car racing for Aston Martin, he moved to Gilera and the fabulous dohc 500-Four.

Under race boss Joe Craig, Norton had earned a hard-nosed reputation which was easier to respect than like. Gilera was a far more homely and sympathetic set-up, quite apart from the relative merits of its kit. 'After two disappointments [one crash, one race blighted by weather] it was great to get that first win for them in '55. The Gilera was a superb bike, especially after they redesigned it in 1954. It was the only bike I rode [in the TT] which didn't really need a steering damper – so we took it off to save weight.' Duke and the Gilera was the perfect pairing, bringing a hat-trick of 500cc world titles.

Titles certainly did not elude the Master, but one landmark did. In the 1955 Senior TT he came agonisingly close to recording the first 100mph TT lap when timekeepers 'rounded down' the speed to a tantalising 99.97mph. Less than a month earlier, at the North-West 200, he had come even closer to the same milestone with a lap at 99.98mph.

Duke's last world title was to be in 1955, not least because he was banned for the first half of the 1956 season for supporting a privateer's strike at the 1955 Dutch TT. (He whiled away the TT as a travelling marshal.) He appeared to withdraw from full-time competition, but returned to the TT in 1958 riding a Junior Norton and Senior BMW, retiring in both events. His last TT was in 1959, when he placed fourth in the Junior, before retiring, aged 36.

Yet, with six wins in just 13 TT starts, six World Championships and the 1951 BBC 'Sportsman of the Year' award, Geoff Duke was an utter natural who became British racing's first pin-up – perhaps partly on account of his 'invention' of tight-fitting one-piece leathers. 'After the war,' he recalls, 'there was such euphoria about having racing back – and really that's carried on ever since.' Duke, now in his mid-80s, lives at Greeba, not far from the TT course and continues to take a keen interest in racing.

JOHN SURTEES
1954–60: 6 TT wins; 38 GP wins*, 7 world titles

It is fashionable now to think that British racers need time to mature into stars, where Italians seem to produce winners almost from the womb. But by the time John Surtees won his first world crown (and TT race) at age 22, he was already a precocious force.

More aloof and less feted than Duke, his predecessor as World Champion, Surtees was one of the most meteoric talents Britain has ever produced. Born in Tatsfield, Kent in 1934, he began racing at Thruxton on a Vincent Grey Flash, aged 17 (he was apprenticed to Vincent at the time). The bike wasn't very competitive, but its rider certainly was, for later in the year he placed a close second to Duke at the same circuit. After a switch to private Nortons, he became the original 'King of Brands'.

Inevitably, it wasn't long before he was snapped up by the Norton factory, but had to sit out the 1953 TT after crashing a 125 in practice. The following year proved equally disappointing, 11th and 15th in Junior and Senior respectively. But one year later he was almost unbeatable.

In 1955, riding Nortons and a 250cc NSU, Surtees won an astonishing 65 races out of 72 starts, including beating the Gilera of World Champion Geoff Duke at Silverstone. When MV offered him a works ride for '56, it was their good fortune to have recruited not only a hugely talented rider, but also a racing technician who was way ahead of his time. He brought to the team the sort of single-minded perfectionism later generations would associate with Kenny Roberts and Mick Doohan.

As a rider, Surtees was (and, amazingly, still is) breathtakingly fast, the man credited with pioneering high-speed drift. He brought MV their first 500cc title in '56 with wins in every race he started before breaking his arm in Germany, including victory in the Senior TT. The following year, when his arm proved slow to heal, he fought doggedly but in vain to retain his title. But the setback was temporary. From 1958 to '60 he won three 350/500cc doubles, most by massive margins. At the TT his results were just as emphatic, winning two Seniors and three Juniors in the same three-year spell. Altogether he rode in 15 TT races, finishing in all save the '56 Junior. In winning the 1960

Senior TT, Surtees averaged 102.44mph, the first 100mph race average. Two months later, at the Ulster GP – then a World Championship event – he lost 3½ minutes fixing a broken gear lever in the pits. Riding consistently at 3mph above lap-record pace, he came second, just yards behind John Hartle's MV.

After winning practically everything two wheels had to offer, Surtees made the move that made him unique in the racing world. Barely one month after winning his last Senior TT, he placed second at the Silverstone car GP to Jack Brabham. After spells with Cooper and Lola, he joined Ferrari in 1963, bringing them the world crown one year later.

In 1979, almost two decades after his last TT lap, Surtees returned to the Island for the Millennium parade. Riding a 500cc MV Agusta, he averaged 95mph from a standing start. Class, as they say, is permanent.

JIM REDMAN
1958–66: 6 TT wins; 45 GP wins*; 6 world titles

Born in Hampstead, London in 1931, Redman emigrated to Rhodesia following the Second World War, where he later began racing. After becoming South African 350cc Champion in 1957, he spent the rest of the year scraping together £1,500 which he had been told 'was enough for a season in Europe – if you didn't eat. By the time we'd bought a van and stocked up with spares, we arrived at Brands Hatch for our first meeting with £50 left.' In other words, he just had to do well – and did – with that special brand of single-mindedness that seems to characterise overseas competitors. Three seasons later injuries to regular rider Tom Phillis gave him an opening in the Honda factory team, and he would go on to win 45 grands prix for them, more than any other rider until Mick Doohan came along.

By 1962, Redman was Honda's leading 250cc and 350cc rider, winning both titles that year and again in '63. Two more 350cc titles followed, along with six TT wins – all 250/350cc doubles, in successive years, 1963–65. Of the Mountain Circuit, he has the same ambivalence of many who survived the Sixties. 'I'd have loved to race the TT as a privateer, but as a works rider there was so much pressure to be fast,' he recalls. The pressure came from the presence on every grid of at least half a dozen factory teams, all pushing the frontiers of technology to put their hardware foremost in the public eye. At the time they called Jim the 'Iron Man'. Tough as old boots, fast, tricky and ruthless, a real hard competitor. But inside, he quivered just like everyone else.

Redman's racing career ended in 1966 following a 125mph crash in the wet at Spa, ironically a circuit on which he was the acknowledged master, when a badly damaged wrist was slow to heal. A successful businessman, he is still active in motorcycling, particularly parading classic racing Hondas.

BRUCE ANSTEY
1996– : 5 TT wins

New Zealander Anstey debuted in the same year as McGuinness, and is the rider who consistently pushes the Lancastrian hardest. One of the most laid-back men in the paddock, as a rider he's totally committed, sometimes looks wild, but has the reputation amongst his peers of being safe and in control.

In 2000 he placed second to Joey Dunlop in the 250cc event, winning the same (rather undersubscribed) race two years later. True success followed with his fairy-tale victory for Triumph in the 2003 Junior race, and the following year he moved to the top-flight TAS Suzuki squad. In successive seasons since then he has taken wins in the Production 1000 and two Superstock races. If his Superbike/Senior performances had never quite matched his heroics on more production-spec machinery, that changed in 2006 when he became only the second man to lap at over 129mph, taking third place after a slow start. Other than emerging talents like Guy Martin, Ian Hutchinson, Cameron Donald and Martin Finnegan, he remains McGuinness's chief rival for major honours.

ALEC BENNETT
1921–32: 5 TT wins

An Irish-Canadian born in Craigantlet, Bennett's was one of the more colourful racing careers of his era. He first came to Britain with the Canadian Army during the First World War, serving as a despatch rider and later a fighter pilot. In his first TT, 1921, he placed fourth on a Sunbeam. His first win came in the Senior 12 months later, also Sunbeam-mounted. In 1924, he rode Nortons, again taking the Senior, in what proved to be the first race won at over 60mph. A further Norton Senior win in 1927, sandwiched between Junior victories for Velocette in '26 and '28, brought his total to what was then a record five TT wins.

Bennett also starred in many Continental grands prix during the Twenties, as well as earning a gold medal as part of the 1923 British ISDT team. He retired from racing in 1929 but made a brief 'holiday' comeback in 1932 when he placed eighth in the Junior event.

CARLO UBBIALI
1950–60: 5 TT wins; 39 GP wins*, 9 world titles

Born in Bergamo in 1929, the little Italian maestro was by any standards a classy, fearless rider of road circuits (and a pretty capable off-road competitor, holder of an ISDT gold medal). Ubbiali's racing career began with MV in 1949, after which he spent two years with Mondial before returning to Count Agusta's fold. His first grand prix win came at the age of 20 in the 1950 125cc Ulster event, and throughout much of the Fifties he was the man to beat in the 125cc and 250cc divisions.

Ubbiali's first TT win came in the 1955 Lightweight 125cc race. A year later he became the first rider from outside the British Isles to post a TT double in taking both 125cc and 250cc honours. In total, he won nine world titles and 39 grands prix, five of which were TT wins. In 13 TT starts, he placed second six times, fifth once, and retired once.

BRIAN REID
1981–94: 5 TT wins

Another quiet Irishman, happy to let his speed do the talking, Dromore's Brian Reid was a specialist in the lighter classes, never happier than when piloting a two-stroke twin at prodigious speed. Although often plagued by unreliable machinery, and noted for riding hard only when completely happy with his bike, for a decade from 1984, if he finished at all, it was generally in a rostrum place.

His Island career began with the 1978 MGP, culminating in second place in the 1980 Senior, before graduating to the TT in 1981. In his second year, 1982, he placed fourth in the Junior, and while the following year brought three DNFs in three rides, by '84 he was a consistent leaderboard rider. His first win came in the 1986 Formula Two race, which he led throughout at race and lap-record speeds. Later in the week he crashed out of the Junior at Ballaugh.

After a succession of disappointing meetings, his second win did not come until the 1990 Supersport 600 TT, followed by yet another year with three retirements in three rides. However, in 1992 he scored his one double, taking Loctite Yamahas to victory in the Supersport 400 and Junior 250 races. His final win came a year later, again in the Junior. In his final outing in 1994 he had one DNF and a second place on the McAdoo Yamaha in the

Junior. Shortly after, he suffered serious arm and leg injuries at the Temple 100 meeting, ending his racing career.

ROBERT DUNLOP
1984–2004: 5 TT wins

Youngest brother to Joey, Robert Dunlop never considered himself a natural motorcycle racer, yet he has established himself as one of the most consistent – and gutsy – riders of recent decades. After a winning debut in the 1983 MGP Newcomers' race, he first rode the TT in 1984, finishing 12th and 14th in the Classic and Senior races. His first win – indeed his first rostrum position, came in the 1989 Ultra-Lightweight race. Twelve months later he repeated that win, also placing third on the JPS Norton in the Formula One TT.

An Ultra-Lightweight/Junior double was secured in 1991. After two more years of solid finishes, Robert's career seemed to end with a sickening crash into a wall at Ballaugh when the rear wheel of his Honda collapsed. Gravely injured and unable to ride for several years, he next competed in 1997 and, despite being barely able to use one arm, placed third in the 125cc TT. In the same event 12 months later, riding with a shin and collarbone broken at the NW200, he had to hobble to his Honda on crutches before storming to his fourth Ultra-Lightweight win on a tricky, drying track. Not surprisingly, the wee man from Ballymoney described this as his 'best TT win, ever. When I was lying in the road at the North-West 200 I didn't think I'd be riding here.' In 2004, his last race before the axing of the 125cc class effectively ended his TT career, he placed an emotional second.

WAL HANDLEY
1922–33: 4 TT wins

Wal Handley, 'the man who couldn't be frightened', began his TT career as a precocious 18-year-old in the 1922 TT. His first experience, however, was unpromising. For his very first practice outing he pointed his OK-Supreme in the wrong direction – turning right on to Glencrutchery Road and roaring flat-out through the mist. 'The marshals fairly danced about the road waving flags at me', he later recalled, 'and the papers were very nasty about my lapse.' 'Comedy of Novice from Birmingham' was what they actually wrote.

'I decided I'd have to show them something,' decided young Wal, and within a week the tough young Brummie was showing his true mettle, adding no less than 5mph to the Lightweight lap record at 51mph on his Blackburne-engined OK-Supreme. A year later he lapped almost 3mph faster, yet still victory eluded him. Success only came when he signed for Rex-Acme a few weeks later, for whom he romped to victory in both the Belgian and Ulster grands prix.

Wal was to earn all three of Rex's TT wins, beginning with the first ever TT double in the Ultra-Lightweight and Junior events of 1925. The following year proved a heroic disappointment when he lost several minutes in the pits on the 500cc Vee-twin Rex, yet still managed second place. Twelve months later he scored a Lightweight win. His final triumph came in the 1930 Senior when he took a 500cc Rudge to Senior victory. Until Mike Hailwood equalled the feat in 1962, this made him the only man to win in all four classic classes: Senior, Junior, Lightweight and Ultra-Lightweight.

Renowned as a tough loner, Wal switched to car racing after breaking his leg in 1933 at the bend which now bears his name, the fearsome, fast left-right chicane after the 11th Milestone. Unsurprisingly, this didn't stop him crashing on the Isle of Man, for he managed to write off a lamp-post in Douglas during the 1934 'Round the Houses' car race. Ironically, he survived all this only to die while serving as a ferry pilot in the Second World War when his Bell Airacobra crashed just after take-off near Carlisle.

FREDDIE FRITH

1936–49: 4 TT wins; 5 GP wins*; 1 world title

Freddie Frith will go down in history as the winner of the 350cc World Road Race Championship in its maiden year, 1949. In total, he won four TT races (plus one MGP), but had it not been for an enforced seven-year lay off due to the Second World War, his achievements might have been so much greater.

His Isle of Man career began in 1930 with the Manx Grand Prix. Victory in the Lightweight Manx in 1935 earned him a Norton factory ride the following year. He did not disappoint his new bosses, becoming the first rider for over a decade to win a TT – the Junior – at the first attempt, also posting a record lap and the first 80mph average race speed. For good measure he placed third in the Senior, behind the illustrious duo of Guthrie and Woods, before scoring a brilliant win in the same race in 1937 during which he set the first 90mph lap over the Mountain Course. In his final pre-war race, the 1939 Senior, he placed third.

Frith's post-war racing got off to the worst of all starts when a practice crash on a Guzzi sidelined him from the 1947 races. He then switched to Velocette, winning back-to-back Juniors over the following two years. After winning the world title Frith retired, aged 40, opening a motorcycle shop in his native Grimsby which, although it no longer exists, continued trading into the 1990s. Of his world title he said that 'the TT was the Blue Riband of racing … worth more than a World Championship to people in the sport.'

TARQUINIO PROVINI

1955–66: 4 TT wins; 20 GP wins*; 2 world titles

Born in Roveleto, Italy in 1933, Provini was one of the classiest riders of his era. Intelligent and easy to work with, he rode Italian machines exclusively, initially Mondial, for whom he brought the 1957 125cc world title. In 1958 he switched to MV, taking the

250cc Championship. After 1959 Count Agusta withdrew from the smaller classes and Provini declined the offer of a 500, preferring to move to Morini, where in his best year, 1963, he recorded four grands prix wins. The following year found him mounted on 250cc four-cylinder Benellis.

In all, the little Italian contested a round dozen TT races. His four wins, including a 125/250cc double in 1957, all came on the Clypse Circuit. His best result over the Mountain Circuit was third place on a Morini in the 1960 Lightweight 250cc class. His final TT appearance came in 1966 when injuries sustained in a crash near Alpine Cottage ended his racing career.

JOHN WILLIAMS
1968–78: 4 TT wins; 1 GP win

Born in Liverpool in 1946, Williams debuted on a Matchless Metisse in the 1968 Senior TT, placing 11th. His first win came three years later when his 500cc Honda led the Production event from flag to flag, a result he repeated 12 months later on a 250cc Honda. In the same year he battled heroically to split the MVs of Agostini and Pagani for much of the race, only to break down on the final lap. His 1974 campaign saw him sidelined by a huge practice crash near Kerrowmoar, but he scored a full house of rostrum places in 1975, including his first big win in the Classic 1000 TT on the 750cc TZ Yamaha.

Williams's reward was a berth in the Suzuki grand prix squad for 1976, the year in which he blew apart the old lap records. Although his fastest lap in winning the Classic 1000 was marginally behind Hailwood's old mark, in the Senior he took speeds into a new realm with 112.27mph – the first 110mph lap, and by some margin. However, his Suzuki stalled almost within sight of the flag, and while he pushed in to an exhausted seventh place, Tom Herron took the winner's laurels. In the same year, Williams recorded his sole grand prix win, at Spa.

After a disappointing 1977 TT, Williams returned to finish second to Hailwood in that fairy-tale Formula One TT of '78, a result he repeated behind Mick Grant's Kawasaki in the Classic 1000 race. Little more than two months later he was dead, killed at the Ulster GP, aged 32 years.

DAVE LEACH
1985–97: 4 TT wins

Leach hailed from Halifax, but became an adopted Irishman later in his career after falling out with the ACU. An engaging character mysteriously known as 'Fred' to the locals, during his road racing heyday he was second in popularity only to Joey Dunlop. Like Geoff Johnson he achieved his best success on production-based machines, although given the chance he was equally fast on lightweight two-strokes. No rider ever lapped a TZ350 faster than Fred.

His four wins came in the 1988 and '89 Production 1,300cc events (the latter by a mere 0.8 seconds from Geoff Johnson), and the Supersport 400 races of 1990 and '91. In 1989, riding an OW01 Yamaha, he set a 750cc Production lap record of 116.91mph which would stand for almost a decade. Leach was gravely injured in a crash in Ireland during 1992 and although he hobbled back to the TT in 1995, he was never the force he had been.

ADRIAN ARCHIBALD
1997– : 3 TT wins

Another product of Ballymoney, 'Scratch' Archibald took over from the late David Jefferies as the mainstay of the TAS Suzuki squad, for which he scored all of his three TT wins. At his best he is supremely fast and safe, but can be inconsistent and invariably struggles to dial-in his best pace on the opening lap, by which time the likes of McGuinness are usually well in control.

Archibald first raced over the Mountain in the 1995 MGP and a year later placed second in both the Junior and Senior races in the same meeting, averaging over 115mph in the latter. His first TT success came with second place in the 2000 Junior, with a new class lap record of 121.15mph.

As a TAS Suzuki rider, he emerged from the tragedy of losing team-mate Jefferies in 2003 with an emotional Formula One/Senior double. The following year he took a slightly fortunate Senior win – and the lucrative Joey Dunlop trophy for the second year running. In 2005 he placed second in the Superbike TT and was desperately unlucky not to win the Superstock race when he ran out of fuel, but was dropped by the team at season's end. Hurriedly drafted back into TAS Suzuki when his replacement Ryan Farquhar was injured, he had an oddly lacklustre 2006 TT.

HAROLD DANIELL
1934–50: 3 TT wins; 1 GP win*

Daniell was the bespectacled little Londoner who resembled a bank clerk far more than a death-defying TT racer. Indeed, during the Second World War, he was turned down as an Army despatch rider on account of poor eyesight, serving instead in 'Dad's Army', the Home Guard.

Daniell was a regular MGP competitor before attempting the TT, winning the 1933 Senior Manx. A year later he rode AJS machines in his first TT, retiring in the Junior and placing ninth in the Senior. Two years later he was a factory Ajay rider, but found himself on the monstrous supercharged Vee-four, on which he must have been relieved to retire. It was an experience which contributed to a switch to private Nortons, a brace of fifth places in Senior and Junior, and the offer of Bracebridge Street works tackle for 1938.

The cammy Nortons launched Daniell on his finest TT years,

for he immediately posted his first win, overcoming a titanic challenge from 'unbeatable' Stanley Woods with consecutive record laps. Overall, his three successes all came in Senior races, and each in alternate TTs: 1938, 1947 and 1949.

By his own admission, a 'steady' starter who took a lap or two to get into his stride, Daniell could nonetheless be blisteringly fast. His 1938 lap record of exactly 91mph, the first lap under 25 minutes (24:52.6), withstood even the supercharged BMWs of 1939 and endured until blown away by a young Geoff Duke in 1950. A jovial character off the track, Daniell was a stubborn, gutsy racer whose determination belied his looks. He's remembered by Duke as a cheerful character who, 'If he'd been a bit slimmer, he'd have been really tough to beat.' After retiring in 1950 Daniell became a Norton dealer in London's Forest Hill. He died in 1967.

RAY AMM

1951–54: 3 TT wins; 6 GP wins*

Rhodesia's Ray Amm was the first notable invader from Southern Africa, a region which was to produce such racing greats as Redman, Hocking, Ekerold and Ballington. Like many such imports, he brought a fierce focus to his racing that few 'home' riders could match. Arriving in Europe in 1951 with wife Jill, meagre funds and a brace of Nortons, his fearless style impressed at once and he was quickly signed by Joe Craig. By 1953, he had replaced the departed Geoff Duke as the Norton squad's star rider. Despite his origins, Amm was defiantly patriotic to Britain, repeatedly turning down offers to ride for Italian factories. During the mid-Fifties, he battled against the all-conquering Gileras, MVs and Guzzis practically alone.

His finest TT year was to be 1953, for he became only the fifth rider to achieve the coveted Senior/Junior double. Victory in the latter was especially delicious, for despite sliding off and snapping a footrest at Sarah's on the last lap, he overtook Duke's Gilera on the road on the way to pulverising the same man's lap record. By then he had already posted an emphatic start-to-finish win on the 350cc Norton.

Amm rounded off the season nicely with third place in the 350cc World Championship before taking the radical Norton kneeler to the Montlhéry speed bowl. His new one-hour world record, 133.71mph, was more than 6mph faster than Piero Taruffi's old mark, set ironically, on a supercharged predecessor of Duke's Gilera.

If the kneeler was eye-grabbing, Amm's mount for the 1954 TT was even more so. Riding the streamlined 'Proboscis' Norton in the Junior he set yet another emphatic lap record (94.61mph) and led comfortably with a lap to go, only for his engine to fail. Amm was more lucky in winning that year's Senior when it was abandoned after four laps, before he had needed to stop for fuel, yet he also set the fastest lap of the race.

Amm finished the 1954 season as runner-up in both the 350cc and 500cc World Championships, despite riding a machine clearly out-paced by its Italian rivals. When Norton pulled out of racing he reluctantly signed for MV for '55, but was tragically killed in his first race, at Imola, on Easter Monday. He was just 29 years old.

BOB McINTYRE
1952–62; 3 TT wins; 5 GP wins*

Although he won only three races during a fitful TT career, the craggy Glaswegian was one of the greatest riders ever to grace the Mountain Course – and the first man to lap at the magical 'ton'. His Isle of Man apprenticeship began in 1952 when, as a complete unknown riding a BSA Gold Star, he placed second in the Junior Clubman's. Three months later he went one better in a stirring Junior MGP dice with Harold Clark during which both shattered the lap record. In the Senior MGP the same week, riding his Junior AJS rather than his 500 Norton, he placed second.

For a while, McIntyre focused more on scrambling than road racing and the next four TTs proved fruitless. In 1953 he retired, but a year later, riding the ill-starred factory AJS Porcupine he could manage only 14th. With no factory Nortons competing in 1955, Bob Mac rode Nortons prepared by Joe Potts to second place in the Junior and fifth in the Senior, followed by yet another year of retirements. Then came his move to Gilera.

Riding the Italian multis, McIntyre shattered the 1957 fields in both Junior and Senior races, winning by more than two and four minutes, respectively. At 97.42mph his new Junior lap record was almost 3mph faster than Ray Amm's old mark. Yet it was his Senior lap at 101.12mph which would go down in history. (In fact in a race extended to eight laps to mark the TT's Golden Jubilee, he lapped at over 100mph four times, despite signals telling him to slow down.) With one race to go he was hot favourite to take that year's 500cc crown, but fell ill and failed to make the Monza grid.

Gilera's withdrawal from racing (along with Guzzi and Mondial) at the end of the '57 season denied the Scot such superb machinery. His one further TT success came in the 1959 Formula One 500cc event. In 1961 he switched to Honda, leading the Lightweight comfortably before retiring, then finishing second to Hailwood's Norton in the Senior. He was also second in the 250cc World Championship. A little over a year later, at the age of 33, he was dead, following a crash on an experimental five-speed Norton at Oulton Park's August Bank Holiday meeting.

LUIGI TAVERI

1955–66: 3 TT wins; 30 GP wins*; 3 world titles

Born in Horgen in 1929, this cheery Swiss was one of the most popular Continental riders of his generation. Although his international career began on 350cc and 500cc private Nortons in 1954, it was in the lightweight classes that he ultimately made his mark, taking the 125cc World Championships for Honda in 1962, '64 and '66. His Isle of Man career began on the Clypse Course in 1955 when, riding factory MVs, he placed second in the 125cc event. In the same year, he sat in as passenger for Hans Haldemann in the sidecar grands prix.

After seasons with Ducati, MZ (for whom he came agonisingly close to winning the 125cc Lightweight TT in 1959) and Kreidler, Taveri signed for Honda in 1961, placing second to Hailwood on the 125cc twin on the full Mountain Circuit. Twelve months later, he went one better, at a race record speed of 89.88mph. In 1964, now riding the 125-four, he won again, with a lap record of 95.5mph. His final victory came one year later when his Honda twin won the 50cc race ahead of the Suzukis of Hugh Anderson and Ernst Degner.

TOM HERRON
1970–78: 3 TT wins; 2 GP wins*

Born in Lisburn in 1948, Tom Herron was the first Irish rider since Artie Bell to make a mark in international racing, an inspiration to compatriots to follow, and something of a mentor to Joey Dunlop. As tough and courageous on the track as he was a party animal off it, Herron's TT career began badly when he crashed at Ballacraine in only his second race, the 1970 Junior. He had no sooner recovered from those injuries than he collected more at the following NW200, so his TT career didn't really begin until 1972 – when he broke down in all three races he began. The following year proved little better, but 12 months later he scored his first rostrum finish, third in the 250cc race, plus two fourth places. In '75 he was third again, this time in the Junior.

Herron's first win came in the 250cc TT of 1976, followed a few days later by victory in the Senior, the last Isle of Man Grand Prix, after John Williams's famous push-in from Governor's Bridge. His final TT win came in the 1978 Senior, with a race-record speed of 111.74mph. He was tragically killed 11 months later when he crashed on Juniper Hill at the NW200 in his native Ulster, aged just 30.

ALEX GEORGE
1970–92: 3 TT wins

This no-nonsense Scotsman is perhaps best remembered for narrowly preventing the great Mike Hailwood from completing a fairy-tale double during his farewell TT, but he was one of the toughest competitors of his day. That result, when he won the £30,000 Schweppes Classic race by a mere 3.4 seconds, stands as one of the great TT contests of all time in what had been billed as 'the richest race in the world'. In the same week he took the Formula One race, also for Honda.

His Isle of Man debut came in the MGP of 1968. In '69 he rode a Yamaha to victory in the Lightweight MGP, before graduating to the TT in 1970, only to retire in ten of his first 11 starts. His first TT win came in the ten-lap Production TT in 1975. Paired with Dave Croxford and the legendary *Slippery Sam* Triumph triple, he posted a record lap at 102.82mph. His best year was 1979 when he won both the Formula One and Classic 1000 TTs, the latter with outright race-record speed. Serious injuries sustained in a hair-raising crash at Ginger Hall in 1982 effectively ended George's competitive career. He raced again in 1987 and 1992, just 'for a bit of fun'.

GRAEME CROSBY
1979–81: 3 TT wins; 2 World F1 titles

Graeme Crosby's TT career may have been brief, but it was certainly memorable. Having made his mark on UK short circuits on the high-handlebarred Moriwaki, the colourful Kiwi made his TT debut on similar machines before joining the official Suzuki squad for 1980 and placing fourth in the Formula One and retiring in the Classic 1000. Twelve months later he was back with a bang, winning the Senior and placing second in the F1, although he again retired in the Classic. Victory at the Ulster GP two months later brought him the World F1 title by two points from Mick Grant, partly thanks to a superb spoiling ride by temporary team-mate Joey Dunlop.

Although 'Croz' rode superbly to take an F1/Classic double in his last Island appearance, the week is largely remembered for its controversy, for he was declared the winner of the F1 race only on protest over two hours after the finish, with Ron Haslam demoted to second (leading to Honda's infamous 'Black Protest'). Although Haslam turned the tables at the Ulster GP and finished level with him on points, the World F1 title again went to the Suzuki man.

A supremely versatile rider, Crosby holds the unique distinction of having won the Daytona and Imola 200s, the Suzuka 8-hour and the TT. In 1982 he concentrated on the 500cc grands prix World Championship, finishing runner-up to Franco Uncini.

GEOFF JOHNSON
1981–90: 3 TT wins

During the 1980s, Johnson, from Richmond, was one of the most popular stalwarts of the TT races. Often strapped for budget, his best results were in Production races where finance spoke less loudly than in the open classes – although, given the kit, he was fast on both. His wins came in the 1984 and '85 1,300cc Production events and the 1987 Production 'B'. In the latter year he joined the Loctite Yamaha squad, for whom he also placed second in the Senior. Luck rarely seemed to follow the Yorkshireman, and in 1988 he set lap records on both 750cc and 1,000cc Production Yamahas without winning either race. He died in 1990 from an embolism, possibly caused by injuries received at Castle Coombe earlier in the year.

ROB McELNEA
1982–84: 3 TT wins

Rob McElnea's TT career was as spectacular as it was brief, and gave the lie to the notion that only veterans can succeed over the Mountain Course. He first rode the Island in 1979 when he was leading the MGP Newcomers' race by 30 seconds only to fall off at Whitegates, climb back on, and finish second. By his TT debut he was, by his own admission, 'less brain out' but, riding a TZ750, 'got really psyched up in dodgy wet and dry conditions, forgot my fuel stop and ran out in Kirk Michael while lying third.'

The following year the Humbersider was a Suzuki factory rider, and evidently a deal more composed, taking his first win in the Senior Classic after a furious battle with Norman Brown and Joey Dunlop. In '84 he bagged a memorable Premier Classic/Senior double, including a new outright lap record at over 118mph. Indeed, after the death of Norman Brown at Silverstone, he seemed to be the one rider who could seriously push Joey Dunlop in his prime. Altogether, in just seven starts, he scored three wins, one third place and three retirements.

McElnea explained his abilities over the Mountain in terms of his regular work riding in GPs. 'I'd come to the TT so sharp, riding so hard, I could go fast at around 85 per cent. I think if I'd stuck my neck out, I could have been crazy fast. But I always thought the law of averages is against you if you do a lot of TTs. I came to my last one, fresh from a front-row grid position at the Nürburgring, and won two races.'

CARL FOGARTY
1986–92: 3 TT wins; 3 World F1 titles; 4 World Superbike titles

Winner of the 1985 Lightweight Newcomers' Manx Grand Prix, Carl Fogarty went on to become British biking's biggest phenomenon since Barry Sheene, and treated us to some of the finest TT tussles of any era.

On debut in 1986 Foggy had three DNFs and two finishes, with a best of 12th. The following year he placed fourth in the Junior, a position he repeated in the 1988 Formula One event on the way to the first of three World F1 titles. His first win came on the RC30 in the 1989 Production race, and one year later he scored a commanding Senior/Formula One double. Although he won nothing in 1991 and '92, his epic battles with Steve Hislop are still talked about with awe. During his last race, riding a 750 Yamaha against Hislop's Norton in the 1992 Senior, he lost by just four seconds, setting an enduring outright record at 123.61mph on the last, nail-biting lap. However, it was his exploits in winning a record four World Superbike titles that truly established the Blackburn man's reputation.

IAN SIMPSON
1989–98: 3 TT wins

A talented short-circuit rider with five British Championships, Dalbeattie's Ian Simpson is the son of Bill who, riding with Chas Mortimer, won the 1976 Production 250cc TT, a rare instance of father and son TT winners. On debut in 1989, Ian placed 15th in the Supersport 600 race, but was then absent until 1993 when he placed fourth and fifth in the Supersport 600 and Senior events respectively.

'Simmo's' first rostrum finish came in 1994 with a second in the Supersport 600 TT. After being sidelined by injury he returned to a disappointing year in 1996, but scored his first win in the 1997 Junior with lap and race records. His final TT outing brought a double victory in the 1998 Senior and Formula One events, plus second place in the Junior. Simpson would surely have added to his tally of three TT wins had his career not then been cut short by serious leg injuries.

CHARLIE COLLIER

1907–14: 2 TT wins

C. R. Collier's place in TT history is assured: the first winner, the creator (jointly with brother Harry) of the first winning machine (a Matchless), and the first TT lap record holder for the single-cylinder class. By the time of that first TT in 1907, Plumstead-born Charlie was already a veteran of three previous International Cup races. It was on the way home from a race in France in 1906, that the brothers happened to travel with the Marquis de Mouzilly de St Mars, who sparked their interest in an inaugural motorcycle TT. Fittingly, the Marquis provided the trophy, now the Senior pot, of which Charlie became the first winner.

In 1908, Charlie placed second to arch-rival Jack Marshall's Triumph, before winning once more in 1910. Twelve months later, in the first bike TT over the Mountain, he originally placed second before being disqualified for refuelling at a non-designated spot. In his final TT, 1914, he retired on the first lap. He remained both a director of AMC, successors to Matchless, and a keen motorcyclist, until his death in 1955.

FREDDIE DIXON

1912–27, 2 TT wins

Freddie Dixon holds the unique distinction of having won TTs on two, three and four wheels and, more bizarrely, of often riding with neither goggles nor gloves. He first contested the races in 1912 and, although obviously fast, he achieved nothing remarkable, other than becoming famed for preferring old-fashioned footboards to racing 'pegs. The 1920s, however, were his heyday, beginning with second place in the 1921 Senior race. Then, when the sidecar race was initiated in 1923, he turned up on something remarkable: a Douglas twin to which was hooked a curious sidecar which could be banked left and right by a system of levers.

Although the concept had been around in American dirt oval racing for some time, race organisers were doubtful. A test was arranged on Glencrutchery Road and Dixon hurtled towards the officials, turning at the last minute at what seemed like breathtaking speed, and terrifying his audience in the process. In the race, he won despite the frame breaking on the final lap, before placing third in the Senior later the same week. Although he contested future sidecar TTs, he never again raced the 'banker', nor did he explain why not. With no sidecar TT held on the Mountain Circuit from 1925 until 1960, Dixon's race and lap records stood for no less than 35 years.

Dixon's solo win came in the 1927 Junior TT when he brought an HRD to victory – reputedly aided by a swig of champagne during his pit stop. He then turned to car racing, winning, amongst other events, both the car TT (then held in Ulster) and the Douglas 'Round the Houses' race.

HOWARD R. DAVIES
1914–27: 2 TT wins

H. R. Davies's TT career began in the last meeting before World War I when, aged just 19, he brought a Sunbeam home in third place behind Pullin's Rudge and Godfrey's Indian. His TT exploits may have gone no further had there been any truth in a report in *Motor Cycling* in 1917 that the erstwhile racer had been killed in action. 'The facts are all correct save the central one,' said the unflappable Davies at the time. 'I am not dead.'

Instead, he survived to lead the 1920 Junior on his AJS before retiring. A year later he took his 'Ajay' to second place in the same race – a feat all the more remarkable because a couple of days later he used precisely the same 350cc machine to win the Senior TT. This was not only the first time a 'Junior' machine had so excelled, but the winning margin was over two minutes. Astonishingly, there was a move to disqualify him for using tyres narrower than those specified for the Senior class, but sensibly this came to nothing.

After a frustrating run of mechanical problems with other maker's machinery, in 1925 Davies resolved to ride a bike he could depend on – his own. The result was almost an historic double when Davies and his eponymous HRD won the Senior but came only a close second in the Junior race. When he retired from racing (and manufacturing) in 1927, his TT tally showed two wins, three second places and nine retirements. In other words, he never finished lower than second. His legacy continued with the HRD company, later to evolve into the mighty Vincent.

ARTIE BELL
1947–50: 2 TT wins: 1 GP win*

The first Ulsterman to win a TT, Belfast-born Bell enjoyed a short but brilliant Island career which saw him finish every race he began, save the first, the 1947 Junior. In the same year, after a scintillating race-long dice with Harold Daniell, he took second in the Senior, having led until slowed while overtaking Lightweight traffic (the two races were held concurrently). A year later he won the Senior and finished third in the Junior, followed by a fourth and third in 1949. In his final TT, 1950, he won the Junior at record speed and with a record lap, also taking second place in the Senior.

Renowned as a tough, uncompromising competitor, Bell's career was cut short by injuries sustained when Les Graham and Carlo Bandirola collided in front of him at the 1950 Belgian GP. Bell hit Graham's sliding AJS Porcupine and cartwheeled into a timing box at almost 100mph. He recovered, but was unable to race again.

BILL LOMAS
1949–56: 2 TT wins; 9 GP wins*; 2 world titles

Bill Lomas was a double World Champion whose career was synonymous with that of Moto Guzzi, and in particular the fabulous Vee-eight. The Milford-born rider also raced factory MV Agustas. Yet his first TT machine could scarcely have been more different, for in the 1949 Junior Clubman's he rode a standard Royal Enfield, at least until it broke down. Twelve months later he suffered another retirement in the Junior TT. His first finish, and first replica, came with fifth place on a Velocette in the 1951 Junior race.

By far his best TT season was 1955, the year of his first world title, when he rode for both Guzzi and MV, taking the Junior and Lightweight respectively. Both were memorable races. On the streamlined 350cc Guzzi single he overcame a fierce challenge from Bob McIntyre on Joe Potts's Norton only on the seventh and final lap. The Lightweight, the first 250cc race to be held on the Clypse Course, developed into an equally stirring dice between his MV and Cecil Sandford's Guzzi, which led for the first seven laps.

In 1956, the year of his second world title, Lomas was due to ride the Vee-eight in the Senior, but the exotic 500 was not ready in time and he rode a Guzzi single into fifth place instead. Two years later injuries sustained in a crash at Imola ended his racing career.

GARY HOCKING
1959–62: 2 TT wins; 19 GP wins*; 2 world titles

Born in Newport, Monmouthshire in 1937, but a Rhodesian national, Hocking's was an all-too-brief but illustrious racing career during which he showed all the fearless commitment we have come to expect from Colonial riders. Riding a Dearden Norton, he placed 12th on debut in the 1959 Junior TT, but returned 12 months later as a fully fledged MV rider, winning the 250cc Lightweight race. Hailwood's triple year, 1961, was a disappointment for Hocking, with a best of second in the Junior. His second and final win came in the Senior in '62, Hocking's golden year. In all he won no less than 12 grands prix that season, finishing as World Champion in both the 350cc and 500cc classes. However, the death of his close friend, Honda star Tom Phillis, brought about his premature retirement from two-wheeled sport. He switched to car racing only to be killed in a South African meeting in December 1962, aged just 25 years.

BILL IVY
1962–68: 2 TT wins; 21 GP wins*; 1 world title

Born in Maidstone in 1942, during the height of his regrettably short career Bill Ivy was the mischievous foil to Yamaha team-mate Phil Read's more transparent ambitions. His TT debut came in 1962, riding a 50cc Chisholm-Itom. A year later he rode a 50cc Sheene Special into seventh place in the same event. His two TT wins came in the 1966 Lightweight 125cc and 1968 Lightweight 250cc races, both as a Yamaha factory rider. His one world title came in 1967 in the 125cc class.

In 1968, he lapped at 100.32mph on the 125, only 5mph slower than Agostini's fastest lap on the 500cc MV, an astonishing performance. Spectators vividly recall the mercurial little rider kicking himself off walls and banks on the screaming liquid-cooled Vee-four. That was the year of the notorious duel with team-mate Read, to whom he was under orders to gift the win. Ivy wasn't about to allow that to pass without making a point, and cruised to a stop at Creg-ny-Baa to 'check' his position.

After 1968 Yamaha withdrew from grands prix racing and in July 1969, Ivy guested for Jawa at the East German GP at the old Sachsenring. He died when the notoriously seizure-prone two-stroke locked up during practice.

JACK MARSHALL
1907–10: 1 TT win

Laconic, cool-headed and always Triumph-mounted, Coventry's Jack Marshall was certainly one of the greats of the TT's early years, winning once and finishing second twice in the first three TTs. Indeed, but for a puncture which cost him at least ten minutes, he might well have won in 1907. A year later his problems were even more acute. Yet despite a crash, another puncture and stopping to change a broken exhaust valve (a rather simpler task then than now), he overcame Charlie Collier to win. In those days, they just didn't know how to quit. In 1909 he was second again, this time to Charlie's brother, Harry.

Marshall abruptly retired from racing after finishing sixth in the 1910 TT – the last to be held on the original St John's course – and so never competed over the Mountain. For many years he was landlord of the Royal Oak at Whitley, near Coventry.

JIMMY SIMPSON
1922–34: 1 TT win

Although he won only one race, Jimmy Simpson could justifiably claim to be the fastest TT rider of his and perhaps even any era. Probably the fates were sown in his debut race, during that vintage year of 1922, when he retired on the first lap when his Scott's fuel tank split.

In 1923, he returned as an AJS rider, setting a new lap record and retiring, a pattern that was to become entrenched. Twelve months later it was more of the same: the first 60mph lap (and by a margin, at 64.54mph), then out. In 1925: Senior lap record, retired; 1926: same again. Having trashed 'Ajays' for most of the 1920s, he switched to Norton in 1929, but even then his fortunes failed to improve. In six consecutive races beginning with the 1927 Senior until the 1930 Junior TT, he retired in every one.

Little wonder that they dubbed him 'record and machine breaker', an appellation he resented, for it seemed fated that, whatever he rode, and however fast, he simply could not win. In a total of 26 rides he finished only 11, and of these he set fastest lap no less than eight times. Remarkably, he holds the distinction of having set the first 60mph, 70mph and 80mph laps (in 1924 Junior, AJS; 1926 Senior, AJS, and 1931 Senior, Norton, respectively). Fittingly, the trophy awarded even today to the rider setting the fastest lap of the week is named after him.

Undoubtedly, Jimmy's final year was his finest, when he grasped that elusive victory riding a Rudge in the Lightweight TT, before placing second in both the Junior and Senior races, after which he promptly retired. As well as road racing, where he won several grands prix, Simpson was highly successful in hill-climbs and sprints.

LES GRAHAM
1938–53: 1 TT win; 8 GP wins*; 1 World GP title

Born in Wallasey, almost within sight of the Isle of Man ferry, Graham first appeared in the 1938 Lightweight race, placing 12th on an OK Supreme. He fared even less well the following year, retiring from the Lightweight race. After the war, he rode the fast but finicky AJS Porcupine. In its best year, 1949, he took the inaugural 500cc world title but broke down while leading the Senior at Cronk-ny-Mona, pushing in to take 10th place.

Switching to MV Agusta for 1951 after a brief flutter with Velocette, Graham placed second in the 1952 Senior, taking his sole TT win in the Ultra-Lightweight event 12 months later, aged 42. Just one day later he was dead, killed when his MV crashed on Quarterbridge Road on lap 2 of the Senior race. A supremely stylish rider, he would surely have won more races had war not intervened. His son, Stuart, is also a TT winner.

H. R. 'REG' ARMSTRONG
1949–55: 1 TT win; 7 GP wins*

Dublin-born Reg Armstrong was a hugely talented racer who suffered a conspicuous lack of Irish luck which even his clover-leaf helmet design couldn't invoke. In the course of riding for no less than six different factories, he was five times a World Championship runner-up, but never once a champion.

His Island career began with the Manx Grands Prix of 1947 and '48 when he scored two fourth places, in the Lightweight and Senior respectively. In his debut TT, still aged only 21, he rode the same private 'Ajay' to fourth place in the Junior (a mere second behind Daniell) and seventh in the Senior event. A switch to factory Velos brought little joy in 1950, nor was an AJS contract any more rewarding the following year. He pushed in to 23rd place in the Junior when his chain snapped at Cronk-ny-Mona while contesting third place, and retired in the Senior TT.

His one success came when partnering Duke in the Norton squad of 1952. The duo shared first and second places, Armstrong taking the Senior at 92.97mph. The same duo switched to Gilera for the next season, initially a frustrating experience for all concerned. When Duke slid off the four-cylinder 500 at Quarter Bridge, Armstrong inherited the lead, but a slipping chain later dropped him to third place. Twelve months later, riding for NSU as well as Gilera, he could manage no better than third place on the 250cc German machine. His swansong was in 1955, placing second to Duke in a Gilera 1–2, the Arcore company's first TT win.

Although Armstrong retired after the 1955 season, seven years later he was back as manager of the Honda Racing team. After enjoying more luck and success as boss than ever he had as a rider, he was killed in a road accident in 1979, aged 52.

PETER WILLIAMS

1966–74: 1 TT win, 1 GP win

Although his solitary TT win appears unremarkable, fellow competitors speak of Peter Williams as one of the great Mountain Course exponents of his era. As fluent on a bike as he was clever off it, his self-imposed handicap was that he always chose British machines in preference to more competitive mounts from overseas. His one grand prix win, at the 1971 350cc Ulster GP, came courtesy of a rare overseas ride for MZ.

Born in 1945 in Nottingham, Williams first rode on the Island in 1964 on a Norton, returning to the MGP a year later to take a Greeves to third in the 1965 Lightweight event. On his TT debut in 1966, he posted a sensational second place on an AJS 7R behind Agostini's new MV-three. Twelve months later he was second again, this time to Hailwood's Honda, on Tom Arter's G50 Matchless, a result he repeated in 1973 on the same machine. His one TT win came in the same year, when he rode the factory Norton Commando in the Formula 750 event. His fastest lap, 107.27mph, was the nearest anyone had come to Hailwood's 1967 record for some years. William's racing career was cut short before he could add to that win, by injuries received in an accident at Oulton Park.

Sidecar riders

DAVE MOLYNEUX
1985– : 11 TT wins

Already the first Manxman to win the Southern 100, 'Moly' first entered the TT in 1985, and two years later actually led one before breaking down. In 1989, after years of struggle with inferior kit (he'd started five TTs before once seeing the chequered flag), a sponsor provided an Ireson's chassis on which he took his first TT win, although 'the bike just didn't suit my style'.

A gifted craftsman and fabricator, when he emphatically established his reputation with a double win in 1993 it was on outfits of his own creation. In 1995 even arch-rival Rob Fisher became a customer, and used DMRs for all his subsequent wins. A constant process of year-by-year development has made these unquestionably the finest TT sidecars money can buy.

For half a decade the 112.76mph lap record set by Moly in 1999 appeared inviolable, until he marginally improved it to 113.17mph during yet another sidecar double in 2004. The benchmark moved to a new order of magnitude in 2005, when he lapped at 115mph in practice before setting a staggering new record of 116.04mph in the second sidecar race (having retired in the first, won by another Manxman, Nick Crowe, inevitably on a DMR outfit). It was his 11th win, the most by any sidecar driver.

Molyneux is now so far ahead of his rivals that it seems that only failure to finish can deny him a win. Last year he scorched round faster still, at 116.224mph during practice, but the following day he and passenger Craig Hallam crashed out spectacularly at Rhencullen, taking no further part in the meeting. Molyneux's reaction from his hospital bed was to announce his retirement from TT racing, only to recant a couple of days later.

ROB FISHER
1993–2002: 10 TT wins

Rob Fisher's TT record is remarkable. In 17 starts he has logged up no less than ten wins, with three second places, one fifth and three DNFs, winning his last five races on the trot. On his debut in 1993 he placed fifth in race 'A', averaging 100.57mph. He failed to finish in race 'B', then recorded a double win 12 months later in only his second outing on the Mountain Course. Using a stock FZR600 engine bought from a breakers' en route to the Island, he posted the week's fastest practice time – an unofficial record at 104.53mph.

Further doubles followed in 1995, 2000 and '02, along with individual race wins in '97 and '99, before he sat out the 2003 races to concentrate on the Superside Championship. Recently retired, the highlights of many of his races have been his duels with Dave Molyneux (who built Fisher's outfits), the only other sidecar driver consistently able to challenge the Workington man. Rick Long, his passenger since 1997 has shared six of his victories.

SIGGY SCHAUZU
1966–76: 9 TT wins; 9 GP wins*

Until eclipsed by Rob Fisher in 2002, Siegfried Schauzu was the most successful sidecar driver in the TT's history, having amassed a total of nine victories (four of which were also grands prix wins) between 1967 and 1975. Born in Passendorf, Germany, Schauzu mainly drove BMW twins but also Helmust Fath's ARO two-stroke flat four. He showed a particular liking for tough road courses, also winning at the old Nürburgring, Spa and Brno. His most memorable win came in 1967 when passenger Horst Schneider fell out at Governor's Bridge on the final lap. Unhurt, he climbed back aboard for the pair to take the win ahead of Klaus Enders. Popularly known as 'Sideways Sid' because of his lurid riding style, Schauzu also scored five TT second places, but never quite managed to clinch a world title.

MICK BODDICE
1966–98: 9 TT wins

Along with Schauzu and Saville, Kidderminster's Mick Boddice shares a tally of nine TT wins, placing him joint second on the all-time list. Son of Bill, another famous sidecar racer, Mick's sequence of wins ran from 1983 to '93. He also placed second six times, and third five.

DAVE SAVILLE
1968–93: 9 TT wins

Dave Saville first raced on the Island as a last-minute replacement driver in the 1968 TT, and went on to become one of the event's biggest stalwarts. Although he recorded nine wins in all, mostly on Sabre outfits of his own making, the first seven of these were class wins, when the F2 and 1,000cc sidecar events were run side by side. His career ended when he crashed a solo at the Creg in the 1993 Manx Grand Prix Classic race, suffering irreparable spinal damage. (He also raced a solo BSA in the 1975 Production TT.) In 2001 he returned to the races to unveil a new 'mobility' lift in the TT grandstand.

JOCK TAYLOR
1978–82: 4 TT wins: 6 GP wins; 1 world title

John Robert 'Jock' Taylor was clearly a class act from the moment he first arrived on the Isle of Man. On debut in 1978 he placed second, adding a third place a few days later.

In 1980 he was joined by a new passenger, Benga Johansson, with whom he would share all subsequent triumphs. The duo scored one first and one second place in that year's TT, going on to take the World Sidecar title and the next year brought a double win and a new lap record at 108.12mph. In what would be their last TT, the

'B' event of 1982, they again won, with a 108.29mph record lap which would not be bettered until 1989. Ten weeks later Jock was dead, killed during the Finnish Grand Prix at Imatra, aged just 28.

ERIC OLIVER
1937–58: 1 TT win; 17 GP wins*; 4 world titles

Born in Stratford-upon-Avon, Eric Oliver was another British rider who won a maiden world grand prix championship in 1949, a title he was to retain for the next three years. However, as a sidecar rider, there was no place for him on the Isle of Man, since the class did not resume until 1954, the year after his last World Championship.

Although Oliver had previously competed on solos in 12 TT races, with a best result of eighth in the 1948 Junior, it was on three wheels that he was supreme. When outfits did return, over ten laps of the Clypse Course, Oliver duly recorded his sole TT win, holding off the mighty BMW twins on a Norton Manx with Les Nutt in the chair. However, there was to be no repeat in '55, the year in which the German boxers began two decades of almost uninterrupted success. Oliver, by then aged 44, retired from racing to open a motorcycle shop in Staines.

Despite having virtually invented the kneeler racing outfit, in 1958 Oliver returned to the TT to ride a Norton Dominator road bike hitched to a standard Watsonian Monaco sidecar – just to show that it could be done. He and his doughty passenger, Mrs Pat Wise, earned a bronze replica for tenth place. Two years later, Oliver and Stan Dibben returned on a proper 'kneeler' machine, only to crash on the Mountain when the front suspension broke. Although neither man's injuries were serious, both took the hint to retire from racing. Oliver suffered a fatal stroke just nine years later, at the age of 68.

Keeping it in the family
Only four father-and-son combinations have won TTs. Tony Jefferies won two TTs during the Seventies, while son David

won nine in recent years. (For good measure, Uncle Nick won one, too.)

British Superbike contender Michael Rutter also emulated the achievements of his father, eight-times winner Tony, when he won the 1998 Junior TT. Les Graham, the 1949 500cc World Champion, won the 1953 Ultra-Lightweight race, while son Stewart also won one TT, the 1967 50cc event. Bill Simpson shared a Production win with Chas Mortimer in 1976, while son Ian took three wins in 1997 and '98.

Others who have come close were George and Carl Fogarty. Carl, of course, won three TTs, while his father was runner-up to Joey Dunlop in the 1977 Jubilee Classic race. Jimmy Guthrie won six TTs during the Twenties and Thirties, and in 1967 his son, also Jimmy, won the Senior MGP. Only one mother/daughter combination has contested TTs: Hilary and Gail Musson.

Winning siblings are equally rare, although they started earlier. Charlie and Harry Collier won in 1907 and 1909 respectively, with Harry going on to win again in 1910. The Twemlow brothers, Eric and Ken, won three between them, each winning one race in 1924 with Eric taking a second 12 months later. In recent years, Joey and Robert Dunlop have shared no fewer than 31 wins, while William, son to Robert and nephew to the late Joey, enjoyed a supremely promising TT debut in 2006.

Race fitness

A Norton factory boss once complained that 'the [factory] riders can be as temperamental as the machines.' Although some racers, such as Stanley Woods, saw the benefit of keeping themselves in good shape, at least one manufacturer felt moved to press its riders to 'live an ascetic life' because 'it was little use spending a lot of money to prepare racing machines unless the jockeys were really fit.' A decade or so later, Graham Walker, editor of *Motor Cycling*, recommended that drinking 'beer or stout before a race will do more good than harm, but lay off the spirits.' Ignoring his own advice, the former TT winner went on to advocate a pre-race breakfast of two eggs beaten with a pint of milk and a large brandy, 'precisely two hours before starting time.' Of course, it wasn't until the Nineties that any sort of dope or alcohol testing was introduced.

Disqualifications

Many riders have been disqualified for breaches of TT rules – notably Trevor Nation and Steve Parrish in the modern era. But, Nation excepted, rarely have they affected the rostrum places. In 1911, Charlie Collier split the marauding Indian twins, only to be thrown out of the results for taking on fuel illegally.

In the Junior race ten years later, even the great Jimmy Guthrie found himself in hot water when it was alleged he had received outside help when re-starting at Hillberry. Race organisers reacted promptly – too promptly, perhaps – having him black-flagged at Ramsey while lying in second place. An angry Guthrie got on the phone, argued his case, and continued to the finish, coming in a provisional fifth. Although Norton's protest was allowed – no witness confirmed the alleged bump-start – Guthrie was stuck with fifth place, although he was awarded second-place prize money and Norton the coveted team prize.

In 1966, after the first TT to be run on a Sunday, Fritz Scheidegger was excluded from first place in the sidecar race for using Esso petrol, rather than the 'official' BP/Shell. In a rare triumph for good sense, he was later reinstated. Less fortunate was Ian Hutchinson, who lost his runner-up spot in the 2006 Junior, his Kawasaki having fractionally excessive valve lift but, according to officials, 'no performance advantage'.

Silver and bronze replicas

For many riders, a TT replica is the most coveted award of their career. Each is a scale replica of the Senior trophy, awarded to riders who finish within a certain proportion of the winner's time. Silver replicas are awarded to every rider finishing within 105 per cent of the winner's time, while 110 per cent is the cut-off for bronze replicas.

Chapter 5

GREAT RACES

In the TT's earliest years, the races were great not so much for what they brought in the way of close finishes, but because they represented one of the greatest challenges for primitive and trouble-prone machines. Most bikes failed to finish at all, and whether they did or not their intrepid riders usually had a tale to tell at the end. From the very first bike TT in 1907, competitors started in pairs at one-minute intervals. But if there was a lack of wheel-to-wheel dicing, riders had quite enough trouble getting themselves and their flimsy machines around ten laps of the St John's Course.

Jack Marshall, second in the Single-cylinder class, described some of the hazards: 'Overtaking, one charged blindly into a cloud of dust and hoped there would be a clear road ahead on the other side.' The first time around the bend after Devil's Elbow on the Kirk Michael to Peel coast road, the Triumph man 'came a bit of a purler ... damaging my knee and bent the machine a bit.' On the second lap he burst a tyre on Ballig Bridge, then a pronounced hump-back, but continued to the finish without further trouble. Or so he thought. It emerged that in order to damp down dust the organisers had sprayed the course with dilute acid. After a couple of days, Marshall's race clothing 'looked as if the rats had been at it.'

As well as being the first motorcycle TT race, 1907 may well go down as one of the longest to reach a conclusion. After the event there was widespread debate as to whether Marshall might have beaten Charlie Collier had his Triumph not punctured. Indeed, Triumph actually advertised their machine as having 'made faster time' than the Matchless. To settle the issue a special race was held at Canning Town race track (a banked oval, and one of Britain's first circuits), but when Marshall's team-mate Frank Hulbert crashed heavily, this 'decider' was abandoned.

For the most part, winning margins were counted in several minutes rather than seconds. Charlie Collier won that first race by over 11 minutes, while in the Twin-cylinder class Rem Fowler's advantage over W. H. Wells was over half an hour, which is still the longest ever. Perhaps the most notable exceptions came in 1913, when Hugh Mason's NUT won by just 46 seconds from W. Newsome's Douglas. On the same Friday, the Senior was even more nail-biting, Tim Wood's Scott edging out the Rudge of A. R. Abbott by a mere five seconds.

Twelve months later, the Senior produced an even closer finish when Oliver Godfrey and Howard Davies dead-heated, albeit for second place. Nonetheless, it must have been a pretty spectacular contest, for the winner, Cyril Pullin, led the pair home by only 6.4 seconds, in a race lasting well over four hours.

In stark contrast to the widespread indifference that had marked the motorcycle races in 1905, by this time the races had captured the imagination of the Manx public to the extent that Friday, the final race day, had become a de facto public holiday. Ironically, this occurred in the very same year that Hall Caine was leading his crusade against the danger and disruption caused by the races. Manx history clearly favoured the masses over the rich novelist, for it wasn't long before the Friday of TT week became an official bank holiday, as it is today.

1923 Junior: STANLEY WOODS

This was a vintage year all round. For the first time there were four races to savour, a sidecar event having been added to the 250cc Lightweight race introduced the year before. All four events were won by relatively narrow margins, and local interests were well served when Manxman Tom Sheard added a Senior win to the Junior honours he had claimed in 1922. But for sheer drama and excitement, it was the 350cc race which drew the public's attention.

Few races have seen as many lead changes as that Junior TT, nor so much incident. As was to become his custom, Jimmy Simpson led after smashing the record on the opening lap, and just as predictably retired his AJS. This gave the lead to Bert le Vack (New Imperial), who in turn, retired on lap five. George Dance now held the advantage, but with less than a dozen miles to the finish his Sunbeam broke down on the Mountain. Improbably, for he was once two minutes down, then even more after sliding off in Ramsey, Stanley Woods's unfancied Cotton now led the field. Throwing up a 'bow wave of dirt and stones' over the rough roads, the great man hung on to record his – and Cotton's – first TT win, with a record lap of 55.74mph. The Irishman's winning margin in a race of attrition which produced only six finishers was over two minutes from the 'Ajay' of H. F. Harris.

Results:

	Rider	Motorcycle	Race time hr min sec	Av speed mph
1	Stanley Woods	Cotton	4.03.47.0	55.74
2	H. F. Harris	AJS	4.06.16.0	–
3	A. H. Alexander	Douglas	4.09.35.0	–
4	J. A. Watson-Bourne	Matador	4.13.41.0	–
5	Vic Anstice	Douglas	4.15.57.0	–
6	Frank Longman	AJS	4.17.33.0	–

1925 Junior and Ultra-Lightweight: WAL HANDLEY

Wal Handley, still only 21 years old, but riding in his fourth TT in 1925, switched from OK-Supreme to Rex-Acme and became the first man to win two races in one week.

Favourites for the Junior race were Howard Davies, Freddie Dixon, Jimmy Simpson, Jock Porter and Paddy Johnston, all of whom had impressed in practice. But after the first of six laps the crowd was startled to learn that Wal lay second, just a single second behind Dixon. One lap later the tables were emphatically turned, for now Handley led by 23 seconds. The tough little Brummie was never again challenged, taking the win at 65.02mph, almost four minutes ahead of Davies and Simpson. If the margin appears comfortable, it didn't seem so from the saddle. On lap 4, still fearing he could be beaten by the distant opposition, he posted a lap record of 65.89mph to widen the gap.

Just six motorcycles were flagged away for Wednesday's Ultra-Lightweight race, with all eyes on the winner of Monday's Junior TT. Five bikes, including Handley's Rex-Acme, were powered by spindly 174cc ohv Blackburne engines, complete with outside bacon-slicer flywheels. The sixth machine was a two-stroke Excelsior.

Handley led easily from the flag, and such was his lead that he slowed by over two minutes on his fourth and final lap. The final finisher, C. S. Barrow on the Excelsior had not even started his last lap by the time Handley had won.

Results: Junior TT

	Rider	Motorcycle	Race time hr min sec	Av speed mph
1	Wal L. Handley	Rex-Acme	3.28.56.4	65.02
2	Howard R. Davies	HRD	3.32.42.0	63.87
3	Jimmy H. Simpson	AJS	3.39.20.0	61.89

Results: Ultra-Lightweight TT

1	Wal L. Handley	Rex-Acme	2.49.27.0	53.45
2	Paddy Johnston	Cotton	2.55.54.0	52.08
3	Jack A. Porter	New Gerrard	2.57.40.0	50.98

1935 Senior: STANLEY WOODS

This event was special not least for what had happened in the previous year's race, contested in the foulest imaginable Manx weather. Riding a Husqvarna Vee-twin, that man Stanley Woods led for almost the entire race, setting an astonishing fastest lap of over 80mph, only seconds slower than his own lap record. Despite sliding off (yet again) at Ramsey Hairpin on the final lap, he still held a narrow lead over the flying Jimmy Simpson and Jimmy Guthrie, both riding for the factory Norton squad which had so comprehensively won the previous three Seniors. Then, when just eight tantalising miles from the finish, the 'Husky' ran out of fuel, giving Norton a 1–2 through Guthrie and Simpson.

If Woods was out for revenge the following year, he had also to be patient, for the Island's fickle weather intervened, causing the race to be postponed to Saturday for the first time. Again, he rode a Vee-twin, but this one said 'Moto Guzzi' on the tank. But when he trailed Guthrie's Norton by 26 seconds after the penultimate lap, it looked like the Hawick man's race.

However, like another Irishman who would become a TT legend 50 years later, Woods was as canny as he was quick. Late in the race feverish activity in the Guzzi pit suggested Woods would be making a second pit stop, but he gambled and howled on through – by which time Guthrie, with a much earlier start number, was already halfway round his final lap. Indeed, when he finished, Guthrie was initially hailed as the winner, since no-one could conceive of Woods clawing back so great a deficit – except, perhaps, the great man himself. On that final circuit he raised the lap record to 85.53mph, almost 3mph up on the mark he had set on a Norton two years before, to snatch victory by a mere four seconds.

It was the first time a twin had won since Scott in 1913, and the first time a sprung-framed bike had ever won. In both respects, it set a marker for the future – if only other factories, and especially British ones, had had a mind to notice.

Results:

	Rider	Motorcycle	Race time hr min sec	Av speed mph
1	Stanley Woods	Moto Guzzi	3.07.10.0	84.68
2	Jimmy Guthrie	Norton	3:07.14.0	84.65
3	Walter Rusk	Norton	3:09.45.0	83.53
4	J. G. Duncan	Norton	3:16.48.0	80.54
5	Otto Steinbach	NSU	3:23.09.0	78.02
6	Ted Mellors	NSU	3:30.32.0	75.34

1938 Senior: HAROLD DANIELL

On the eve of the 1938 Senior race, Stanley Woods was the all-time TT great, having just a couple of days earlier taken a factory Velocette to his ninth TT win in the Junior event. Indeed, his reputation went before him much as another mercurial Irishman's would 50 years later. Woods rode an experimental 500cc factory Velo developed from the all-conquering cammy 350. In his shadow, but only just, was Freddie Frith, twice victorious, and the first man to lap the course at 90mph in winning the Senior the previous year, the first seven-lap race completed in under three hours.

Confronting this illustrious duo was a chubby, short-sighted Londoner, whose previous best position was fifth. After three laps, Harold Daniell, a notoriously slow starter, riding a factory Norton for the first time, was averaging 88.2mph, faster than any previous Senior TT. Yet such was the pace of the favourites that he lay only third, 32 seconds behind Woods with Frith in second place. At his fuel stop, the message from no-nonsense race boss Joe Craig was clear: 'You're a good half-minute behind and had better do something about it.'

Daniell did just that. 'Really driving the model', as he later put it, he set about clawing back the deficit. After setting a new lap record on the penultimate lap – 25m 57s, the first sub-26 minute lap – his signal read '1+4': he led, but by a mere four seconds. Using 'maximum permissible revs', and possibly a few more, his final tour was faster still, 25:52.6, exactly 91.00mph. Daniell won from Woods by 15.2 seconds, finishing with so little petrol that there was barely enough for a scrutineering sample. His record lap stood until 1950.

Results:

	Rider	Motorcycle	Race time hr min sec	Av speed mph
1	Harold Daniell	Norton	2.57.50.6	89.11
2	Stanley Woods	Velocette	2:58.05.8	88.99
3	Freddie Frith	Norton	2:58.07.4	88.98
4	John White	Norton	3:01.52.0	87.14
5	Jock West	BMW	3:04.27.0	85.92
6	Ted Mellors	Velocette	3:07.10.0	84.67

1939 250cc Lightweight: TED MELLORS

TTs are not always won by the fastest rider, but by the one with the best racing nous. In the 1939 Lightweight race, Ted Mellors showed that even the redoubtable Stanley Woods can be out-thought. In his first practice on the new Benelli single, Chesterfield's Mellors lapped within seconds of Kluge's 1938 record, set when the German won by no less than 11 minutes from Woods's Excelsior.

At over 12 stones, Mellors was hefty for a 250cc rider, but his 30bhp Benelli was fast, clocking 110mph on the flat on TT gearing, and was capable of lapping as quickly as most of the 350s. Conditions were poor at the start, and deteriorated markedly during the seven-lap race. Anticipating the conditions, Mellors had put extra cuts in his tyres. After one lap, Omobono Tenni led by eight seconds from Woods, with Mellors a further half-minute behind, but the Benelli man, believing the blown Guzzi would not last the distance, let them go. On the second lap Tenni slowed, while Woods endured an agonising six-minute pit stop. Mellors was never headed again, and his judgement was proved correct when first Tenni, then Woods, retired, and Kluge's hard-charging DKW developed sulky spark plugs.

Results:

	Rider	Motorcycle	Race time hr min sec	Av speed mph
1	Ted Mellors	Benelli	3.33.26.0	74.26
2	Ewald Kluge	DKW	3:37.11.0	72.97
3	H. G. Tyrell Smith	Excelsior	3:40.23.0	71.91
4	Les Martin	Excelsior	3:50.08.0	68.87
5	Siegfried Wunsche	DKW	3:50.25.0	68.78
6	Charlie Manders	Excelsior	3:56.48.0	66.93

1947 Senior: HAROLD DANIELL

The clear favourite to win the 1947 Senior, the first after the war, was lap-record holder Harold Daniell. Wherever the challenge might come from, few expected that a rookie Ulsterman, Artie Bell, riding in his first TT, would be it. And yet Bell would give Daniell the race of his life and come agonisingly close to a shock win.

Curiously, the two riders started at opposite ends of the field: Bell number 41 (the Lightweight TT was held concurrently, and had set off first with numbers up to 40), with Daniell wearing 82 and the last away. They never saw each other once during the race, but Harold certainly read all about Artie's exploits each time he passed the pits.

After one lap, the novice led by four seconds. Then Daniell, ever a steady starter, got into his stride and turned the tables. As he passed the pits after two laps, Daniell, got a '+7' – normality was restored. But one lap later came another signal that wasn't in the plan. Daniell's factory Norton was '–3' on the Ulsterman. At the fuel stop four laps into this ding-dong battle, the veteran had redressed the balance: the upstart was again behind.

Positions remained the same after five laps, and perhaps Daniell thought he could relax. But not a bit of it. After six laps, with one to go, Bell led again: '+1'. Harold must have thought it was 1938 again, and that prodigious battle with Stanley Woods. Just as he had then, the portly Londoner dug deep, winning by the hardest-fought 22 seconds of his career. Bell would go on to win the following Senior by a far less precarious margin – more than ten minutes from Bill Doran.

Results:

	Rider	Motorcycle	Race time hr min sec	Av speed mph
1	Harold Daniell	Norton	3.11.22.2	82.81
2	Artie Bell	Norton	3:11.44.2	82.66
3	Percy Goodman	Velocette	3:12.11.0	82.46
4	Ted Frend	Norton	3:14.17.4	81.57
5	G. Newman	Norton	3:19.00.0	79.64
6	E. R. Evans	Norton	3:23.02.8	78.05

1950 Lightweight: DARIO AMBROSINI

Dario Ambrosini, 250cc World Champion in 1950, seemed to specialise in close finishes and was surely a man who would have become one of the TT greats had he only lived longer. In total, he contested just three TTs, the Lightweight events of 1949, '50 and '51. On debut he crashed out at Governor's on the first lap, but 12 months later took the Benelli single to victory in the Lightweight TT – a duel made all the more dramatic for having a massed start.

Carrying extra fuel in a seat tank to ride the seven-lap race non-stop, the Italian started steadily, lying fifth after one lap, a minute down on Maurice Cann's Guzzi. Steadily upping his pace, with a lap to go Ambrosini was a mere 15 seconds behind the leader. Three hours into what must have been by far the longest race of his career, he caught Cann on the road, then passed him on the final rush down the Mountain. At the finish timekeepers gave the Benelli man victory by just 0.2 seconds, although from contemporary photographs it was a matter of a few yards and must have been even less. It was the closest TT finish on record, made all the more memorable for being conducted in 'real time'.

In 1951, Ambrosini returned to the Island, but this time he was on the wrong side of a nail-biting finish when his mis-carburetted

Benelli lost to Tommy Wood's Guzzi by just 8.4 seconds. He was killed six weeks later when he skidded on wet tar during practice for the French Grand Prix at Albi.

Results:

	Rider	Motorcycle	Race time hr min sec	Av speed mph
1	Dario Ambrosini	Benelli	3.22.58.0	78.08
2	Maurice Cann	Moto Guzzi	3.22.58.2	78.07
3	Ronnie A. Mead	Velocette	3.29.38.0	75.60
4	Roland Pike	Rudge	3.33.45.0	74.14
5	Len Bayliss	Elbee Special	3.41.33.0	71.53
6	A. W. Jones	Moto Guzzi	3.42.41.2	71.17

1953 Senior: RAY AMM

Few riders in TT history have battled quite so hard as Southern Rhodesia's Ray Amm. Renowned for his lurid and fearless riding, for the 1953 Senior the factory Norton rider was expected to be a distant onlooker to hot favourite Geoff Duke, riding the Gilera for the first time. Although the Italian four lacked the impeccable handling of the British single, it had a power advantage of the best part of 20bhp.

None of this impressed Amm, who arrived on the Senior grid in excellent shape, having led the Junior from start to finish with record race and lap speeds. To the alarm of spectators he thundered after Geoff Duke's Gilera like a man on a mission, making up in sheer commitment what his Norton lacked in outright speed. Forcing all the way, he caught and passed Duke on the Mountain, until eventually even the peerless Duke was forced into error and crashed out. Amm himself slid off at Sarah's on the final lap, breaking a footrest. At 97.41mph, his third and fastest lap was almost 3mph faster than Duke's 1952 record. In the process he had become only the fifth rider to achieve the coveted Senior/Junior double.

Twelve months later, with the redesigned Gilera now handling well and the Norton even more out-classed than before, he gained the advantage of missing a pit stop in a race abandoned after four laps to beat Duke and the Gilera once again. In fact, he only narrowly failed to score a 'double double' when his 'Proboscis' Norton (so named for its peculiarly shaped forward-projecting frontal fairing), broke down while leading the Junior on the last lap, but not before he had set a new record lap at 94.61mph.

Results:

	Rider	Motorcycle	Race time hr min sec	Av speed mph
1	Ray Amm	Norton	2.48.51.8	93.85
2	Jack Brett	Norton	2:49.03.8	93.74
3	Reg Armstrong	Gilera	2:49.16.8	93.62
4	Rod Coleman	AJS	2:50.49.6	92.77
5	Bill Doran	AJS	2:54.25.0	90.86
6	P. A. Davey	Norton	3:02.13.0	86.97

1963 Lightweight 250: JIM REDMAN

On the face of it, the 1963 Lightweight TT was just one of many won by a succession of Honda fours and sixes, but it also marked the opening salvos in the technological warfare between Yamaha and Honda during the mid-Sixties. Yamaha had first competed in 1961 with the 125cc RA41 and 250cc RD48. Both were simple piston-ported air-cooled parallel twins but, in contrast to Suzuki's embarrassing lack of horsepower at the time, passably quick. They were, however, fragile and ill-suited to the Mountain Course. Their best finisher that year, Fumio Ito, placed sixth on the 250.

Yamaha had sat out the 1962 TT, preferring to develop their machinery instead, before returning in 1963 with the vividly fast RA55 and RD56 twins, the latter producing over 40bhp at 11,000rpm. By this time Honda was undisputed king of the Lightweight classes, yet to widespread amazement, in only their second year on the Island, Yamaha claimed a 1–2 after the opening lap. In blisteringly hot conditions, however, surely the fragile strokers couldn't last? Yet even after two laps, Itoh was still showing Redman's, Robb's and Taveri's fours a clean pair of heels. A major surprise looked possible, but Tony Godfrey crashed out and Ito lost precious time in a disorderly pit stop, handing the Rhodesian Redman the win by 27 seconds.

Perhaps if they had signed Phil Read a year earlier, it might have been a different story. Or perhaps not. Although Read took the 250cc world title in 1964 and '65, winning 12 grands prix along the way, his Yamaha was never quite up to the demands of the TT course. Year after year the seven-speed twin showed that it had the legs on the Hondas, only to break down. In 1964, Read set the fastest lap before slowing, then retiring, and twelve months later the Yam's crank broke, but not before it had been speed trapped at 143mph – practically as fast as the 350cc Honda four. Only when they adopted liquid-cooling did Yamaha truly cut the Manx mustard, but the game of technological leapfrog which began in 1963 was something to behold.

Results:

	Rider	Motorcycle	Race time hr min sec	Av speed mph
1	Jim Redman	Honda	2.23.13.2	94.85
2	Fumio Ito	Yamaha	2.23.40.4	94.55
3	Bill Smith	Honda	2.29.05.2	91.12
4	H. Hasegawa	Yamaha	2.33.41.4	88.39
5	Tommy Robb	Honda	2.44.10.2	82.75
6	John Kidson	Moto Guzzi	2.44.10.6	82.74

1965 Senior: MIKE HAILWOOD

This is one of those races TT fans still talk about, whether they are old enough to remember it or not. In 1965, Mike Hailwood was joined in the factory MV squad by a 22-year-old Italian hot-shot named Giacomo Agostini. A complete TT novice, Ago had to endure a compulsory 'sighting' lap courtesy of a Crossley's Tours bus before he was allowed to compete. His first practice lap, in wet conditions, was completed at a leisurely 75mph.

If Ago wondered what he had let himself in for, come Senior day, it didn't show. Indeed, he had already placed an impressive third in the Junior, behind Redman and Read, when his team-mate retired. Unfortunately, Senior day was wet, but the Italian still went for it. On the second lap, rounding Sarah's Cottage, he slid off. Precisely 37.73 miles later, Hailwood binned his MV at the very same spot. While Ago retired from the race after his spill, Hailwood kicked his mangled MV straight and despite an oil leak, broken screen and flattened exhaust, and two lengthy pit stops, went on to win from Joe Dunphy's Norton. Hailwood's fastest lap, at just over 95mph, gives an indication of how bad conditions were. Although there seems to have been no great controversy at the time, Hailwood restarted the Agusta illegally by rolling it downhill at Sarah's, a single-handed push start being quite impossible against the steep incline.

Twelve months later, the same duo were at it again, although this time Hailwood was back with Honda in the year they resolved to win rider and Manufacturers' World Championships in all five solo classes. (They lost out on only the 50cc and 500cc riders' titles.) This time, both riders stayed on, but the winner was the same: Hailwood, by over 2½ minutes, to give Honda their first Senior win.

Results:

	Rider	Motorcycle	Race time hr min sec	Av speed mph
1	Mike Hailwood	MV Agusta	2.28.09.0	91.69
2	Joe Dunphy	Norton	2.30.28.8	90.28
3	Mike Duff	Matchless	2.34.12.0	88.09
4	Ian Burne	Norton	2.35.01.6	87.63
5	Selwyn Griffiths	Matchless	2.36.08.6	87.00
6	Billy McCosh	Matchless	2.36.19.4	86.90

1967 Senior: MIKE HAILWOOD

The battle between Hailwood on the Honda and Agostini on the MV in the Diamond Jubilee Senior is said by many to have been the greatest TT race ever run. Again, Hailwood rode the RC181, the machine largely developed by Jim Redman, who had been forced to retire through injury the previous year. But while the Rhodesian always considered the 500 one of his favourite race bikes, Hailwood loathed the brutal handling of the 85bhp four. He was, nonetheless, firm favourite to make it five Senior wins on the trot.

Inevitably, the race boiled down to a duel between Hailwood and his former pupil, the precocious Giacomo Agostini, on the MV Agusta. Their hardware was certainly evenly matched, the Honda clocking 154.8mph through the Highlander speed trap, compared to 152.5mph for the MV-three.

The first lap went resoundingly to Italy, as Ago celebrated his birthday by pulling out a 12-second advantage over Hailwood with a record lap at 108.38mph. After two laps, the lead was down to 8.6 seconds. By the halfway pit stop, Hailwood had trashed even the new lap record with another at 108.77mph, and was now a mere two seconds in arrears. But the Honda's twist grip came loose. During an agonising 44-second pit stop Hailwood himself reached for a hammer to bang it back on to the clip-on, as Ago's MV roared towards Bray Hill. Despite struggling with a twist grip attempting to fall off the 'bar, on a bike he was already convinced was trying to spit him off, Mike chipped away at the Italian's lead, passing him on corrected time at Ramsey on lap five.

But Ago wasn't finished yet. Over the Mountain he regained the lead, and was two seconds ahead at the Bungalow, only for his chain to break two miles later at Windy Corner on the fifth lap. Although his signals allowed him to cruise on the final anticlimactic lap, Hailwood had taken the Honda to a race record which was faster than any previous Senior TT by more than three minutes. It was a record which would stand for a decade – almost until the great man himself returned in 1978.

Results:

	Rider	Motorcycle	Race time hr min sec	Av speed mph
1	Mike Hailwood	Honda	2.08.36.2	105.62
2	Peter Williams	Matchless	2.16.20.0	99.64
3	Steve Spencer	Norton	2.17.47.2	98.59
4	John Cooper	Norton	2.18.20.4	98.20
5	Fred J. Stevens	Paton	2.19.34.6	97.32
6	John Hartle	Matchless	2.19.50.0	97.14

1976 Senior 500cc: TOM HERRON

1976 should have been John Williams big year, for he arrived on the Island as a full member of the Suzuki grand prix team, with equipment comparable to that of team-mate Barry Sheene. The Senior began exactly according to plan. From a standing start Williams broke the lap record, went faster still (112.27mph) on the second lap, and after almost six laps had victory in his grasp, despite riding with no clutch for most of the race. Then, in the agonisingly slow turn into Governor's bridge, the RG500 stalled and refused to re-start (although contemporary reports had it that it ran out of fuel).

In the Senior four years earlier the Liverpudlian had ridden heroically on his out-paced G50 to split the MV pairing of Agostini and Pagani, only to run out of petrol on the Mountain. Although he eventually finished in 28th place he was excluded from the results for taking on fuel from a spectator. This year he was just as determined, paddling and pushing the Suzuki up the deceptively cruel climb to the Glencrutchery Road, with the grandstands baying in encouragement as his five-minute lead dwindled with every ragged step. Sadly, it was not to be, for as he collapsed exhausted over the line, he had dropped to seventh place.

Even then, another drama was unfolding, for in the battle of TZs that followed, Tom Herron took the win by a mere 3.4 seconds ahead of Ian Richards, racing's fastest Buddhist and in more recent years a top mechanic in the Castrol Honda squad. Neither man realised he was in with a chance of winning until he passed the pushing Williams. Victory capped a spectacular week for the popular Irishman, who had already won the Lightweight 250cc race. For Williams consolation came in the final race of the week, when he won the Classic 1,000cc TT on the GT750-based Suzuki with the added satisfaction of setting new race and lap records of 108.18mph and 110.21mph.

Results:

	Rider	Motorcycle	Race time hr min sec	Av speed mph
1	Tom Herron	Yamaha	2.09.10.0	105.15
2	Ian Richards	Yamaha	2.09.13.4	105.11
3	Billy Guthrie	Yamaha	2.09.33.0	104.84
4	Takazumi Katayama	Yamaha	2.09.38.2	104.77
5	Roger Nicholls	Yamaha	2.10.15.6	104.27
6	Jon Ekerold	Yamaha	2.11.12.4	103.52
7	John Williams	Suzuki	2.11.36.8	103.20

1978 Formula 1: MIKE HAILWOOD

The Formula One TT was the first event of the week, held in glorious weather before record-breaking crowds. It was little Ducati versus mighty Honda. Hailwood versus Read. If there was a god up there somewhere, there could surely be only the one result.

Honda, naturally, had other ideas, having won the same event the year before. Their main man, Read, would be Mike's main rival over six laps of the Mountain Course. He started the race 50 seconds ahead of Hailwood (and alongside a young Joey Dunlop), whose plan was to ride nine-tenths until he received his first signals at Gooseneck, then take it from there. In the event his board showed that he was already leading, but narrowly, from Tom Herron (who had actually led at Ballacraine), with Read third. Mike pushed harder, posting a record 110.62mph on lap 2, then

110.32mph on lap 3, giving him a seemingly unassailable margin when Herron retired with broken rear suspension on the same lap.

After two laps the two old stagers were almost level on the road, meaning Mike enjoyed a comfortable 50-second advantage. Yet even now there was drama. Read's half-distance pit stop was the faster, and the big four fired up right away. Mike's bike, meanwhile, didn't seem to want to start. With the massed grandstand on tenterhooks, the Ducati finally roared into life and set off in pursuit.

Hailwood set about re-catching Read, willed on by the biggest TT crowd for years. Every wall, every bank, every front garden, was crammed with fans yelling, encouraging, waving whatever came to hand. Then the Honda started smoking. Early on the fifth lap, with Hailwood only yards behind, Read – covered in oil and already chastened by a couple of big slides – pulled in at the 11th Milestone. Victory was assured. As Hailwood cruised down the Mountain for the last time, grown men wept tears of joy. The Island, the entire motorcycling universe, was having fits of ecstasy.

What no-one realised at the time, other than possibly Hailwood himself, was that as it crossed the line the Ducati had stripped the bevel gears which drove its camshafts, wrecking the pistons and bending con-rods and valves. Despite contemporary reports that it 'never missed a beat', the bike literally couldn't have gone another yard under its own power.

Results:

	Rider	Motorcycle	Race time hr min sec	Av speed mph
1	Mike Hailwood	Ducati	2.05.10.2	108.51
2	John Williams	Honda	2.07.09.6	106.81
3	Ian Richards	Kawasaki	2.08.07.6	106.01
4	Helmut Dahne	Honda	2.08.26.8	105.74
5	Alex George	Triumph	2.08.28.2	105.72
6	Chas Mortimer	Suzuki	2.10.50.4	103.81

1979 Schweppes Classic: ALEX GEORGE

With some £30,000 in prize money, the 1979 Classic TT was billed as the 'richest race in the world', and if such a sum could guarantee a race to remember, it was richly rewarded. The race boiled down to a glorious head-to-head between Alex George, the no-nonsense Scotsman, riding a 998cc factory RCB Honda, and Mike Hailwood on an ex-factory 1978 Suzuki RG500 square four on which he had already won that year's Senior with race and lap-record speeds.

Throughout a captivating race, the lead yo-yoed between the two combatants, never separated by more than a few seconds on corrected time. After five laps Hailwood led George by less than one second, but the Scot dug deep as Hailwood was baulked by a couple of slower riders, recording a new lap record of 114.18mph. At the finish, after 226 miles of the fiercest racing, the Honda won by just 3.4 seconds, with third-placed Charlie Williams 3½ minutes adrift. It was not only the richest, but the fastest TT ever run.

In the winner's enclosure, the 39-year-old Hailwood generously accepted that 'Alex went too quick for me ... I didn't want to stick my neck out any further', before observing that this was the first time he had ever finished second in a TT race – exactly 21 years after his Island debut. He then announced, 'finally and irrevocably' his retirement from racing. As farewells go, it was hard to forget.

Results:

	Rider	Motorcycle	Race time hr min sec	Av speed mph
1	Alex George	Honda	2.00.07.0	113.08
2	Mike Hailwood	Suzuki	2.00.10.4	113.02
3	Charlie Williams	Yamaha	2.03.29.4	109.99
4	Jeff Sayle	Yamaha	2.04.00.0	109.53
5	Graeme McGregor	Yamaha	2.04.10.4	109.38
6	Joey Dunlop	Yamaha	2.04.39.2	108.96

1980 Classic: JOEY DUNLOP

This was the win that truly launched Dunlop's career, yet it had looked so unlikely. In practice he had managed no better than sixth, with a best lap at 108.54mph. Throughout the week he had struggled with the big Yamaha's handling, only to notice at the last minute that the rear wheel spacers were in back-to-front, throwing the wheel alignment out. Then, on the night before the race Joey himself had worked until 2.30am changing the crankshaft.

Three inches extra welded onto the fuel tank 'at a place in Ballasalla at 1 o'clock on the night before the race' gave a monstrous eight gallons capacity and the prospect of only one pit stop. It also made it 'the ugliest thing you've ever seen.'

Worse still: 'It was a bit of a monster for a little guy like me,' Joey explained after the race, 'especially as I couldn't find a screen tall enough to cover the tank and my helmet.' At Ballacraine on the first lap, two of the tank straps broke. Joey spent the rest of the race trying to hold it on with his knees and fearful that it would pull the fuel pipes off the carbs.

But the wee Ulsterman hung in there, and even though he took his time during his one fuel stop, with two stops to make, even Honda's high-tech quickfill system, worth over half a minute, could not turn it around for Mick Grant. Leaving Ballacraine for the last time, Joey led by just 0.3 seconds, but a record final lap at 115.22mph put the result beyond doubt. Grant, struggling to use top gear on his overgeared 1,062cc works Honda, was 20.4 seconds in arrears at the finish.

It is difficult now to appreciate the enormity of what Joey and his crew had achieved. If his 1977 win was in something of a second division TT, this was the real thing. And it was a triumph for innocent Irish enthusiasm over the might of the factory Hondas. For the rest of his career Joey would nominate this win as his most satisfying TT victory. Some of its appeal, for a man practically living on the breadline, was its £8,000 payout; much was the fact of 'beating all the factory riders by fooling them.' But of equal importance was being able to dedicate his triumph to the memory of his greatest racing friend, Merv Robinson, killed at the NW200 just the previous month.

Results:

	Rider	Motorcycle	Race time hr min sec	Av speed mph
1	Joey Dunlop	Yamaha	2.00.29.8	112.72
2	Mick Grant	Honda	2.00.50.2	112.40
3	Ron Haslam	Honda	2.03.02.6	110.39
4	Chas Mortimer	Suzuki	2.04.19.2	109.25
5	Steve Cull	Suzuki	2.05.21.2	108.35
6	Sam McClements	Honda	2.05.30.2	108.22

1981 Classic: GRAEME CROSBY

In the early Eighties, Suzuki and Honda battled for TT supremacy in the larger classes, a rivalry that came to a head after Saturday's Formula One TT. Initially, it seemed that Honda's Ron Haslam had won the race. Then Suzuki's Martyn Ogborne put in a protest, as a result of which Graeme Crosby was credited with time lost on the grid and installed as the winner 2½ hours after the race had finished.

The Honda camp, with some justification, was livid. Rumours of protest flew around the Island, but none quite captured the bizarre reality that lined up for Friday's Classic TT. No longer was Honda Britain red, white and blue. Not only the bikes, but the rider's kit was as black as Honda's corporate mood.

Whatever Honda's pleas to the contrary, their riders looked patently embarrassed by the whole affair. But if it affected Joey Dunlop's riding, it didn't show. Trailing Crosby by five seconds after lap one, Joey took 1.8 seconds off his own record next time around. By the Bungalow on lap 3, he had edged into a narrow lead at an even more furious pace. But the extra speed exacted a cruel price as he ran out of fuel on the climb from Hillberry. Joey part coasted, part pushed to the pits.

Refuelled and pumped up with adrenaline, Joey set off to recapture lost time. From Ballacraine to Ballacraine he recorded a time of 19m 22s – around 117mph, way inside the record. (His 'official' lap record was 115.40mph.) But the chase was too much. Leaving the Gooseneck on lap five the Honda's cam chain broke.

The result was that the black protest, far from convincing observers of Honda's case, had simply drawn more attention to errors in their race strategy. To compound the team's misery, Haslam went out with ignition troubles when lying third, leaving Crosby and Mick Grant, winner of the Senior race, to display-ride to an easy Suzuki 1–2. Only third-placed Alex George was left to fly Honda's black flag. Team boss Barry Symmons blamed the miscalculation on the race's furious pace: 'We reckoned on 9.2 litres per lap ... even our most pessimistic calculations gave him enough to complete three laps non-stop ... but we didn't reckon on three 115mph laps.'

Results:

	Rider	Motorcycle	Race time hr min sec	Av speed mph
1	Graeme Crosby	Suzuki	1.59.34.8	113.58
2	Mick Grant	Suzuki	2.00.04.8	113.11
3	Alex George	Honda	2.02.14.0	111.12
4	John Newbold	Suzuki	2.05.23.4	108.32
5	Alan Jackson	Suzuki	2.05.34.0	108.17
6	Bernard Murray	Yamaha	2.05.36.2	108.14

1983 Senior Classic: ROB McELNEA

This was the race that inspired Steve Hislop, a spectator at the 11th Milestone, to take up TT racing. If the results suggest a comfortable first win for Rob McElnea by almost two minutes, they also hide the furious contribution of two Irishmen, both at the peak of their form.

One, of course, was Joey Dunlop, who despite his Honda's handling problems, made his customary blistering start and led early on, until slowed by a blocked fuel breather pipe. The same 850cc Vee-four had won the Formula One race earlier in the week, but the Classic's extra fuel load transformed it into an ill-handling 'monster'. Looking at the Honda's broken screen after the race, Joey suggested that he had 'spent more time on top of the screen than underneath it.'

The other Irishman was Norman Brown, son of a Newry publican and winner of the Senior the year before (and backed by the same Hector Neill who now heads the TAS Suzuki squad). Brown was on a mission that day, lapping at a staggering 116.19mph from a standing-start on Neill's RG500, only to run out of fuel on lap 3, leaving him coasting at Kate's. 'When Norman and Joey came through,' Hislop remembered many years later, 'I nearly fell backwards off the bank in surprise. Boy, look at that! It was that moment that made me want to do it, too.'

Dunlop's troubles passed the lead to McElnea, who went on to secure a relatively untroubled maiden TT win at 114.81mph, the fastest TT ever run to that date. Had Dunlop and Brown not had their problems, who knows what that figure might have been.

Results:

	Rider	Motorcycle	Race time hr min sec	Av speed mph
1	Rob McElnea	Suzuki	1.58.18.2	114.81
2	Con Law	Suzuki	2.00.13.6	–
3	Joey Dunlop	Honda	2.00.24.4	–
4	Charlie Williams	Honda	2.01.31.4	–
5	Mick Grant	Suzuki	2.01.32.0	–
6	Bernard Murray	Kawasaki	2.03.26.2	–

1984 TT: Formula One, Senior and Premier Classic: ROB McELNEA and JOEY DUNLOP

This duel lasted for the whole of race week, leaving spectators spell-bound as records were smashed seemingly lap by lap. The proponents were Joey Dunlop, fresh from a double win at the NW200 and just coming into his prime, and the redoubtable Rob McElnea, then riding in his third and last TT. The pair were in a class of their own. A radar trap part way through Rhencullen bends clocked both at 118mph, fully 8mph faster than the best of the rest.

The opening skirmish, the Formula One TT, went to Joey, but not without problems. On lap 3, he stopped in a cloud of smoke at Braddan, then again at Union Mills. Thinking the rear wheel had jammed, he gave it a cursory kick before noticing that the exhaust pipe was jamming against the tyre. By this time his 50-second lead had become a 24-second deficit to Reg Marshall, suffering exhaust and fuel problems of his own, and a 115.89mph lap record regained him the lead. It was a race Honda seemed desperate to lose, but luckily for them Suzuki were trying even harder. Grant's Suzuki gearbox broke, and McElnea's broke its steering damper and then seized.

McElnea turned the tables in the Premier Classic event, making just one pit stop to Dunlop's two to win by 14 seconds from the 920cc Honda. Again there was a new lap record, this time to the Humbersider, at 117.13mph.

The Senior would be the decider, and Dunlop was in the mood. Riding the 500cc Honda two-stroke triple, on every one of the first five laps he set a new lap record, leaving it at a staggering 118.47mph. Then, cruelly, he ran out of fuel (although contemporary reports spoke of a broken crank), coasting to a halt at Mountain Hut within ten miles of the finish when leading by 40 seconds. McElnea, scarcely loitering himself, with a best lap at 118.23mph on the RG500, hung on to take Suzuki's seventh consecutive Senior TT.

Results: Formula One

	Rider	Motorcycle	Race time hr min sec	Av speed mph
1	Joey Dunlop	Honda	2.01.37.0	111.68
2	Roger Marshall	Honda	2.01.57.2	111.37
3	Tony Rutter	Ducati	2.04.07.0	109.43

Results: Premier Classic

1	Rob McElnea	Suzuki	1.56.58.2	116.12
2	Joey Dunlop	Honda	1.57.12.4	115.88
3	Mick Grant	Suzuki	1.58.26.2	114.68

Results: Senior

1	Rob McElnea	Suzuki	1.57.26.2	115.66
2	Roger Marshall	Honda	2.00.34.0	112.65
3	Trevor Nation	Suzuki	2.01.13.2	112.05

1988 Production 'A': DAVE LEACH

It is rare that a Production race warrants such star billing, but the heroics with which the top riders wrestled the biggest, meanest road bikes around the Mountain deserves special mention. If ultimately it ended in tragedy, it also produced some stirring spectacles, and none more so than Dave Leach's win in 1988. Slowed on the final lap when his worn chain began jumping the sprockets, the Halifax man clung on to win by just 0.8 seconds from Geoff Johnson, riding a similar FZR1000 Yamaha. Johnson's final-lap charge gave him a new record of 116.55mph.

Bikes such as the FZR1000 and GSX-R1100 Suzuki were ferocious things to ride, steering and handling with nothing like the precision of their modern equivalents. And yet the speeds attained by the likes of Johnson, Leach and Nick Jefferies were mind-boggling in the extreme. Jefferies, riding the fast but flabby CBR1000 Honda, remembers filling the rear shock absorber with 80-weight gear oil to make the best of its inadequate ground clearance and never being so happy to see the finishing line.

Twelve months later, after the tragic deaths of Mez Mellor and Steve Henshaw, the Production event was scrubbed only to be revised in 1996 with a new generation of sports superbikes.

Results:

	Rider	Motorcycle	Race time hr min sec	Av speed mph
1	Dave Leach	Padgett Yamaha	1.19.12.2	114.32
2	Geoff Johnson	Loctite Yamaha	1.19.13.0	114.30
3	Kevin Wilson	Suzuki	1.19.33.8	113.81
4	Phil Mellor	Heron Suzuki	1.20.22.6	112.65
5	Robert Hayes	Kawasaki	1.20.55.0	111.90
6	Nick Jefferies	Honda	1.21.00.8	111.77

1990 Junior: IAN LOUGHER

Lougher's start in Island racing could scarcely have been more auspicious. In the 1983 MGP he shared the 250cc Newcomers' rostrum with Robert Dunlop and Steve Hislop; 'Lucky' Lougher placed third.

Revenge, as they say, is a dish best eaten cold. But it was in one of the hottest TTs ever witnessed that 'Lucky' put Hislop in his place, overhauling the Scot on the final lap to win the 1990 Junior by a mere 1.8 seconds. After years of struggling for competitive machinery, it was the first time the Welshman had enjoyed a new race bike capable of making a serious challenge. He clicked at once with the 250cc Yamaha, finishing second at the NW200, then unofficially breaking the class lap record by fully 18 seconds during TT practice.

Nonetheless, Honda Britain's Hislop remained the clear race favourite, a fact which seemed to take some of the pressure off Lougher, whose best previous performance had been a second place to Robert Dunlop in the 1989 125cc TT. In the groove from the minute the flag dropped, 'Lucky' took another 20 seconds off the lap record during the race, beating a man then considered almost untouchable over the Mountain Course. Hislop admitted that failing ever to win a 250cc race was the biggest disappointment of his TT career, and he never came closer than on that day. The pace was so fierce that it would be another nine years before any 250 went faster than the new lap record – 117.80mph, an astonishing 3.76mph up on Eddie Laycock's 1989 mark.

Nor was the rest of the opposition remotely feeble. The pace of the front two utterly blew away riders of the calibre of Eddie Laycock, Carl Fogarty, Johnny Rea and Phil McCallen. Imagine it: Foggy fourth, by almost two minutes – some race.

Results:

	Rider	Motorcycle	Race time hr min sec	Av speed mph
1	Ian Lougher	Yamaha	1.18.37.6	115.16
2	Steve Hislop	Honda	1.18.39.4	115.12
3	Eddie Laycock	Yamaha	1.20.24.0	112.62
4	Carl Fogarty	Honda	1.20.27.2	112.55
5	Johnny Rea	Yamaha	1.20.35.2	112.36
6	Phillip McCallen	Honda	1.21.07.6	111.61

1991 Formula 1: STEVE HISLOP

Individual TT races are often remembered as Classics, but in 1991 Steve Hislop and Carl Fogarty treated us to a mesmerising week-long duel in the sun. The press, inevitably, made much of their bitter rivalry, although the truth was that the Honda team-mates were on the best of terms. From their adjacent rented cottages in Union Mills, they would emerge each day to do battle on a brace of 145bhp RVF Hondas – and in the process take some of the edge off Yamaha's 30th TT birthday celebrations.

Throughout practice week the pair swapped fastest laps. On a bike he had only previously ridden at an airfield, Hislop startled even himself with an opening session at 121.54mph. A day later, Fogarty retorted with 122.06mph, only for Hislop to trump that 24 hours later with a 'totally out-of-control' 122.81mph. Spectacular, yes. Epoch-making, certainly. But this was also getting silly.

At 2.39pm on the Thursday, Fogarty delivered the coup de grace – 123.66mph, the fastest lap ever recorded over the Mountain Circuit. The Blackburn man looked pleased, if not downright smug. 'Beat that, Hizzy', was the message. Precisely 30.8 seconds later, Hislop did just that, with a lap at 124.36mph (the first 200kph lap, incidentally, and not bettered until 1999).

Hislop, it seemed, had all the answers but Foggy's never-say-die reputation had many thinking he would go for broke. From Honda race boss Mr Oguma downwards, they were beginning to rue the day they had initiated this face-off by bringing two RVFs to the Island. Hislop, they trusted; Fogarty, they feared for. Orders were issued: 'Don't go mad.' But this was racing, not a card game. Could a racer as competitive as Foggy possibly hold back?

Between themselves the two friendly rivals hatched a deal: whoever led at the first pit-stop would be allowed to win. But until then, the gloves were off. To everyone's relief, Fogarty kept his cool. After a lap he knew Hizzy had him beaten, and after two he tried to indicate as much to Hislop in the pits. The 1–2 decided, the pair put on a display of formation flying – lapping together at close to 122mph – which can rarely have been exceeded for sheer precision by two men at the peak of their craft on machines hand-crafted for the purpose.

Results:

	Rider	Motorcycle	Race time hr min sec	Av speed mph
1	Steve Hislop	Silkolene Honda	1.52.15.0	121.01
2	Carl Fogarty	Silkolene Honda	1.53.31.0	119.65
3	Brian Morrison	Loctite Yamaha	1.55.26.4	117.66
4	Phillip McCallen	Silkolene Honda	1.55.38.0	117.46
5	Steve Ward	Honda	1.57.21.6	115.73
6	Bob Jackson	Honda	1.58.25.6	114.69

1992 Senior: STEVE HISLOP

Twelve months later, Foggy and Hizzy were at it again – and not a factory Honda in sight. The Senior race, in gloriously sunny conditions, was one of the all-time greats, even eclipsing the duo's duel of the previous year. Riding a 588cc rotary Norton dragged out of retirement, Hislop's only serious opposition came from Fogarty – but what opposition it was! Fogarty, riding the same 750cc OW01 Yamaha which Hislop had earlier been contracted to ride, led three times in a race which never saw more than seven seconds separating the leading two riders. After 226 mercurial miles, the margin was a mere 4.4 seconds, with both riders charging furiously for the flag. Fogarty had the consolation of an outright lap record at 123.62mph, 1.2 seconds faster than Hislop's 1991 record aboard the works RVF750 Honda.

Hislop, after a week which had seen him set fastest lap in three races without winning any of them, was jubilant in victory: 'I'm really pleased to have done it for Norton. It's a bit of history.' The last man to win the Senior for Norton was Mike Hailwood in 1961. Thirty-one years later, the born-again British marque had done it again. The win followed Hislop's second place to Ireland's Phillip McCallen on a Honda RC30 in the previous week's Formula One TT, after Fogarty pulled out with gearbox problems.

Norton team boss, Barry Symmons, observed wryly that, after last year's win from 'a million dollar Honda, it wasn't a bad effort for a bike built in a shed in Lichfield.' To compound Norton's joy, Robert Dunlop took a second Norton to third place.

If it was the end of an era for Norton, the 1992 Senior would also mark Hislop and Fogarty's last TT duel. As spectators thrilled to video pictures of the leading bikes snaking and weaving over the Isle of Man's bumps, Hislop confirmed that this would 'definitely' be his last big bike TT. 'It's actually stupidity riding 750s round here. You are out of control most of the time. The 600s are fast enough.' Two years later he was back.

For his part Fogarty, Hislop's partner in the Kawasaki France endurance team, confirmed that this would be his last TT before concentrating on World Superbike racing, at which he went on to make a point or two. But he was second best on that glorious Manx day in June 1992.

Results:

	Rider	Motorcycle	Race time hr min sec	Av speed mph
1	Steve Hislop	588 Norton	1.51.59.6	121.28
2	Carl Fogarty	750 Yamaha	1.52.04.0	121.20
3	Robert Dunlop	588 Norton	1.54.02.6	119.10
4	Nick Jefferies	750 Honda	1.54.33.2	118.57
5	Mark Farmer	750 Yamaha	1.54.47.6	118.32
6	Robert Farmer	750 Yamaha	1.57.03.6	116.03

1996 Lightweight 250cc and Ultra-Lightweight 125cc: JOEY DUNLOP

After the departure of Hislop and Fogarty, the larger classes lost some of their sheen, and much of the interest focused on the smaller machines, and not least the improbable exploits of a middle-aged man from Ballymoney: Joey Dunlop. 'Yer Maun's' double win in 1996 – giving him 21 TT victories in all – neatly illustrated why he had been so good and for so long.

As was so often the case, Dunlop had struggled in practice – sixth in the Lightweight, fourth in the 125 – giving little hint of the success to come. Indeed, the major talking point seemed to be that Joey, a renowned gasper, had recently quit smoking.

The Lightweight race, postponed to Tuesday, gave us perhaps the most thrilling dice of the week. Phillip McCallen, fresh from victory in Saturday's Formula One event, again started strongly, but after a lap led by a mere 0.2 seconds from team-mate Dunlop. One lap later the margin had stretched – to a paltry 1.9 seconds – but a slow pit stop handed the advantage back to Dunlop. With

McCallen unable to respond due to a holed exhaust, it was left to late-charging Jim Moodie to harry Dunlop home as the Ulsterman eked out his fuel to last the distance.

Weather again intervened for the concurrent Ultra-Lightweight and single-cylinder TTs, which were delayed by over six hours and shortened to a two-lap sprint. Dunlops – either Joey or brother Robert – had won the 125cc event every year but one since its reintroduction in 1989. Despite Joey's indifferent practice times, he had a history of getting it right on race day.

Slowed by traffic on lap 1, the master took a while to get into his stride. But when he did, his 20 years of TT experience gave him the winning edge. He and Gavin Lee reached Ramsey Hairpin neck-and-neck second time around, but the Ulster veteran's trackcraft paid off as he forged a 3.8-second advantage through treacherous banks of mist on the Mountain. At 107.62mph, this proved to be the fastest lap of the race.

Results: Lightweight 250cc

	Rider	Motorcycle	Race time hr min sec	Av speed mph
1	Joey Dunlop	Honda Britain	1.18.31.5	115.31
2	Jim Moodie	Honda	1.18.37.2	115.17
3	Jason Griffiths	Morris Honda Britain	1.20.11.4	112.92

Results: Ultra-Lightweight 125cc

1	Joey Dunlop	Honda	42.34.6	106.33
2	Gavin Lee	Honda	42.38.4	106.18
3	Glen English	Beale Honda	42.47.3	105.81

1997 Junior 600cc: IAN SIMPSON

In 1997, it had not seemed that long since we were speculating on the first 120mph lap on a full-on racing machine (in fact it was Steve Hislop in 1989), and yet suddenly, here was Ian Simpson – at the time probably the classiest contender never to have won a TT – coming so tantalisingly close on a souped-up roadster middleweight. Yet even though he topped the leaderboard, the Scot's practice performance, at just 117mph, gave little hint of what was to come.

It wasn't, in truth, a great contest. 'Simmo' led from start to finish, and it was the sheer pace of his ride that impressed. His new lap record, 119.86mph, eclipsing the mark set by McCallen the previous year. From Ramsey to Ramsey on laps 2 and 3, he was unofficially timed at over 120mph. The Dumfries man also established a new race record at 118.41mph.

Ironically, Simpson was drafted into the V&M squad only after regular rider Iain Duffus pulled out due to injuries received at Snetterton the previous month. His victory came 21 years after his father, Bill, scored his only TT win on a 250 Yamaha in 1976. Ian was a six-year-old spectator that day.

Phillip McCallen scored a brave second place despite a badly swollen left hand, a legacy of a horrifying crash at Quarry Bends in the Lightweight race. 'Every time I came through [Quarry Bends]' he said afterwards, 'I could see my tyre marks from Monday. I was too cautious.'

Results:

	Rider	Motorcycle	Race time hr min sec	Av speed mph
1	Ian Simpson	V&M Honda CBR600	1.16.28.3	118.41
2	Phillip McCallen	Honda	1.16.57.8	117.65
3	Michael Rutter	V&M Honda	1.17.21.7	117.05
4	Derek Young	Anderton Honda	1.17.21.9	117.04
5	Joey Dunlop	Harris Honda	1.17.42.6	116.52
6	Bob Jackson	McAdoo Honda	1.17.51.6	116.30

1998 Lightweight 250cc: JOEY DUNLOP

This went down as the event which produced some of the keenest competition for years, despite a catalogue of injuries to the top riders. It was remarkable, too, for Robert Dunlop's feat in taking the 125cc race yet again, despite the twin handicaps of a broken leg and having to use a left-handed front brake, a legacy of crashing into a Ballaugh cottage wall in 1994 when his rear wheel collapsed. But most memorable of all was his wily big brother's performance in the Lightweight race.

Joey Dunlop arrived on the Island mangled from a crash at Tandragee early in May. Although his injuries included a broken left hand and collarbone, cracked pelvis and missing half his ring finger, he pronounced himself fit for the Island, if too sore to ride anything bigger than a 250. Just turning up at all showed just how much guts and bloody-minded toughness matter, and that Joey had both in abundance. If he needed an excuse not to fight the pain over 150 miles of the toughest course in the world, the Manx weather obliged. It blew and it poured down. But far from giving it a miss, Dunlop confounded everyone by splashing through the puddles to win his 23rd TT.

In pain or not, Joey Dunlop still knew how to out-fox his opponents. As the 250cc race began it was scheduled to be run over three laps (reduced, because of time pressure, from four), which for most riders meant one pit stop. While many of his rivals elected to pit after lap 1, Joey held on in the worst weather many riders could remember. Sure enough, the race was further reduced to two laps as more muck rolled overhead. By that time, the likes of Simpson and even hard man Moodie had already pulled out.

But not Joey. Mangled hand or not, he teased out a convincing lead over his nearest rival, so Joey's wet-weather smoothness would probably have given him the win, anyway. For even had he pitted, it is unlikely that 'Yer Maun' would have failed to win. His margin of victory was a gaping 43.1 seconds, and his fastest lap – 100.50mph – was comfortably the quickest of the race. Asked afterwards whether he had had any problems, he simply replied: 'Och, I didn't go fast enough.'

	Rider	Motorcycle	Race time hr min sec	Av speed mph
1	Joey Dunlop	Honda Britain RS250	46.51.8	96.61
2	Bob Jackson	DTR Spondon Yamaha	47.34.7	95.16
3	John McGuinness	Team Vimto Honda	47.48.6	94.69
4	James Courtney	MSR Honda	48.08.0	94.06
5	Jason Griffiths	Webb Honda UK	48.32.4	93.27
6	Gavin Lee	DTR Yamaha	48.40.6	93.01

2000 Formula One: JOEY DUNLOP

In 1999, for the first time anyone could remember – well, since 1981, anyway – not a single Irishman won a race at the Isle of Man TT. Whether Joey Dunlop resolved to return things to normality for the year 2000, we can only guess, but the great man's final TT was a week to remember.

The records show that Dunlop scored three wins that year, his third hat-trick, but it was the first that meant the most to him, and to his thousands of fans. On Saturday, 3 June, we witnessed something as close to a fairytale as such a fast and frenzied sport ever gets. At 48 years of age, and a dozen years after the last one, Joey Dunlop had won yet another Formula One TT.

Riding a factory-engined SP-1 and with Honda president Mr Kawashima looking on, Joey blasted into a lead he would relinquish only briefly throughout the six-lap race held on a daunting mix of wet and dry roads. If conditions that day suited him better than anyone else in the field, that is only to say that he was also the field's most complete road racer. For a brief period during lap 4 the lead passed to David Jefferies' R1 Yamaha, before slick work by the Honda pit crew put Dunlop back ahead. Then, with conditions continuing to improve on lap 5, the V&M machine's clutch basket exploded, sidelining 'DJ' at Ballig Bridge. At the finish Dunlop led by almost one minute from Michael Rutter's Yamaha, with John McGuinness's SP-1 a further 23 seconds behind in third.

Even before the finish, it was delirium. As Joey left the pits for his final stint, not only the grandstands stood and roared in exultation, but most of the other pit crews did too. Across the Glencrutchery Road, the cub scouts manning the antique scoreboard couldn't resist cheers and waves of their own. After the race, the finishing enclosure was more like a rugby scrum, and even the man himself seemed surprised by the emphatic nature of his victory, not to mention all the fuss. Sheer speed wasn't the issue so much as sustaining a high pace over six gruelling laps. 'I never thought I'd win another F1 race,' he admitted amidst emotional scenes, 'but I've never had a bike this good.'

'Yer Maun' may have been magnificent over the Mountain, but he struggled to open his 24th bottle of TT celebratory champagne. McGuinness and Rutter were already in full spray by the time Joey opened his – and was left with the cork in his hand while the bottle ricocheted to the floor. One month later he was dead.

Results:

	Rider	Motorcycle	Race time hr min sec	Av speed mph
1	Joey Dunlop	Honda VTR SP1	1.52.15.3	120.99
2	Michael Rutter	V&M Yamaha R1	1.53.14.9	119.93
3	John McGuinness	Vimto Honda SP1	1.53.38.0	119.53
4	Ian Lougher	Yamaha 1000	1.54.22.8	118.75
5	Jim Moodie	Honda Britain FireBlade	1.55.08.6	117.95
6	Jason Griffiths	Cowles Yamaha 1000	1.55.44.1	117.36

2002 Senior: DAVID JEFFERIES

The Standard Bank Offshore Senior of 2002 certainly wasn't a great race in the sense that the lead was hotly challenged. David Jefferies' utter domination on the TAS GSX-R1000 Suzuki saw to that. But it was memorable for the sheer speeds of the leading riders, for in this one race no less than eight men achieved something only a handful had managed before, averaging 120mph over the full six laps. Rarely can the TT course have suffered such a working over.

Way out in front of them all was that man Jefferies, recording his ninth TT win and, uniquely, his third consecutive treble. Slowing for his pit stop on lap 2, he lapped at 127.29mph, which turned out to be only one of three sub-18 minute laps. At 124.74mph his race average speed was the fastest ever, and to cap it all, no less a legend than Giacomo Agostini presented him with the Senior trophy. TAS team boss Hector Neill, exactly 20 years after tasting Senior victory with Norman Brown, wore a grin two decades wide.

Results:

	Rider	Motorcycle	Race time hr min sec	Av speed mph
1	David Jefferies	1000 TAS Suzuki	1.48.53.1	124.74
2	Ian Lougher	1000 TAS Suzuki	1.49.15.2	124.32
3	John McGuinness	954 Honda	1.50.01.3	123.45
4	Richard Quayle	1000 Suzuki	1.51.18.6	122.02
5	Richard Britton	1000 O'Kane Suzuki	1.51.30.7	121.80
6	Adrian Archibald	954 Red Bull Honda	1.52.19.1	120.93
7	Ryan Farquhar	1000 McAdoo Yamaha	1.52.27.0	120.78
8	Chris Heath	1000 Yamaha	1.53.05.1	120.11

Tax haven?

From 1922 until the 1960s, visiting vehicles were obliged to buy a temporary Manx driving licence (for 5p) and pay Manx road tax, or what was euphemistically known as an 'Exemption Registration Document' (race machines were exempt). In 1949, the Manx Parliament even considered a tax on private temporary grandstands, but this was never levied.

Another Island peculiarity was the requirement to sound your horn when approaching a crossroads, which landed Jimmy Guthrie with a ten-shilling fine after one practice session.

Unthinkable now, but riders were also occasionally charged with riding unsilenced machines to practice.

The Manx kitty was then so low that when the ACU pressed for better grandstand and race control facilities in the late 1940s, it was to be another four decades before their ambitions bore fruit.

Practice

Until 1927, riders practised on open roads, contending with whatever Manx traffic threw at them and obeying normal driving laws. Indeed, riders could start their lap anywhere they chose – so Scott's workshop, for instance, was in Ramsey, while Douglas (the motorcycle company) favoured Peel.

Then the inevitable happened, and Archie Birkin collided fatally with a delivery vehicle at Rhencullen on the outskirts of Kirk Michael and subsequent practice sessions were held on closed roads. Yet even this did not entirely prevent incidents. Jimmy Guthrie was prosecuted for shooting a red light during the first-ever evening practice session in 1937. Then there was the case of Phil Read, out for a bit of unofficial practice on open roads in 1978. When he crashed his RG500 at Brandish, he found himself facing charges for no road tax, no insurance and two bald tyres – the police don't take kindly to slicks.

At the other extreme, and despite the valiant efforts of police and marshals, there are sometimes still vehicles to hit. In the postponed Formula One TT of 1994 both Joey Dunlop and Phil McCallen narrowly missed a Manx Highways truck backing out of a driveway near the 13th Milestone.

Cancellations

Although it is commonplace for races to be postponed, and more rarely for them to be halted and restarted, outright cancellations are rare.

Bad weather in 1935 causes postponement of the Senior TT from Friday to Saturday, causing chaos for the 11,000 fans who had sailed across supposedly for the day. With just four telephone lines linking the Island to England, making alternative plans wasn't simple.

A Seamen's strike caused the 1966 TT to be postponed. Eventually run from 28 August to 2 September, that first date was a Sunday, a day which had never seen TT racing before, and required a special act by Tynwald. The Manx Grand Prix was rescheduled to follow immediately after the TT, offering the best part of a month of continuous racing.

In 1987, Honda's brand-new CBR600 looked poised for victory in Production class C, having taken every one of the first ten practice places. Yet it was not to be. A prolonged spell of bad weather caused the Production 'A' and 'C' events to be dropped, and seriously threatened that year's Senior TT, too.

Sidecar race 'A' in 1998 was cancelled. Or was it Sidecar 'B'? Race 'A' was rained off on Saturday and again on Sunday. Then, on Monday, race 'B' – or was it still race 'A'? – succumbed to the mists of Man. The combined 'A + B' event finally got underway on the Tuesday of race week.

Manx Radio

Prior to TT commentary hitting the airwaves, the only news most spectators had as racing took place came from one of a handful of public address speakers dotted around the course, or from the progressively less frequent BBC bulletins. Manx Radio first covered the races in 1965, from a Portacabin alongside the timekeeper's hut on the Glencrutchery Road. The man with the mike that first day – and for the next 35 years – was Peter Kneale, destined to become 'the voice of the TT'. By 1967 Peter had moved to a position in the grandstand (meaning he could now actually see the scoreboard whilst on air). Following Peter's death in January 2002 – ironically after the year in which there was no racing – Geoff Cannell and then Charlie Lambert, with a roving team including Chris Kinley and Charlie Williams, took over the helm of Radio TT.

Chapter 6

RISK AND TRAGEDY

'I loved it, absolutely loved it. Real nerve-wracking, yeah, but such an adrenalin rush – and what else do you ride bikes for? It was the big test. You needed a big mental commitment. And to be honest I never had any moments when I thought I'd run out of road – just the sort of scares you get landing crossed-up off a jump at 160mph. And that time the steering damper exploded ...'

That's how Rob McElnea summed up his TT experiences: the biggest test, and the one with the biggest risks.

Risk is an ever-present partner to all forms of motorcycle racing, from trials to desert rallies. Risk is the principal element in the adrenalin rush that makes racing so attractive for those who take part. That is not to say that it is the sole element, for competition, dreams of glory, or simply reaching personal milestones, all play their part, too. But danger is as much a part of motorcycle racing as are the engines in the bikes themselves.

Few TT riders freely articulate the connection between danger and potential death, but it is there. Few riders, indeed, will permit themselves the luxury of even thinking of the myriad things that might go horribly wrong. Some of the time your body – or maybe your subconscious – is better informed. As the seconds tick down to the start your mouth is dry, your pulse racing. Your stomach is doing hand-springs and the blood in your veins feels to fizz. Some riders are monosyllabic and unreachable, others seem to jabber faster than words will fit. Then the flag drops, and by the top of Bray Hill the anxiety is forgotten, replaced by a rush which gives no time for introspection. As a racer, this is why you're here.

But the same attribute that gives road racing its tremendous allure for those who take part, can also lead to death. Norton's

Gilbert Smith summed up the cruel appeal of the TT in the Thirties when he suggested that 'the TT is the manifestation of every human emotion ... of victory ... of triumph ... but sometimes of tragedy and pathos.'

Perhaps it is miraculous, given the unforgiving nature of the Mountain Course, that more get-offs don't have tragic results. Almost everyone who has ridden it will have slid off at least once. Yet remarkably, the majority of riders survive their spills, often walking away with just a few bruises. Given the races' long history, the odds are that wherever anyone might bale off, another will have died at much the same spot. There's no sense to it, and little point seeking any: it is something of a lottery out there.

Mick Grant had more TT crashes than most TT riders, yet emerged from 17 years of Manx racing unscathed. During each TT he was as taciturn as the rest of them, but can admit now to being 'always frightened daft going to the Island, and relieved to get away. But I actually enjoyed the experience. I first went because that's what you did, and anyway, plenty of other grands prix were on road circuits, too – Spa, Brno, Imatra.'

If there's an apparent incongruity between enjoyment and being frightened daft, then Mick is no more illogical than the rest. A decade ago both Hislop and Fogarty were suggesting that the bikes had become too fast. Yet if you had offered either another 50 horsepower, they would have trampled you to get it for themselves. That is not hypocrisy, it is simply the mentality which makes a racer what he is.

From an outside viewpoint, the same mind-set can often appear callous. Few top riders have not lost at least one close friend to racing, yet most pull down the emotional shutters and carry on, almost as if nothing had happened. Inside, they all feel it, but to do anything else would cripple them as racers, too.

Jim Redman, one of racing's true hard men, remembers the awful death toll of those times, during which he won six TTs. 'The statistic was six per year [in all top road race competition].

Imagine now, going back five or ten years, and ticking off 60 grand prix riders who are no longer around, including the likes of Dale and McIntyre. It was no respecter of talent.'

'Nineteen sixty-two was a really bad year. I was really knocked up when Tom Phillis was killed. We'd lived and dreamed together as part of the same Honda team. The guy who got me through it was Bob McIntyre. He said: "If you're going to go, let it be quick like that, against the wall at Laurel Bank." Then two months later he was dead, too, killed at Oulton Park. That was hard – really hard. That season, the 350 championship seemed to be between Tom, Bob, Gary Hocking, Mike Hailwood and me. By the end of the year, the first three were dead and Takahashi had nearly died. What a way to win! You'd give the championship away to get the guys back if you could.'

If racing and risk are synonymous, then it is self-evident that the risk should be reduced to the absolute minimum. And times change. Fatalities at the rate they occurred in the Sixties would be wholly unacceptable today. That is one reason racing and – above all – race circuits have changed so much. Not just the world at large, but the riders themselves cried 'enough'. Until 30 years or so ago, as Mick Grant observed, the Mountain Circuit was not significantly more dangerous than any other. But today, 'pure' road circuits inevitably stand out.

Equally, in the days when the TT was also the British Grand Prix, the moral balance was different from today's. Factory riders then were more or less obliged to take part in races on a circuit which was notoriously difficult to learn, and equally unforgiving of mistakes. Most of them, in an age in which few wielded personal power to anything like the extent that they do now, were ill-equipped to resist. Only riders of the status of Agostini had sufficient clout to say: 'No, this isn't for me' and keep their jobs. The rest, particularly in the Sixties, were so much fodder to corporate ambition (and, in truth, glad of the chance). Redman frankly admits the TT scared the shit out of him. 'I'd have loved to have ridden there just for myself, but as a factory rider, the pressure was immense.' By today's standards that was indefensible.

Ireland, far more than the Isle of Man, has suffered a tragic catalogue of losses in recent years. Yet the attitude there seems to be that so long as riders wish to road race, the will to accommodate them will persist. In a free society, surely there is no other way?

Someone, somewhere, may keep a running total of the number of racer's lives the Mountain courses have claimed. Certain newspapers say they do, and in any event, the number now must exceed 200, since Rudge's first visit to the Island ended so tragically when Victor Surridge became the first fatality when he crashed at Glen Helen in practice for the 1911 TT.

The first racing death occurred three years later. In 1914, the TT start was near the petrol station at St Ninian's traffic lights. Riders turned right here on to Bray Hill, having left the current circuit at Cronk-ny-Mona on the 37½-mile 'Four Inch' Course. In the Junior, Frank Walker rounded the final corner to find the road blocked with celebrations for the winner, Cyril Pullin. Walker bravely laid his Royal Enfield down to avoid them and suffered fatal injuries in sliding to third place. Rope barriers were introduced the following year.

Another overdue measure was taken after the death of Archie Birkin, when in 1927, in only his second TT, he collided with a delivery cart at the bends later named after him, while practising on open roads. In 1928, road closures for practice were introduced. Five years earlier the Manx Grand Prix claimed its first victim, in its maiden year, when Ned Brew was killed, also during open roads practice. However, these early years of racing were comparatively safe, since speeds were much lower.

There is no pecking order of TT deaths. Whether the victim is some obscure hopeful or a household name, racing's real victims – their families – feel it just the same. Nonetheless, it is usually true that the loss of the big names has the greatest impact. The first World Champion to die on the Island was Les Graham, on 12 June 1953. The 1949 500cc title holder had already won the Lightweight 125cc race earlier in the week. On the second lap of the Senior, he crashed at around 130mph beyond Ago's Leap. George Brown riding close behind on his Norton, saw Graham battle to control his wayward MV, before hitting the wreckage and being flung into a tree. Brown promptly abandoned road racing in favour of sprinting.

Nine years later, Australia's Tom Phillis, then reigning 125cc World Champion and a Honda factory rider, was killed at Laurel Bank. The loss caused even hard men like Jim Redman to consider quitting. Gary Hocking publicly did, giving voice to what many were thinking: that the factory's ambitions were causing riders to race too hard. The Welsh-born Rhodesian switched from bike to car racing and in the cruellest of ironies, was killed in a car race a few months later, aged just 25.

The Grand Prix Riders Association was formed in 1969, aiming principally to improve safety and increase prize money – with good reason on both counts. The winner of the 1930 Senior TT won £200 in prize money, a figure which did not increase one penny until 1971. Race organisers – in Britain and abroad – knew that most riders, dictated either by ambition or factory contracts, had little choice but to compete, and had no compunction about holding them to ransom in this way. But by now star riders, in particular, were beginning to flex their muscles, much as professional soccer players had done a decade earlier in their campaign to abolish the maximum wage.

If the TT had a particular problem, it wasn't that it was run over normal public roads. At the time, road circuits were commonplace in grands prix. Both Spa and Assen were still 'pure' roads, as was Brno and most of the rest. The Ulster Grand Prix, over the Dundrod circuit, was still a World Championship event. By modern standards, each was pretty much as dangerous as the other.

What set the TT apart was its sheer length and remoteness, the difficulty of reaching injured riders (although a rescue helicopter had been introduced in 1963), and the unpredictability of conditions around the course. This discontent reached a head in 1970, when no less than six riders were killed during practice and racing, most notably the Spaniard, Santiago Herrero.

Two years later, on 9 June 1972, came the TT's watershed event when, in atrocious conditions, Morbidelli rider Gilberto Parlotti was killed at the Verandah on the second lap of the Ultra-Lightweight race. The Italian was only competing because his main rival, Angel Neito, had refused to ride, giving him a chance to gain an edge in the World Championship. Giacomo Agostini, a close friend of Parlotti, was ready to boycott that afternoon's Senior, but conditions improved and Agostini won the race. It was to be his last TT.

Agostini and others, including Phil Read and Rod Gould, contended that the TT had become too dangerous. A greater number quietly kept their counsel and simply stayed away. In what looks with hindsight uncannily like a cynical attempt at bribery, the prize for a Senior win, frozen at £200 for four decades until the previous year, soared to £1,000. Twelve months later, the TT's overall budget was doubled. So, ironically, by staying away the Grand Prix Riders Association had had at least part of its desired effect.

After the 1976 TT, when all the top 500cc riders declined to race in the British Grand Prix, the FIM stripped the races of their World Championship status. Instead, the TT was awarded its own world series, the Formula Championship, which proved popular with the factories. This, and a continued escalation in prize money, did much to preserve the status of the racing. And yet, as the Formula series prospered and widened to include races elsewhere, the old moral dilemma re-emerged: was it right to pressure riders to take part?

In the event, it is hard to think of a single rider killed after being enticed against his better judgement to contest one of these events. Many have died, but their attendance was truly voluntary. For all that we remember 1978 mostly for Hailwood's comeback, it was particularly bleak. Mac Hobson and passenger Kenny Birch were killed when the popular Geordie lost control of his outfit over a raised manhole on Bray Hill, just yards from where Ernst Trachsel died later in the same event. Within a few days the career of Suzuki works star Pat Hennen, the first American to win a 500cc GP, ended when he was critically injured at Bishopscourt, shortly after becoming the first man to lap in under 20 minutes (113.83mph). Although the American survived, he would be severely disabled for the rest of his life.

A circuit over 37 miles long is impossible to make safe, and even safety measures can backfire. In 1984, Ireland's Gene McDonnel was killed when he struck a pony, panicked by the arrival of the rescue helicopter to pick up Brian Reid at Ballaugh.

In 1989, the 1,300cc production class claimed the lives of Mez Mellor and Steve Henshaw at Doran's Bend and the Quarries, respectively. Yet other riders have binned it at Quarries and lived to tell the tale: Steve Hislop, convinced (mistakenly) that he could get a 250 Honda through there flat-out; James Whitham, whose get-off contributed to Henshaw's accident; and Phillip McCallen. All three remarked that you slide for an awfully long time – every second of which could be your last.

Four riders died in 1996: Robert Holden, Aaron Kennedy, Mick Lofthouse and Steve Tannock. Popular Lancashire man Lofthouse died at Milntown Cottage after presumably being blinded by early morning sun, while New Zealander Holden died during the same practice session after hitting the wall at the left-hander before Glen Helen. At the time, both topped their class leaderboards and were tipped as likely race winners.

Another four arrived to race in 1999, never to return home: Simon Beck, Bernadette Bosman, Terry Fenton and Stuart Murdoch. Beck, a burley roads specialist from Leyland, Lancashire, was riding a Honda Britain RC45 and was looking forward to his most competitive TT when he died at the 33rd Milestone. Worse was to come in 2003 when David Jefferies died at Crosby Corner during practice, robbing the event of its outright lap record holder and leading light, as well as calling into question the quality of marshalling. Two years later the death of Gus Scott after colliding with a marshal at Kirkmichael during the Senior race further precipitated a review of safety procedures and training.

Yet despite the fact that TT '06 was statistically the safest for many years (for racers and visitors alike), the reality is that the Mountain Course is dangerous. To suggest otherwise is delusional. Rarely a year goes by without at least one death. The Mountain has claimed six riders I counted as personal friends. While their exploits enriched my life, and perhaps yours too, we were not entitled to expect it from them, any more than we should condemn those who choose to race elsewhere. But all of them rode fully aware that fatalities are an inevitable fact of Manx racing life. All were equally convinced that nowhere else was so sensationally exhilarating to ride. Were it otherwise, I believe the TT would already be long gone. That is its only possible defence.

Chapter 7

THE FESTIVAL

If Island racing offers something uniquely dramatic for the riders, in the days of morning practice, it also guaranteed TT spectators a similar treat, and never more so than at 4.30am in the hush of a pre-dawn opening practice day. In the far, drowsy distance a crowd of revellers clatter their unsteady way home through Douglas's Strand Street. Nearer by, one who didn't quite get that far snores gently from the discomfort of a shopping trolley.

Somewhere up the hill to the left, a racing engine barks into life, stalls into eerie silence, then chatters back into a revvy roar. The culprit, a sidecar outfit, appears at the foot of Mona Drive, slithers right as its slick tyres scrabble across the tram lines, and accelerates along the deserted promenade. As the noise ricochets off a regiment of Victorian boarding houses, a chip wrapper flutters oddly in its wake.

Forty-five minutes later at Appledene it is light – just – but witching-hour dark under the trees. Hedgerows trill to the pre-dawn chorus, as little feathered fellows stake territorial claims they're about to surrender. The first bike is felt, rather than heard – a remote, reedy vibration in the air. The sound is momentarily muffled as its source climbs the hill out of Crosby, then bursts louder over the leap by the old Halfway House. The bike is in sixth gear now, still a mile away but screaming, growing on the plunge past the Highlander. As you peer expectantly through the half-light, the hairs begin to prickle on the back of your neck.

The engine cogs down twice – that'll be Greeba Castle – quietens briefly, then emerges from the left-right bend with a howl. The rider – he's in sight now – tracks down the right-hand gutter and hurls the bike on its side over the bridge. The 'bars shake violently in protest, the gas comes back on, and the wail recedes through the leafy kinks towards Greeba Bridge. For the birds, it's going to be one of those days. For the rest of us, it is one of those glorious fortnights. Another TT has begun.

Morning practice is no more, but if Bunuel had created a race meeting, this celebration of the surreal would be it. Each June, the faded gentility of Mannan's holiday seafronts hosts a riot of leather and primary colours. Its lanes and byways, normally the preserve of blue-rinsed old biddies in antique Metros, reverberate to the brightest, fastest motorcycles in creation. The population soars by 50 per cent, as bikers of every hue, creed and persuasion return to their Isle of Man.

Go to any grand prix and you'll need a camera lens like a bazooka to capture even a distant glimpse of the action. On the Island you can practically tap the racers on the shoulder with your Instamatic as they hustle past. For gravel traps and run-offs read dry stone walls and trees and pretty little rose-clad cottages and lamp-posts and pubs and iron railings and other hard, immovable stuff. For 'purpose-built' read precipitous cambers and kerbs and bumps and grids and manhole covers of a circuit paved more with history than tarmac. For 'grid' read Glencrutchery Road, and a backdrop of suburban bungalows just down the road from the Governor's gaff. For starting lights read a funny old chap with a tiny flag, stood on a wooden box. And for computerised digital scoreboard read bloke with paintbrush, aided by the distinctly analogue 1st Douglas Cub Scouts.

They call it 'The Last of the Great Road Races'. Once, Europe was awash with similar events. But what the TT has, and the rest never did, is the greatest festival of motorcycling on Earth, held on biking's very own island (which the locals have thoughtfully looked after since last year). Imagine the Bol d'Or at its wildest. Stretch it from two days to two weeks. Lay on pubs, nightclubs that don't close until 4am, and trials and motocross and meet your mates at Glen Maye and 20,000 other mates you never knew you had. And a quick lap at dawn and drag racing and bands and wet T-shirt competitions. And bungee jumping, beach racing and Busheys Brew Pub and blow me, if that isn't the tastiest special I've ever seen. And a mile of prom lined with two-wheeled tackle, idiots doing donuts and 75mph monowheeling streakers and … and how the hell am I going to fit it all in?

Then there's Sunday, but not just any old Sunday. The first Sunday of race week is Mad Sunday. To the untrained eye it is little different from Mental Monday, Crazy Tuesday or Frantic Friday. But Sunday is the day when the 12-mile mountain section of the circuit, from the Gooseneck to Creg-ny-Baa, becomes one-way. And it's free. Well, if you don't wreck your bike it is. Douglas is littered with mangled bikes supporting notices: 'Third-party insurance only. Please give generously.' Mostly, people do.

If Sunday is Mad, Tuesday is just as traditionally Crazy. On Tuesday, the Island moves up the coast from Douglas to Ramsey. Ramsey is The Sprint, more custom shows, Manx ice-creams and beer, falling asleep in the sun, and shredding what little of your hearing various rock bands have left unscathed. Ramsey is the Vintage Club gathering, Angels in cut-offs, placid as grazing cows in the bike-rich air. Then there's the Triumph, BMW, Kawasaki, Harris and Norton get-togethers, or whatever it is this year, the Red Arrows RAF display team, a snatched fish and chips and … oh my God, there's still the TT trial at Santon to squeeze in …

That's what's wrong with the TT Festival: it only lasts two weeks.

Chapter 8

THE FUTURE

Nothing is more certain than the fact that the TT races will end; everything does. The Roman Empire eventually succumbed, as did the British, 1,500 years later. Yet if the TT lasts even half as long as Ancient Rome, your grandchildren will still be enjoying it come the 22nd century. On the other hand, 'the last of the great road races' may be just a racing memory, albeit a vivid one, a decade from now. For the truth is that no-one knows. Anything else is wish-fulfilment.

But it is equally true that barely a year goes by without the issue of Manx road racing's future being raised. A persistent rumour in recent years has been of 'plans' to allow the bike races to reach their centenary in 2007, then let them disappear. Such a notion may be at the back of a few influential minds, but I know of no such agenda. Above all, the announcement in December 2003 of the Island being granted a contract to run the races on its own behalf until at least 2023, should go some way to allaying such fears, although it is by no means a cast iron guarantee. From 2004, rather than being run directly by the ACU, the TT will be in the hands of the Manx Motor Cycle Club, which already organises the Manx Grand Prix. However, there are 'no plans' to unite the two events.

Amongst race fans the question of the races' future is typically phrased along the lines of 'When will they ban it?' Sometimes, the identity of the 'they' is unclear, but often it represents something 'Across', as the Manx like to call the UK. In years when racing fatalities are unusually high, or other news is slack, UK newspapers throw in their three penn'orth – invariably with a sensational and negative bent. 'Manx Carnage' is generally the consensus, 'Ban it' the ill-considered response.

Equally invariably, the Island's reaction to such tirades is timorous and defensive. Typically, these amount to a comparison with something else such as horse riding or mountaineering, which, from time to time, also claims lives. Alternatively, it is maintained that racing over the Mountain is safe in terms of fatalities per mile, disregarding the fact that Manx races can be five times as long as other grands prix. On both counts this is self-serving and disingenuous. As an epitaph to dead riders, it is callous.

Barry Sheene, whose 'attacks' on the TT actually amounted to little more than pithy but off-hand remarks that it wasn't for him, was for three decades a major Manx bête noire. The truth is that for most of this time he wasn't particularly bothered either way. Indeed, it is possible to make a slim case for Sheene as a TT supporter, for on several occasions he loaned bikes on which other riders raced the TT. Certainly, as his performances at Spa, Brno and elsewhere showed, he had no shortage of road-race bottle.

The timidity of the Manx response is strange on several counts. On the one hand media attacks rarely linger and are forgotten within days as Fleet Street moves on to something else. While on the other, one can only be puzzled as to what they might achieve. Let us not forget that racing first came to the Isle of Man precisely because it was not under the control of Westminster, which is as true now as it was in 1904. Put simply, the only body with the authority to ban the TT is the Isle of Man government.

The day may come when the Manx authorities do decide that the TT has run its course, although let us hope that time is not soon. If it does, the impetus will surely come from the Island itself, and not from 'Across'. In recent years rumblings of discontent have emanated from the financial community (particularly the 'Comeovers' it employs) and undoubtedly many Island residents are inconvenienced by road closures. Early in 2004, the Island's Chamber of Commerce called for the races to be scrapped (along with the Department of Tourism and Leisure, which is responsible for the TT). Ultimately perhaps, such objections might become hard to resist, but for the present they are little more than familiar background noise.

But of course, none of this is new. 'Isle of Manslaughter' rang out in UK headlines urging that the 1908 car TT be banned. Even four years earlier, before the first motorsport event was held on the Island, the organisers feared that by calling it a 'race' at all, they would invite hostile publicity.

Today, the greatest threat to the races comes from changes in the wider motorcycling world. As racing becomes ever more confined to purpose-built tracks with elaborate safety provisions (and spectators so remote from the action that they may as well watch on TV), road racing in all its forms becomes a growing anachronism. But then so is crossing the ocean by yacht when perfectly good aeroplanes fly overhead.

However, these changes have had an enormous impact on road racing. Even before the TT lost its grand prix status in 1976, the top factories and many top riders were already giving it a wide berth. Yet there is far more to this than the preferences of the men involved. As the two sports – pure road racing and 'the shorts' – have grown apart, so has the machinery required for each.

During the last 100 years the bike TT grew from a sideshow patronised by a few enthusiasts to become the premier motorcycle event of any kind, anywhere, during the 1920s and '30s. In its years as a grand prix it attracted the top riders and top machines, and Mr Honda himself saw it as the one race he had to win. Imagine now if Messrs Rossi, Pedrosa and their ilk turned up to ride on the Island every June …

That, of course, isn't going to happen. Today, the TT is essentially a production race contested by road-race specialists. Since the demise of the 125cc TT, the machines bear no serious resemblance to those campaigned in grands prix. The Formula One (now Superbike) event has, since its inception, been for roadster-based machines, and in recent years the same bikes have dominated the Senior. To some, this is an erosion of the TT's status. That may be so, but perhaps it is also a process which is returning the races to their roots. What could be more appropriate than a road bike being pitted against the toughest road on Earth?

And what of future speeds? From the end of the Fogarty–Hislop era until the arrival of David Jefferies, the outright lap record was rarely troubled. Indeed, throughout the 1990s it rose by less than 2mph. True, there have been such droughts before. Due to the war and its aftermath, records were stationary throughout the 1940s, and again for almost a decade after the withdrawal of the Japanese factories from 1967. But from 1999 Jefferies brought new vitality to the event, as he pushed the record beyond 127mph, only to die in pursuit of something more. Many of us feared that the record – and the event – might become moribund again, only for John McGuinness to inherit his friend's mantle. Last year the affable Lancastrian pushed the record beyond 129mph. With the major road 'improvements' planned for Brandish corner, the TT's centenary could well witness the first 130mph lap.

Nonetheless, we will surely never again witness anything like the 1920s and '30s, both decades in which the record soared by 18mph, give or take. Between 1923 and '26 alone the lap record leapt by over 10mph. Since then, as if by an inevitable law of diminishing returns, the increase has lessened: 10mph through the 1950s, 7.6mph in the '60s, and just 5.4mph a decade later. Perhaps we will come to regard the 1980s, during which the outright record leapt by 8.4mph, as the vintage era of modern times. Like that other 'Golden Age', the Twenties, it witnessed a quantum leap in the technology of race machinery, coinciding with significant improvements in the course itself.

On almost any other circuit, this would be of little consequence. But on the Island, where the concept of man and machine against the Mountain is so very pronounced, it counts for a lot. If the outright lap record is unthreatened, the event loses much of its lustre. The TT needs men who push the frontiers, men like Jefferies, McGuinness – and perhaps Martin, Hutchinson, Finnegan and their young ilk in future years.

The truth is that the races have declined in recent times. Entries, press releases are happy to inform us, are as high as ever. But the calibre of both riders and machinery has undoubtedly declined. Whatever special plans are made for 2007, the prospect of true factory machines regularly racing each other over the Mountain is remote, because the races count for less than they once did to the world at large. The media corps which used to descend on the Island en masse, a Who's Who of Fleet Street and beyond, has now shrivelled to almost nothing. Even *Motor Cycle News* is represented by just one freelance writer.

Nor have the Manx authorities always done as much to foster the races as they might. The decision to abandon the event during the Foot and Mouth epidemic of 2001, in which the influence of the Island's farming lobby was a major factor, was probably a mistake. If nothing else it showed such British importers as still supported the event, that their absence did not have a major effect on sales. Astonishingly, in 2002, not one representative from Suzuki GB was on the Island to witness David Jefferies's Formula One win.

In 2003, in the aftermath of Jefferies's death, many teams were angered and bewildered by what they saw as insensitive and high-handed treatment by senior officials. This, in turn, highlighted issues of safety, machine specifications and professionalism already bubbling beneath the surface. Most of these teams had as their yardstick the British Superbike series, a comparison which did no favours for the conduct and management of the TT.

In presenting the findings of a major consultation exercise on 18 December 2003, the Hon David Cretney, Minister for Tourism and Leisure, acknowledged that there may previously have been too much pettiness and officiousness, of which he hoped to see less in the future. The major thrust of the *Report on the Future of the TT Races* was to reduce all races to not more than four laps (later rescinded), abandon morning practice except in emergencies (partly due to the difficulty of recruiting sufficient marshals), and above all, to try to heal the wounds of 2003. 'The only way forward', he asserted, 'is for us all to work in partnership.'

Other safety-related issues included the immediate adoption of BSB-type oil catch tanks for 2004, formal risk assessment of different sections of the Mountain Course, the use of more air-fence crash barriers and the abolition of wet races. 'It is wrong', said the Minister, a former MGP competitor, 'to unnecessarily add risks to what we acknowledge is a risk sport.'

The death of Gus Scott after hitting a jaywalking marshal during the 2005 Senior did nothing to improve the event's image. In the same week a near miss between a policeman and a sidecar outfit caused the Manx Constabulary to adopt a less active role. Nor have sensational and questionably-informed articles in *Motor Cycle News* helped. Whilst considerable efforts have been made, before and since, to improve safety in general and marshalling in particular, it remains a thorny issue. Simply manning such a long course extends volunteer resources to the limit. It is conceivable that this and associated liability issues, rather than external opposition, could be the races' Achilles Heel.

In an attempt to improve the quality of entries, tighter qualifying times were introduced, and while the authorities would continue to encourage top flight racers to compete, Cretney conceded that 'we should not encourage riders to race here against their better judgement ... they should do so because they want to do so.' Such a statement would have been unthinkable a few decades ago. But the quality of entries as a whole is now demonstrably far higher that it was just three years ago, when the slowest riders were lapping at barely 90mph. The slowest rider in last years' Junior TT *averaged* 106mph.

Perhaps the single biggest factor influencing the quality of the top of the field is the TT's perennial clash with one or other British Superbike round, which invariably sees the TT losing out. Such conflicts affect not only the machinery, riders and budgets available to contest the TT, but also trade and industry presence at the wider festival. Several teams are as unhappy about this state of affairs as are the TT organisers, and it is known that during the 2006 season at least two major manufacturers emphatically told BSB organisers that there should be no such clash in 2007.

As it enters its eleventh decade, the TT is more of a racing anachronism than ever before. On the one hand this diminishes its global relevance and the industry support it attracts. On the other, it makes the event increasingly unique – not less attractive, but more, to fans and riders weary of the over-clinical ambience of other forms of racing. They will need no persuading that the TT truly is, if not the last, the greatest of the great road races.

TT TIMELINE

1904	International Cup race trials for cars, over a 52-mile course including the current Mountain section.
1905	International Cup race trials: motorcycles included for first time. First TT races, for cars.
1906	First motorcycle TT race, St John's Course, with both single and twin-cylinder classes.
1907	'Four Inch' Course introduced for cars.
1909	Fuel restriction removed, and all machines combined in a single class. Now 83 entries, compared with just 25 two years before. Harry Collier raises the lap record to over 50mph (52.27mph).
1911	Motorcycle TT moves to the 'Four Inch' Course. Senior (500cc) and Junior (350cc) classes introduced, but larger capacity permitted for twins. First 50mph motorcycle 'Mountain' lap: Frank Philipp (Scott), 50.11mph. First TT fatality: Victor Surridge, during practice, at Glen Helen. Silencers no longer compulsory.
1912	Handicapping of singles abolished, Classic Senior (500cc) and Junior (350cc) classes come in force. Senior day becomes a de facto national holiday, later made official.

1913   The races are spread over two days for the first time. On the first day Junior and Senior machines compete over two and three laps respectively. On the second, the survivors in both classes race over another four laps. Class colours introduced: a red waistcoat for the Senior, blue for the Junior. A team award is presented for the first time, to Rover.

1914   Frank Walker becomes the first racing fatality when he crashes valiantly trying to avoid celebrating spectators in the Senior, having earlier placed third in the Junior. Crash helmets become compulsory.

1920   The Signpost and Governor's Bridge sections, and the present start/finish, are included for the first time.

1922   The course assumes its present form when the then private road from Parliament Square to May Hill and Cruikshanks replaces the former detour through Ramsey. The Lightweight (250cc) is introduced, competing for the Motor Cycle Cup. The first silver and bronze TT replicas are awarded (instead of the previous gold medals). Tim Sheard becomes the first Manxman to win a TT, in the Junior event. The last IoM car TT is held, after which the event moves to Northern Ireland.

1923   First sidecar TT. The event is discontinued after three years, only reappearing in 1954. The first 'amateur TT', initially the MARRC race, is held in September the same year.

1924   Ultra-Lightweight TT introduced, for 175cc machines. The class survives only two years. The

1924 race has the first TT mass start, an experiment not repeated until 1948. Freddie Dixon (Douglas) records the first 60mph lap at 63.75mph in the Senior – but Jimmy Simpson has got there first, lapping at 64.65mph two days earlier on his Junior AJS.

1925   First double win, Wal Handley, Junior and Ultra-Lightweight (175cc) races.

1926   The TT reverts to the three 'classic' classes – Senior, Junior and Lightweight – until 1947. Alcohol fuels are banned, but Jimmy Simpson still sets the first 70mph lap, on his Senior AJS at 70.43mph.

1927   Archie Birkin is killed after colliding with a cart at Rhencullen (later Birkins Bends) during open roads practice. The *TT Special* first appears, edited by former race winner Geoff Davison, who continued in post until his death in 1966.

1928   Closed-road early morning practice introduced (so machines are no longer required to be taxed, insured and silenced).

1930   For the first time the Manx Government contributes directly to the racing, and TT winner's prize money is set at £200 (paid to the entrant). MARRC races are revised and re-named Manx Grand Prix.

1931   Jimmy Simpson again cracks a milestone, lapping at 80.82mph on his Senior Norton.

1933   A sidecar race is planned, but abandoned when only 14 entries are received.

1935   A warm-up period is allowed before each race. Previously, engines started from cold. A TT race is postponed for the first time when the Senior is delayed to Saturday by bad weather. Travelling marshals introduced. *No Limit*, the classic George Formby TT movie, is filmed during the races.

1937   Freddie Frith breaks the 90mph barrier, lapping at 90.27mph on his Senior Norton. Evening practice sessions introduced (but not until 1946 for the MGP).

1939   The outbreak of the Second World War causes the Manx Grand Prix to be cancelled on the day before practice is due to start.

1946   Racing resumes after the war, with the Manx Grand Prix.

1947   First post-war TT. Clubman's TT races introduced.

1948   Mass start reintroduced for Lightweight TT. Commentary speakers first sited at key points around the course.

1949   The TT becomes the British Grand Prix within the new FIM World Championship.

1951   First Lightweight 125cc TT, over two laps of the full Mountain Circuit. TT Riders' Association formed.

1954	Sidecars return, now on the Clypse Course, along with Lightweight 125cc TT. Both now have mass starts. Inge Stoll-Laforge becomes the first woman to contest a TT, as passenger to fifth-placed Jaques Drion. Soichiro Honda first visits the Isle of Man.
1955	Lightweight TT moves to Clypse Course. Clubman's TT reduced to two classes, Senior and Junior, and moves to Clypse Course for just one year.
1956	Clutch starts introduced, for sidecars. Last running of Clubman's TT, now in the week after the 'proper' TT. In winning both the Junior and Senior classes, Bernie Codd becomes the first rider to take a Clubman's double.
1957	Bob McIntyre (Gilera) becomes the first rider to lap the Mountain Circuit at over 100mph (101.12mph) in the Golden Jubilee Senior TT. Lengthened to eight laps, this is the longest grand prix ever run, at 301.84 miles.
1958	MV Agusta win all four solo classes.
1959	Formula One TT introduced, essentially for 350cc and 500cc production machines. 'Seeding' replaces the ballot system of numbering, giving the top riders earlier start times. Honda's first TT.
1960	Clypse Course abandoned. Derek Minter, riding a Steve Lancefield Norton, becomes the first man to lap at 100mph on a single-cylinder machine.

Above: *At over £10,000 Honda's RC30 was expensive for a road bike, but race-kitted versions of the 750cc Vee-four reigned supreme. The bike took a unique TT treble in 1988. (Author)*

Right: *Mick Grant, wearing his familiar number '10' and the 'JL' helmet logo in tribute to his early sponsor, powers the Formula One Suzuki up May Hill in 1983.*

Below: *Joey Dunlop at Braddan in 1988 on the brilliant RVF750. (Phil Masters)*

Top: *Steve Hislop checks on the whereabouts of team-mate Carl Fogarty as the duo round Governor's Bridge during that epic RV750 battle in the 1991 Formula One TT.* (Author)

Below: *Hislop on the Norton rotary with which he scored a famous Senior victory in 1992 – Norton's first win since the 1973 Formula 750 TT.* (Phil Masters)

Opposite: *Phillip McCallen flings his 250 Honda into Creg-ny-Baa in 1994. Running out of fuel denied him the win.* **(Author)**

Opposite top: *Delighted fans cheer Joey through the Gooseneck as he blasts through to a tearful victory in the 2000 Formula One TT.* (Phil Masters)

Opposite bottom: *David Jefferies hugs the wall at Guthries on his way to winning the 2002 Production 1,000cc race at record speed.* (Phil Masters)

Right: *Geoff Duke, flanked by his grandchildren, at a blustery ceremony in 2003 when the 32nd Milestone was renamed in his honour.* (Author)

Below: *The fabulous Honda Six. This is one of George Beale's £200,000 replicas of the 297cc RC174, created in 2003.* (Author)

Left: *Dave Molyneux and Craig Hallam slither their DMR Honda into Bungalow in 2003. They won the waterlogged Sidecar race 'B' after faulty wheel bearings sidelined them in Race 'A'.* (Phil Masters)

Below: *Honda Day, Peel, 2003, and fans turn out in their thousands for a typical celebration of TT silliness, the Purple Helmets display team.* (Author)

Above: *Adrian Archibald at the Gooseneck on the TAS Suzuki GSX-R600 in 2005. All the Ballymoney rider's three wins have come in the larger classes.*

Right: *Dromore-based Welsh veteran Ian Lougher at Braddan Bridge on the way to his seventh TT victory in the 2005 Supersports Junior Race 'A'.*

Below: *The modern master: John McGuinness on the Superstock CBR100RR at Gooseneck in 2006. Unlike his other HM Plant Hondas, which all won, the Superstock Fireblade was outpaced.*

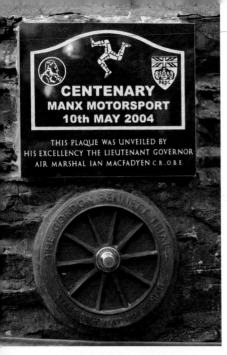

Left: *The other centenary: the plaques on the gatepost next to the site of the Quarter Bridge Hotel commemorating (top) 100 years of Manx motorsport and (bottom) the 1904 Gordon Bennett Cup eliminating trial.*

Below: *Bruce Anstey hustles the TAS Suzuki GSX-R1000 through Braddan on the way to winning the 2006 Superstock race for the second year in succession, his fifth TT win overall.*

1961	Mike Hailwood becomes the first rider to win three TTs in one week, winning the 125 and 250 races for Honda (also their first wins), and riding a Norton in the Senior race. Age limit of 55 introduced.
1962	50cc TT introduced. It lasts until 1968.
1963	Start money introduced (£10 to £25), although prize money remains unchanged from its 1930 level of £200 for a Senior win. Rescue helicopter introduced.
1964	Mountain section of course first made one-way for 'Mad Sunday'.
1965	First 100mph lap by a 250, Phil Read, Yamaha – although Redman's Honda 250-six won the race. Manx Radio begins TT broadcasting.
1966	A seamen's dispute causes the TT to be postponed until late August, finishing on 2 September.
1967	Production TT, with massed Le Mans-style start, introduced in Diamond Jubilee year, commemorated by special medals (and a pigeon TT race). Steve Spencer becomes the first rider to lap at 100mph on debut when placing third in the Senior on the Lancefield Norton.
1968	750cc Sidecar class introduced, contesting the Fred Dixon Trophy. One year later the 500cc and 750cc chairs each have their own three-lap race. First 100mph lap on a 125: Bill Ivy (100.32mph), Yamaha.

1969 Malcolm Uphill sets the first 100mph (100.37mph) Production lap on a Triumph Bonneville. His Dunlop K81 tyres are renamed 'TT 100'.

1970 FIM regulations limit 50cc machines to one cylinder, 125 and 250s to two, and 350 and 500s to four.

1971 Formula 750 class introduced (becoming Classic 1,000cc in 1975). Prize money is at last increased from the levels set in 1930, with £750 for a Senior win (rising to £1,000 12 months later).

1973 Agostini and others boycott the TT following the death of Gilberto Parlotti a year earlier. Early-morning practice abolished, but resumes the following year. Siggy Schauzu scores the first sidecar 'double'.

1974 The Senior is ousted from prime spot as the F750 race concludes TT week. Jack Findlay's Suzuki is the first TT machine to use slick tyres.

1975 More top 500cc GP riders boycott the TT. Production TT extended to a ten-lap, two-rider event, but is dropped from the programme altogether after 1976. 1,000cc Sidecar class introduced. Lightweight 125cc class dropped. Clutch starts for 'Classic' event, which replaces F750.

1976 The last running of the TT as a grand prix World Championship event. Top 500cc GP riders boycott the Senior, won by Tom Herron. Riding a RG500 Suzuki, John Williams comfortably records the first 110mph lap with a record of 112.27mph.

1977	TT race budget increased to £150,000, of which two-thirds goes to riders and teams, making it comfortably the richest event in motorcycling. New Formula World Championships for road-based machines (F1, F2, F3). Production race dropped. Prodigal son Phil Read wins Senior and F1. Dick Greasely records the first 100mph sidecar lap, although George O'Dell lapped faster (102.80.mph) later in the same race, the first of the now identical 1,000cc Sidecar events. Joey Dunlop wins the Jubilee TT.
1978	Mike Hailwood makes a triumphant return, winning the Formula One TT on the Sports Motorcycles Ducati, his 13th TT win, a record. Senior victory a year later takes his tally to 14 wins.
1984	Production TT reintroduced, then dropped again after a double fatality in 1989. Historic TT takes place for the one and only time, creating in Dave Roper the first (and only) American TT winner.
1989	Supersport 600 class introduced. Steve Hislop (Honda RC30) becomes the first 120mph-lapper with a record at 121.34mph in the Formula One race.
1993	Joey Dunlop takes his 15th TT win, an outright record, in the Lightweight 125cc event.
1994	Singles TT introduced. It lasts until 2000.
1996	Production TT reintroduced again. Phillip McCallen becomes the first rider to win four TTs in a week, riding Hondas to victory in the Formula One,

Junior, Production and Senior races. Dave Molyneux and Pete Hill post the first 110mph sidecar lap, with a circuit at 111.02mph.

2000   Joey Dunlop wins his 26th and last TT race. He is killed one month later in Estonia. David Jefferies takes the V&M Yamaha R1 to the first 125mph lap (125.69mph).

2001   Due to the UK Foot and Mouth epidemic, all Manx racing is cancelled for the first time since the Second World War.

2002   David Jefferies records a triple win for the third TT in succession, a unique feat, raising the lap record to 127.49mph in the process.

2003   David Jefferies becomes the first outright lap-record holder to be killed in the races when he crashes at Crosby during practice. Two months later, Steve Hislop dies in a helicopter accident.

2004   100th anniversary of the first race over the Mountain.

2005   Following a major review, the races get new solo programme: Superbikes, Supersports Junior (600cc), Superstock and Senior (open to all three classes). It's the end for two-strokes. For this year only, the longest race is of only four laps.

2007   100th anniversary of the motorcycle TT.

RESULTS

The pioneer races

The first races on the Isle of Man were qualifying trials to select the British team for the International Cup. These were for cars only, and were held in May 1904. Twelve months later, selection trials were also held for motorcycles, and in September 1905 the first car TT took place. May 1907 saw the first motorcycle TT. The IoM car TT continued intermittently until 1922.

Results: Cars

Year	Class	Winner	Machine	Speed
1904	International Cup Trials	C. Jarrott	Wolseley	–
1905	International Cup Trials	C. Earp	Napier	–
	TT	J. Napier	Arrol-Johnston	33.9
	Fastest lap	J. Napier	Arrol-Johnston	34.2
1906	TT	C. S. Rolls	Rolls-Royce	39.6
	Fastest lap	C. S. Rolls	Rolls-Royce	39.9
1907	TT overall	E. Courtis	Rover	28.8
	Fastest lap	L. Coatalen	Hillman-Coatalen	37.5
	Heavy Touring Cars	G. Mills	Beeston-Humber	28.7
	Fastest lap	C. Sangster	Ariel	33.7
1908	TT	W. Watson	Hutton	50.25
	Fastest lap	A. George	Darracq	52.0
1914	TT	K. L. Guinness	Sunbeam	56.44
	Fastest lap	C. Riecken	Minerva	59.3
1922	TT overall	J. Chassagne	Sunbeam	55.78
	Fastest lap	Maj H. Seagrave	Sunbeam	57.7
	1,500cc	Sir A. Guinness	Talbot Darracq	55.30
	Fastest lap	Sir A. Guinness	Sunbeam	55.15

Results: Motorcycles

1905	International Cup Trials	J. S. Campbell	Ariel	29.0

Motorcycle TT race results by year

ST JOHN'S COURSE: 1907–10
Course length: 15.81 miles
Race distance: 10 laps/158.1 miles
Lap record: from 41.81mph (C. R. Collier, 1907) to 53.15mph
 (H. H. Bowen, 1910)
Main bikes: Matchless, Norton, Triumph, BAT
Top riders: C. R. and H. A. Collier, Rem Fowler, J. Marshall

Men such as the Collier brothers and Jack Marshall were the true pioneers of the TT. Many were veterans of the International Cup races on the Isle of Man and elsewhere, doughty individuals who fully expected roads to be rough and their bikes even rougher. Almost the entire course comprised coarse gravel, dusty when dry, muddy and slippery when wet. Speeds may not have been high, but punctures and crashes were commonplace.

Their machines were primitive in the extreme. Most had one or two cylinders (although the odd four also appeared), with single-speed transmission driving the rear wheel by a riveted leather belt. So feeble was the power output that many were pedal-assisted, and even the most modest hill was a daunting challenge. On the descent, the brakes (at the rear only) were equally frail. Silencers were compulsory until 1911.

Results: Motorcycle TT

1907				
Class	**Winner**	**Machine**	**Laps**	**Speed**
Singles	C. R. Collier	Matchless	10	38.22
Fastest lap	C. R. Collier	Matchless		41.81
Multi-cylinder	H. R. Fowler	Norton	10	36.22
Fastest lap	H. R. Fowler	Norton		42.91

1908

Class	Winner	Machine	Laps	Speed
Singles	J. Marshall	Triumph	10	40.40
Fastest lap	J. Marshall	Triumph		42.48
Multi-cylinder	H. Reed	DOT	10	38.50
Fastest lap	W. J. Bashall	BAT		42.25

1909

Overall	H. A. Collier	Matchless	10	49.01
Fastest lap	H. A. Collier	Matchless		52.27

1910

Overall	C. R. Collier	Matchless	10	50.63
Fastest lap	H. H. Bowen	BAT		53.15

OVER THE MOUNTAIN: 1911–20

Course length: 'Four Inch' Course, 37 miles
Race distance: 4 to 7 laps; 148 to 259 miles
Lap record: from 50.11mph (F. Phillips, 1911) to 55.62 (G. Dance, 1920)
Main bikes: Scott, Indian, Rudge, Douglas
Top riders: Eric Williams, Tim Wood, Frank Applebee, W. H. Bashall

A decade much abbreviated by the Great War saw the bikes tackle the Mountain for the first time, over the 37-mile 'Four Inch' Course as first used by the cars in 1908. Course conditions remained very poor, with even Bray Hill just a hedge-lined dirt track and the loop from Cronk-ny-Mona even worse. The Mountain road, rutted and pot-holed in places, was more like an enduro than a road-race course. In wet weather, riders slithered on mud, or choked on dust when it was dry. During practice, the first rider through had to open gates, and livestock was a constant hazard. As if that weren't enough, in 1913 Suffragette demonstrators littered the course with broken glass.

Although most bikes were now chain-driven and two or three-speed (the last belt-driven machine to contest the TT was Norman Black's Norton in 1920), chassis remained archaic, with front brakes a rarity as late as 1914. While Peugeot had an outstanding dohc four by the same year, TT machines were mainly singles and Vee-twins, typically side-valve or i.o.e., plus the innovative Scott liquid-cooled two-stroke twin which became the dominant force after Indian's Vee-twin won in 1911.

1911

Class	Winner	Machine	Laps	Speed
Senior 500cc	O. C. Godfrey	Indian	5	47.63
Fastest lap	F. Philipp	Scott		50.11
Junior 350cc	P. J. Evans	Humber	4	41.45
Fastest lap	P. J. Evans	Humber		42.00

1912

Senior 500cc	F. A. Applebee	Scott	5	48.69
Fastest lap	F. A. Applebee	Scott		49.44
Junior 350cc	W. H. Bashall	Douglas	4	39.65
Fastest lap	E. Kirkham	Douglas		41.76

1913

Senior 500cc	H. O. Wood	Scott	7	48.27
Fastest lap	H. O. Wood	Scott		52.12
Junior 350cc	H. Mason	NUT	6	43.75
Fastest lap	H. Mason	NUT		45.42

1914

Senior 500cc	C. G. Pullin	Rudge	6	49.49
Fastest lap	H. O. Wood	Scott		53.50
Junior 350cc	E. Williams	AJS	5	45.58
Fastest lap	E. Williams	AJS		47.57

No racing due to First World War

Class	Winner	Machine	Laps	Speed
Senior 500cc	T. C. de la Hay	Sunbeam	6	51.48
Fastest lap	G. Dance	Sunbeam		55.62
Junior 350cc	C. Williams	AJS	5	40.74
Fastest lap	C. Williams	AJS		51.36

THE GOLDEN AGE: 1921–29

Course length: 37.73 miles
Race distance: 5 to 7 laps; 188 to 264 miles
Lap record: from 56.4mph (F. G. Edmond, 1921) to 73.55mph
(C. J. P. Dodson 1929)
Main bikes: AJS, Sunbeam, HRD, Norton, Velocette, New Imperial,
Rex-Acme
Top riders: Wal Handley, C. and E. Williams, Tommy de la Hay,
Alec Bennett, Stanley Woods, Jimmy Simpson

Benefiting from the technological boost given by the Great War, the Twenties began with a huge boom in motorcycle registrations and became known as racing's 'Golden Age'. Although singles were predominant, machinery was faster and more reliable than ever, with ohv the norm, albeit with exposed valvegear. In 1922, Alec Bennett's Sunbeam became the last side-valver to win a TT, before the 'Big Port' AJS and four-valve Rudges took over. The first serious Continental challenge came in 1926 when Garelli, Bianchi and Guzzi all competed. By decade's end, ohc Nortons and Velocettes were achieving success, but Rudge still dominated. Friction-type steering dampers appeared, foot gear change began to replace hand-change, and Douglas and later Velocette used disc brakes.

This was also a decade of great riders. In 1922 alone, Stanley Woods, Wal Handley and Jimmy Simpson all made their debuts, remaining leading TT lights into the Thirties. Woods, in particular, was arguably to become bike racing's first superstar.

Even early in the Twenties the race's organisers were proudly proclaiming this the most important road race in the world, and by decade's end this was not seriously in dispute: the TT had become the world's premier motorcycle race. Its timetable had evolved into something recognisable today, with racing on Monday, Wednesday and Friday, but preceded by nine early morning (4.15 to 8am) practice sessions spread over ten days, culminating in the Saturday which now sees the Formula One event. So entrenched was early morning practice that at least one hotel offered 'practice calls at 3.45am, with refreshments'.

1921

Class	Winner	Machine	Laps	Speed
Senior 500cc	H. R. Davies	AJS	6	54.49
Fastest lap	F. G. Edmond	Triumph		56.40
Junior 350cc	E. Williams	AJS	5	52.11
Fastest lap	E. Williams	AJS		55.15

1922

Class	Winner	Machine	Laps	Speed
Senior 500cc	A. Bennett	Sunbeam	6	58.31
Fastest lap	A. Bennett	Sunbeam		59.99
Junior 350cc	T. M. Sheard	AJS	5	54.75
Fastest lap	H. le Vack	New Imperial		56.46
Lightweight 250cc	G. S. Davison	Levis	5	49.89
Fastest lap	W. L. Handley	OK-Supreme		51.00

1923

Class	Winner	Machine	Laps	Speed
Senior 500cc	T. M. Sheard	Douglas	6	55.55
Fastest lap	J. Whalley	Douglas		59.74
Junior 350cc	S. Woods	Cotton	6	55.73
Fastest lap	J. H. Simpson	AJS		59.59
Lightweight 250cc	J. A. Porter	New Garrard	6	51.93
Fastest lap	W. L. Handley	OK-Supreme		53.95
Sidecar 500cc	F. W. Dixon/W. Perry	Douglas	3	53.15
Fastest lap	H. Langman	Scott		54.69

1924

Class	Winner	Machine	Laps	Speed
Senior 500cc	A. Bennett	Norton	6	61.64
Fastest lap	F. W. Dixon	Douglas		63.75
Junior 350cc	K. Twemlow	New Imperial	6	55.67
Fastest lap	J. H. Simpson	AJS		64.65
Lightweight 250cc	E. Twemlow	New Imperial	6	55.44
Fastest lap	E. Twemlow	New Imperial		58.28
Ultra-Lightweight	J. A. Porter	New Gerrard	3	51.20
Fastest lap	J. A. Porter	New Gerrard		52.61
Sidecar 500cc	G. H. Tucker	Norton	4	51.31
Fastest lap	F. W. Dixon	Douglas		53.23

1925

Class	Winner	Machine	Laps	Speed
Senior 500cc	H. R. Davies	HRD	6	66.13
Fastest lap	J. H. Simpson	AJS		68.97
Junior 350cc	W. L. Handley	Rex-Acme	6	65.02
Fastest lap	W. L. Handley	Rex-Acme		65.89
Lightweight 250cc	E. Twemlow	New Imperial	6	57.74
Fastest lap	W. L. Handley	Rex-Acme		60.22
Ultra-Lightweight	W. L. Handley	Rex-Acme	4	53.45
Fastest lap	W. L. Handley	Rex-Acme		54.12
Sidecar 500cc	L. Parker	Douglas	4	55.22
Fastest lap	F. W. Dixon	Douglas		57.18

1926

Class	Winner	Machine	Laps	Speed
Senior 500cc	S. Woods	Norton	7	67.54
Fastest lap	J. H. Simpson	AJS		70.43
Junior 350cc	A. Bennett	Velocette	7	66.70
Fastest lap	A. Bennett	Velocette		68.75
Lightweight 250cc	C. W. Johnson	Cotton	7	63.20
Fastest lap	P. Ghersi	Moto Guzzi		63.12

1927

Class	Winner	Machine	Laps	Speed
Senior 500cc	A. Bennett	Norton	7	68.41
Fastest lap	S. Woods	Norton		70.90
Junior 350cc	F. W. Dixon	HRD	7	67.19
Fastest lap	W. L. Handley	Rex-Acme		69.18
Lightweight 250cc	W. L. Handley	Rex-Acme	7	60.30
Fastest lap	A. Bennett	OK-Supreme		64.45

1928

Class	Winner	Machine	Laps	Speed
Senior 500cc	C. J. P. Dodson	Sunbeam	7	62.98
Fastest lap	J. H. Simpson	AJS		67.93
Junior 350cc	A. Bennett	Velocette	7	68.65
Fastest lap	A. Bennett	Velocette		70.28
Lightweight 250cc	F. A. Longman	OK-Supreme	7	62.90
Fastest lap	F. A. Longman	OK-Supreme		64.65

1929

Class	Winner	Machine	Laps	Speed
Senior 500cc	C. J. P. Dodson	Sunbeam	7	72.05
Fastest lap	C. J. P. Dodson	Sunbeam		73.55
Junior 350cc	F. G. Hicks	Velocette	7	69.71
Fastest lap	F. G. Hicks	Velocette		70.95
Lightweight 250cc	S. A. Crabtree	Excelsior	7	63.87
Fastest lap	P. Ghersi	Moto Guzzi		66.63

THE THIRTIES: 1930–39

Course length: 37.73 miles

Race distance: 7 laps; 264 miles

Lap record: from 76.28mph (W. Handley, 1930) to 91.00mph
(H. Daniell, 1938)

Main bikes: Norton, Velocette, Rudge, BMW, Guzzi

Top riders: Stanley Woods, Jimmy Guthrie, Freddie Frith, Harold Daniell,
Jimmy Simpson

Although marred by the global Depression in the second half of the decade, when entries fell to fewer than 30 per race, this was another classic era. On the machine front, valve enclosure became common, four-speed transmission the norm. Although the superiority of multi-cylinders over singles became widely accepted, singles clung doggedly to success. Equally, four-valve engines (notably Rudge) did well, but most winners were two-valve ohc, with Norton pre-eminent. Later, AJS, Velocette and BMW fielded supercharged machines, of which only the German marque enjoyed success. Few bikes used tachometers, riders using ear and 'feel' to gauge revs. Until Guzzi won the 1935 Senior, sprung rear ends were practically unknown, the 'standard' set-up being rigid rear ends and girder forks. Riders wore body belts to help reduce the jarring suffered over the rough Manx roads.

If the Thirties did not have quite the range of machinery that characterised the Twenties, it saw a startling array of TT talent going head-to-head. Stanley Woods (ten wins) and Jimmy Guthrie (six) were the most successful, but perhaps most mercurial of all was Jimmy Simpson. In a career spanning 13 years he won only one TT, the 1934 Lightweight for Rudge in his last Manx outing. But he set numerous records including, remarkably, being the first man to lap at 60mph (1924), 70mph (1926) and 80mph (1931). This was the decade in which the top factories began to corner the best riders, making it increasingly difficult for smaller factories to compete, and the authorities encouraged overseas riders to take part.

1930

Class	Winner	Machine	Laps	Speed
Senior 500cc	W. L. Handley	Rudge Whitworth	7	74.24
Fastest lap	W. L. Handley	Rudge		76.28
Junior 350cc	H. G. Tyrell Smith	Rudge Whitworth	7	71.08
Fastest lap	G. E. Nott	Rudge		72.02
Lightweight 250cc	J. Guthrie	AJS	7	64.71
Fastest lap	W. L. Handley	Rex-Acme		66.86

1931

Class	Winner	Machine	Laps	Speed
Senior 500cc	P. Hunt	Norton	7	77.90
Fastest lap	J. H. Simpson	Norton		80.82
Junior 350cc	P. Hunt	Norton	7	73.94
Fastest lap	P. Hunt	Norton		75.27
Lightweight 250cc	G. W. Walker	Rudge	7	68.98
Fastest lap	G. E. Nott	Rudge		71.73

1932

Class	Winner	Machine	Laps	Speed
Senior 500cc	S. Woods	Norton	7	79.83
Fastest lap	J. H. Simpson	Norton		81.50
Junior 350cc	S. Woods	Norton	7	77.16
Fastest lap	S. Woods	Norton		78.62
Lightweight 250cc	L. H. Davenport	New Imperial	7	70.48
Fastest lap	W. L. Handley	Rudge		74.08

1933

Class	Winner	Machine	Laps	Speed
Senior 500cc	S. Woods	Norton	7	81.04
Fastest lap	S. Woods	Norton		82.74
Junior 350cc	S. Woods	Norton	7	78.08
Fastest lap	S. Woods	Norton		79.22
Lightweight 250cc	S. Gleave	Excelsior	7	71.59
Fastest lap	S. Gleave	Excelsior		72.62

1934

Class	Winner	Machine	Laps	Speed
Senior 500cc	J. Guthrie	Norton	7	78.01
Fastest lap	S. Woods	Husqvarna		88.05
Junior 350cc	J. Guthrie	Norton	7	79.16
Fastest lap	J. Guthrie	Norton		80.11
Lightweight 250cc	J. H. Simpson	Rudge	7	70.81
Fastest lap	J. H. Simpson	Rudge		73.64

1935

Senior 500cc	S. Woods	Moto Guzzi	7	84.68
Fastest lap	S. Woods	Moto Guzzi		86.53
Junior 350cc	J. Guthrie	Norton	7	79.14
Fastest lap	W. F. Rusk	Norton		79.96
Lightweight 250cc	S. Woods	Moto Guzzi	7	71.56
Fastest lap	S. Woods	Moto Guzzi		74.19

1936

Senior 500cc	J. Guthrie	Norton	7	85.80
Fastest lap	S. Woods	Velocette		86.98
Junior 350cc	F. L. Frith	Norton	7	80.14
Fastest lap	F. L. Frith	Norton		81.94
Lightweight 250cc	A. R. Foster	New Imperial	7	74.28
Fastest lap	S. Woods	DKW		76.20

1937

Senior 500cc	F. L. Frith	Norton	7	88.21
Fastest lap	F. L. Frith	Norton		90.27
Junior 350cc	J. Guthrie	Norton	7	84.43
Fastest lap	= F. L. Frith/J. Guthrie	both Norton		85.18
Lightweight 250cc	O. Tenni	Moto Guzzi	7	74.72
Fastest lap	O. Tenni	Moto Guzzi		77.72

Class	Winner	Machine	Laps	Speed
Senior 500cc	H. L. Daniell	Norton	7	89.11
Fastest lap	H. L. Daniell	Norton		91.00
Lightweight 250cc	E. Kluge	DKW	7	78.48
Fastest lap	E. Kluge	DKW		80.35
Junior 350cc	S. Woods	Velocette	7	84.08
Fastest lap	S. Woods	Velocette		85.30

Class	Winner	Machine	Laps	Speed
Senior 500cc	G. Meier	BMW	7	89.38
Fastest lap	G. Meier	BMW		90.75
Junior 350cc	S. Woods	Velocette	7	83.19
Fastest lap	H. L. Daniell	Norton		85.05
Lightweight 250cc	E. A. Mellors	Benelli	7	74.25
Fastest lap	S. Woods	Moto Guzzi		78.16

THE FORTIES: 1940–49

Course length: 37.73 miles
Race distance: up to 7 laps; 264 miles
Lap record: no improvement on Daniell's record of 91.00mph from 1938
Main bikes: Norton, Velocette, Moto Guzzi
Top riders: Harold Daniell, Freddie Frith, Artie Bell, Manliff Barrington

Manx racing resumed after the Second World War with the 1946 Manx Grand Prix, the TT following in 1947. Although attendances were high from a war-weary public keen to enjoy itself, the factories were cash-strapped. The 1949 Junior, for instance, saw just three marques taking part: Norton, Velocette and AJS. Practically all the machines raced were from the 1930s, causing one wag to dub the 1947 TT 'The greatest vintage meeting of all time'. The line-up was further decimated by the FIM's decision the previous winter to ban supercharging. Riders were obliged to use 'Pool' petrol, notionally rated at just 72 octane, with a consequent reduction in compression ratios and performance. Rigid or sprung hub rear ends and girder forks predominated, but swing-arms and telescopic forks slowly crept in, with Norton's famous 'Roadholders' debuting in 1947.

By today's standards, racing tyre technology was equally low-key. Slicks were still 25 years away, nor were there any such things as wets. Riders used one pair of tyres in practice and, if they had the wherewithal, an identical set for the race. Alloy rims, on the other hand, were just beginning to oust steel.

Many of the top riders were men who had made their name pre-war, but the introduction of the World Championship in 1949 would bring a new generation of racers and factories to the TT.

1940–46

No racing due to Second World War

1947

Class	Winner	Machine	Laps	Speed
Senior 500cc	H. L. Daniell	Norton	7	82.81
Fastest lap	= A. J. Bell/ P. Goodman	Norton/ Velocette		84.07
Junior 350cc	A. R. Foster	Velocette	7	80.31
Fastest lap	M. D. Whitworth	Velocette		81.61
Lightweight 250cc	M. Barrington	Moto Guzzi	7	73.22
Fastest lap	M. Cann	Moto Guzzi		74.78
Senior Clubman's	E. E. Briggs	Norton	4	78.67
Fastest lap	E. E. Briggs	Norton		80.02
Junior Clubman's	D. Parkinson	Norton	4	70.74
Fastest lap	D. Parkinson	Norton		72.92
L'weight Clubman's	W. McVeigh	Triumph	3	65.30
Fastest lap	W. McVeigh	Triumph		65.95

1948

Class	Winner	Machine	Laps	Speed
Senior 500cc	A. J. Bell	Norton	7	84.97
Fastest lap	O. Tenni	Moto Guzzi		88.06
Junior 350cc	F. L. Frith	Velocette	7	81.45
Fastest lap	F. L. Frith	Velocette		82.45
Lightweight 250cc	M. Cann	Moto Guzzi	7	75.18
Fastest lap	M. Cann	Moto Guzzi		76.72
Senior Clubman's	J. D. Daniels	Vincent HRD	4	80.51
Fastest lap	G. Brown	Vincent HRD		82.65
Junior Clubman's	R. J. Hazlehurst	Velocette	4	70.33
Fastest lap	R. Pratt	Norton		73.76
L'weight Clubman's	M. V. Lockwood	Excelsior	3	64.93
Fastest lap	M. V. Lockwood	Excelsior		66.40

1949

Class	Winner	Machine	Laps	Speed
Senior 500cc	H. L. Daniell	Norton	7	86.93
Fastest lap	A. R. Foster	Moto Guzzi		89.75
Junior 350cc	F. L. Frith	Velocette	7	83.15
Fastest lap	F. L. Frith	Velocette		84.23
Lightweight 250cc	M. Barrington	Moto Guzzi	7	77.96
Fastest lap	= R. H. Dale/	both		80.44
	T. L. Wood	Moto Guzzi		
1,000cc Clubman's	D. G. Lashmar	Vincent HRD	3	76.30
Fastest lap	C. Horn	Vincent HRD		85.57
Senior Clubman's	G. E. Duke	Norton	3	82.97
Fastest lap	G. E. Duke	Norton		83.70
Junior Clubman's	H. Clark	BSA	3	75.81
Fastest lap	H. Clark	BSA		75.81
L'weight Clubman's	C. V. Taft	Excelsior	2	68.10
Fastest lap	C. V. Taft	Excelsior		68.71

THE FIFTIES: 1950–59

Course length: 37.73 miles (plus Clypse Course, 10.79 miles)
Race distance: 4 to 8 laps; 151 to 302 miles
Lap record: from 93.33mph (G. Duke, 1950) to 101.18 (J. Surtees, 1959)
Main bikes: Norton, Gilera, MV Agusta, Moto Guzzi, Mondial, NSU
Top riders: Geoff Duke, John Surtees, Bob McIntyre, Bill Lomas, Ray Amm

This was the era in which Italy took over from Britain as the driving force of motorcycle racing. In the smaller classes, Benelli, Guzzi and Mondial were dominant when the decade began, but it was not long before exotic ohc Italian multis took over in the larger classes, too, although it would be Germany's NSU which redefined power outputs. Five-speed transmissions became obligatory (some Montesas even had six). Telescopic forks and swing-arm rear ends were the norm, mostly with hydraulic dampers, although Guzzi persisted with their pre-war friction damping arrangement. On the other hand, many machines still used exposed primary drives, and often finished races with one side of the tyre smeared with oil.

The Fifties was also about aerodynamics, again led by the Italians and German NSUs. Eventually, aluminium 'dustbin' bodywork enclosed both wheels and most of the bits in between, the only requirement being that they should not be capable of trapping a rider should he fall off. One-piece racing leathers were also introduced.

Most of the top riders were still British or Colonial, but Duke, McIntyre, Surtees and the rest increasingly migrated to foreign factories. Before Norton pulled out after 1954, Rhodesia's Ray Amm was almost single-handedly waving the Union flag. From then until 1960, every single solo TT (excluding Clubman's) would be won by an Italian machine. In 1957, all the major factories except MV pulled out of racing, leaving the Galarate machines practically unchallenged until Honda's emergence as a major force.

Class	Winner	Machine	Laps	Speed
Senior 500cc	G. E. Duke	Norton	7	92.27
Fastest lap	G. E. Duke	Norton		93.33
Junior 350cc	A. J. Bell	Norton	7	86.33
Fastest lap	A. J. Bell	Norton		86.49
Lightweight 250cc	D. Ambrosini	Benelli	7	78.08
Fastest lap	D. Ambrosini	Benelli		80.91
1,000cc Clubman's	A. Philip	Vincent HRD	4	78.58
Fastest lap	A. Phillip	Vincent HRD		81.01
Senior Clubman's	P. H. Carter	Norton	4	75.60
Fastest lap	I. B. Wicksteed	Triumph		79.48
Junior Clubman's	B. A. Jackson	BSA	4	74.25
Fastest lap	B. A. Jackson	BSA		76.12
L'weight Clubman's	F. Fletcher	Excelsior	3	66.89
Fastest lap	F. Fletcher	Excelsior		67.48

Class	Winner	Machine	Laps	Speed
Senior 500cc	G. E. Duke	Norton	7	93.83
Fastest lap	G. E. Duke	Norton		95.22
Junior 350cc	G. E. Duke	Norton	7	89.90
Fastest lap	G. E. Duke	Norton		91.38
Lightweight 250cc	T. L. Wood	Moto Guzzi	4	81.39
Fastest lap	F. Anderson	Moto Guzzi		83.70
Lightweight 125cc	W. C. McCandless	Mondial	2	74.85
Fastest lap	W. C. McCandless	Mondial		74.85
Senior Clubman's	I. K. Arber	Norton	4	79.70
Fastest lap	I. B. Wicksteed	Triumph		81.06
Junior Clubman's	B. G. Purslow	BSA	4	75.36
Fastest lap	K. R. V. James	Norton		76.55

1952

Class	Winner	Machine	Laps	Speed
Senior 500cc	H. R. Armstrong	Norton	7	92.97
Fastest lap	G. E. Duke	Norton		94.88
Junior 350cc	G. E. Duke	Norton	7	90.29
Fastest lap	G. E. Duke	Norton		91.00
Lightweight 250cc	F. Anderson	Moto Guzzi	4	83.82
Fastest lap	B. Ruffo	Moto Guzzi		84.82
Lightweight 125cc	C. C. Sandford	MV	2	75.54
Fastest lap	C. C. Sandford	MV		76.07
Senior Clubman's	B. J. Hargreaves	Triumph	4	82.45
Fastest lap	B. J. Hargreaves	Triumph		83.05
Junior Clubman's	E. Housely	BSA	4	78.92
Fastest lap	R. McIntyre	BSA		80.09

1953

Class	Winner	Machine	Laps	Speed
Senior 500cc	W. R. Amm	Norton	7	93.85
Fastest lap	W. R. Amm	Norton		97.41
Junior 350cc	W. R. Amm	Norton	7	90.52
Fastest lap	W. R. Amm	Norton		91.82
Lightweight 250cc	F. Anderson	Moto Guzzi	4	84.73
Fastest lap	F. Anderson	Moto Guzzi		85.52
Lightweight 125cc	R. L. Graham	MV	3	77.79
Fastest lap	R. L. Graham	MV		78.21
1,000cc Clubman's	G. P. Douglas	Vincent HRD	4	81.54
Fastest lap	G. P. Douglas	Vincent HRD		82.80
Senior Clubman's	R. D. Keeler	Norton	3	84.14
Fastest lap	R. D. Keeler	Norton		84.50
Junior Clubman's	D. T. Powell	BSA	4	80.17
Fastest lap	D. T. Powell	BSA		80.96

1954

Class	Winner	Machine	Laps	Speed
Senior 500cc	W. R. Amm	Norton	4	88.12
Fastest lap	W. R. Amm	Norton		89.82
Junior 350cc	R. W. Coleman	AJS	5	91.51
Fastest lap	W. R. Amm	Norton		94.61
Lightweight 250cc	W. Haas	NSU	3	90.88
Fastest lap	W. Haas	NSU		91.22
*Lightweight 125cc	R. Hollaus	NSU	10	69.57
Fastest lap	R. Hollaus	NSU		71.53
Senior Clubman's	A. King	BSA	4	85.76
Fastest lap	A. King	BSA		87.02
Junior Clubman's	P. Palmer	BSA	4	81.83
Fastest lap	D. A. Wright	BSA		83.05
*Sidecar 500cc	E. S. Oliver/L. Nutt	Norton	10	68.87
Fastest lap	E. S. Oliver/L. Nutt	Norton		70.85

1955

Class	Winner	Machine	Laps	Speed
Senior 500cc	G. E. Duke	Gilera	7	97.93
Fastest lap	G. E. Duke	Gilera		99.97
Junior 350cc	W. A. Lomas	Moto Guzzi	7	92.33
Fastest lap	W. A. Lomas	Moto Guzzi		94.13
*Lightweight 250cc	W. A. Lomas	MV	9	71.37
Fastest lap	W. A. Lomas	MV		73.13
*Lightweight 125cc	C. Ubbiali	MV	9	69.67
Fastest lap	C. Ubbiali	MV		71.65
*Senior Clubman's	W. E. Dow	BSA	9	70.73
Fastest lap	J. Drysdale	BSA		72.53
*Junior Clubman's	J. Buchan	BSA	9	68.23
Fastest lap	D. Joubert	BSA		69.78
*Sidecar 500cc	W. Schneider/ H. Strauss	BMW	9	70.01
Fastest lap	W. Noll/F. Cron	BMW		71.93

1956

Class	Winner	Machine	Laps	Speed
Senior 500cc	J. Surtees	MV	7	96.57
Fastest lap	J. Surtees	MV		97.79
Junior 350cc	T. K. Kavanagh	Moto Guzzi	7	89.29
Fastest lap	T. K. Kavanagh	Moto Guzzi		93.15
*Lightweight 250cc	C. Ubbiali	MV	9	67.05
Fastest lap	H. Baltisberger	NSU		69.17
*Lightweight 125cc	C. Ubbiali	MV	9	69.13
Fastest lap	C. Ubbiali	MV		70.65
Senior Clubman's	B. D. Codd	BSA	3	86.33
Fastest lap	B. D. Codd	BSA		86.52
Junior Clubman's	B. D. Codd	BSA	3	82.02
Fastest lap	B. D. Codd	BSA		82.33
*Sidecar 500cc	F. Hillebrand/ M. Grunwald	BMW	9	70.03
Fastest lap	W. Noll/F. Cron	BMW		71.72

1957

Class	Winner	Machine	Laps	Speed
Senior 500cc	R. McIntyre	Gilera	8	98.99
Fastest lap	R. McIntyre	Gilera		101.12
Junior 350cc	R. McIntyre	Gilera	7	94.99
Fastest lap	R. McIntyre	Gilera		97.42
*Lightweight 250cc	C. C. Sandford	Mondial	10	75.80
Fastest lap	T. Provini	Mondial		78.00
*Lightweight 125cc	T. Provini	Mondial	10	73.69
Fastest lap	T. Provini	Mondial		74.44
*Sidecar 500cc	F Hillebrand/ M. Grunwald	BMW	10	71.89
Fastest lap	F. Hillebrand/ M. Grunwald	BMW		72.55

1958

Class	Winner	Machine	Laps	Speed
Senior 500cc	J. Surtees	MV	7	98.63
Fastest lap	J. Surtees	MV		100.58
Junior 350cc	J. Surtees	MV	7	93.97
Fastest lap	J. Surtees	MV		95.42
*Lightweight 250cc	T. Provini	MV	10	76.89
Fastest lap	T. Provini	MV		79.90
*Lightweight 125cc	C. Ubbiali	MV	10	72.86
Fastest lap	C. Ubbiali	MV		74.13
*Sidecar 500cc	W. Schneider/ H. Strauss	BMW	10	73.01
Fastest lap	W. Schneider/ H. Strauss	BMW		74.07

1959

Class	Winner	Machine	Laps	Speed
Senior 500cc	J. Surtees	MV	7	87.94
Fastest lap	J. Surtees	MV		101.18
Junior 350cc	J. Surtees	MV	7	95.38
Fastest lap	J. Surtees	MV		97.08
*Lightweight 250cc	T. Provini	MV	10	77.77
Fastest lap	T. Provini	MV		80.22
*Lightweight 125cc	T. Provini	MV	10	74.06
Fastest lap	L. Taveri	MV		74.99
Formula1 500cc	R. McIntyre	Norton	3	97.77
Fastest lap	R. McIntyre	Norton		98.35
Formula 1 350cc	A. King	AJS	3	94.66
Fastest lap	A. King	AJS		95.27
*Sidecar 500cc	W. Schneider/ H. Strauss	BMW	10	72.69
Fastest lap	W. Schneider/ H. Strauss	BMW		73.32

*Races marked thus were run on the Clypse Course.

THE SIXTIES: 1960–69

Course length: 37.73 miles

Race distance: up to 6 laps; 226 miles

Lap record: from 104.08mph (J. Surtees 1960) to 108.77mph
  (S. M. B. Hailwood, 1967)

Main bikes: MV Agusta, Honda, plus Yamaha, Suzuki and Benelli in the
  smaller classes

Top riders: Mike Hailwood, Giacomo Agostini, Jim Redman, Phil Read,
  Bill Ivy, Gary Hocking, Luigi Taveri, Carlo Ubbiali

No other time witnessed quite the riot of new technology which
marked the Sixties as racing's most prolific decade, although the
bias was heavily towards engine development. For four-strokes
this game of leap-frog culminated in Honda's 250cc and 297cc
six-cylinder machines, their dohc 24-valve engines spinning to
over 17,000rpm and putting out more power than singles twice
their size. Two-strokes made similar strides, culminating in
screaming 125cc and 250cc Vee-fours from Suzuki and Yamaha
with peaky powerbands and as many as 12 gears. Although chassis
received far less attention, on the tyre front, Avon introduced
grippy low-hysteresis rubber, while Dunlop developed the
radically 'triangular' profile.

If the bikes were 'vintage', so were the Sixties' leading riders,
with Hailwood unquestionably leading a very high-calibre field.

With new class regulations looming, Honda pulled out of
grands prix in 1968, with Suzuki and Yamaha following within the
year. Again, this left the way open for MV (and Agostini) to
dominate, but after the furious pace of the preceding decade,
their victories would have a hollow ring. Never once was Agostini
pushed to go anywhere near the 108mph lap he had accomplished
while battling with Hailwood in 1967. In 1969, he won both the
Junior and Senior races by around ten minutes while in the
Lightweight race, Kel Carruthers enjoyed similar superiority on
the 250cc Benelli-four.

1960

Class	Winner	Machine	Laps	Speed
Senior 500cc	J. Surtees	MV	6	102.44
Fastest lap	J. Surtees	MV		104.08
Junior 350cc	J. Hartle	MV	6	96.70
Fastest lap	J. Surtees	MV		99.20
Lightweight 250cc	G. Hocking	MV		93.64
Fastest lap	C. Ubbiali	MV		95.47
Lightweight 125cc	C. Ubbiali	MV	3	85.60
Fastest lap	C. Ubbiali	MV		86.10
Sidecar 500cc	H. Fath/ A. Wohlgemuth	BMW	3	84.10
Fastest lap	H. Fath/ A. Wohlgemuth	BMW		85.79

1961

Class	Winner	Machine	Laps	Speed
Senior 500cc	S. M. B. Hailwood	Norton	6	100.60
Fastest lap	G. Hocking	MV		102.62
Junior 350cc	P. W. Read	Norton	6	95.10
Fastest lap	G. Hocking	MV		99.80
Lightweight 250cc	S. M. B. Hailwood	Honda	5	98.38
Fastest lap	R. McIntyre	Honda		99.58
Lightweight 125cc	S. M. B. Hailwood	Honda	3	88.23
Fastest lap	L. Taveri	Honda		88.45
Sidecar 500cc	M. Deubel/E. Horner	BMW	3	87.65
Fastest lap	M. Deubel/E. Horner	BMW		87.97

1962

Class	Winner	Machine	Laps	Speed
Senior 500cc	G. Hocking	MV	6	103.51
Fastest lap	G. Hocking	MV		105.75
Junior 350cc	S. M. B. Hailwood	MV	6	99.59
Fastest lap	S. M. B. Hailwood	MV		101.58
Lightweight 250cc	D. W. Minter	Honda	6	96.68
Fastest lap	R. McIntyre	Honda		99.00
Lightweight 125cc	L. Taveri	Honda	3	89.88
Fastest lap	L. Taveri	Honda		90.13
50cc	E. Degner	Suzuki	3	75.12
Fastest lap	E. Degner	Suzuki		75.52
Sidecar 500cc	C. Vincent/E. Bliss	BSA	3	83.57
Fastest lap	M. Deubel/E. Horner	BMW		90.70

1963

Class	Winner	Machine	Laps	Speed
Senior 500cc	S. M. B. Hailwood	MV	6	104.64
Fastest lap	S. M. B. Hailwood	MV		106.41
Junior 350cc	J. Redman	Honda	6	94.91
Fastest lap	J. Redman	Honda		101.30
Lightweight 250cc	J. Redman	Honda	6	94.85
Fastest lap	J. Redman	Honda		97.23
Lightweight 125cc	H. R. Anderson	Suzuki	3	89.27
Fastest lap	H. R. Anderson	Suzuki		91.32
50cc	M. Itoh	Suzuki	3	78.81
Fastest lap	E. Degner	Suzuki		79.10
Sidecar 500cc	F. Camathias/ A. Herzig	BMW	3	88.38
Fastest lap	F. Camathias/ A. Herzig	BMW		89.42

1964

Class	Winner	Machine	Laps	Speed
Senior 500cc	S. M. B. Hailwood	MV	6	100.95
Fastest lap	S. M. B. Hailwood	MV		102.51
Junior 350cc	J. Redman	Honda	6	98.50
Fastest lap	J. Redman	Honda		100.76
Lightweight 250cc	J. Redman	Honda	6	97.45
Fastest lap	P. Read	Yamaha		99.42
Lightweight 125cc	L. Taveri	Honda	3	92.14
Fastest lap	L. Taveri	Honda		93.53
50cc	H. R. Anderson	Suzuki	3	80.64
Fastest lap	H. R. Anderson	Suzuki		81.13
Sidecar 500cc	M. Deubel/E. Horner	BMW	3	89.12
Fastest lap	M. Deubel/E. Horner	BMW		89.63

1965

Class	Winner	Machine	Laps	Speed
Senior 500cc	S. M. B. Hailwood	MV	6	91.69
Fastest lap	S. M. B. Hailwood	MV		95.11
Junior 350cc	J. Redman	Honda	6	100.72
Fastest lap	J. Redman	Honda		102.85
Lightweight 250cc	J. Redman	Honda	6	97.19
Fastest lap	J. Redman	Honda		100.09
Lightweight 125cc	P. W. Read	Yamaha	3	94.28
Fastest lap	H. R. Anderson	Suzuki		96.02
50cc	L. Taveri	Honda	3	79.66
Fastest lap	L. Taveri	Honda		80.83
Sidecar 500cc	M. Deubel/E. Horner	BMW	3	90.57
Fastest lap	M. Deubel/E. Horner	BMW		91.80

1966

Class	Winner	Machine	Laps	Speed
Senior 500cc	S. M. B. Hailwood	Honda	6	103.11
Fastest lap	S. M. B. Hailwood	Honda		107.07
Junior 350cc	G. Agostini	MV	6	100.87
Fastest lap	G. Agostini	MV		103.09
Lightweight 250cc	S. M. B. Hailwood	Honda	6	101.79
Fastest lap	S. M. B. Hailwood	Honda		104.29
Lightweight 125cc	W. D. Ivy	Yamaha	3	97.66
Fastest lap	W. D. Ivy	Yamaha		98.55
50cc	R. Bryans	Honda	3	85.56
Fastest lap	R. Bryans	Honda		86.49
Sidecar 500cc	F. Scheidegger/ J. Robinson	BMW	3	90.76
Fastest lap	F. Scheidegger/ E. Horner	BMW		91.63

1967

Class	Winner	Machine	Laps	Speed
Senior 500cc	S. M. B. Hailwood	Honda	6	105.62
Fastest lap	S. M. B. Hailwood	Honda		108.77
Junior 350cc	S. M. B. Hailwood	Honda	6	104.68
Fastest lap	S. M. B. Hailwood	Honda		107.73
Lightweight 250cc	S. M. B. Hailwood	Honda	6	103.07
Fastest lap	S. M. B. Hailwood	Honda		104.50
Lightweight 125cc	P. W. Read	Yamaha	3	97.48
Fastest lap	P. W. Read	Yamaha		98.36
50cc	S. Graham	Suzuki	3	82.89
Fastest lap	S. Graham	Suzuki		85.19
Production	W. A. Smith	250 Bultaco	3	88.63
Fastest lap	W. A. Smith	250 Bultaco		89.41
Production	N. Kelly	500 Velocette	3	89.89
Fastest lap	N. Kelly	500 Velocette		91.01
Production	J. Hartle	750 Triumph	3	97.10
Fastest lap	J. Hartle	750 Triumph		97.87
Sidecar 500cc	S. Schauzu/ H. Schneider	BMW	3	90.96
Fastest lap	G. Auerbacher/ E. Dein	BMW		91.70

Class	Winner	Machine	Laps	Speed
Senior 500cc	G. Agostini	MV	6	101.63
Fastest lap	G. Agostini	MV		104.91
Junior 350cc	G. Agostini	MV	6	104.78
Fastest lap	G. Agostini	MV		106.77
Lightweight 250cc	W. D. Ivy	Yamaha	6	99.58
Fastest lap	W. D. Ivy	Yamaha		105.51
Lightweight 125cc	P. W. Read	Yamaha	3	99.12
Fastest lap	W. D. Ivy	Yamaha		100.32
50cc	B. Smith	Derbi	3	72.90
Fastest lap	B. Smith	Derbi		73.44
Production	T. E. Burgess	250 Ossa	3	87.21
Fastest lap	T. E. Burgess	250 Ossa		87.89
Production	R. L. Knight	500 Triumph	3	90.09
Fastest lap	R. L. Knight	500 Triumph		91.03
Production	R. Pickrell	750 Dunstall	3	98.13
Fastest lap	R. Pickrell	750 Dunstall		99.39
Sidecar 500cc	S. Schauzu/ H. Schneider	BMW	3	91.09
Fastest lap	K. Enders/ R. Englehardt	BMW		94.00
Sidecar 750cc	T. Vinicome/ J. Flaxman	BSA	3	85.85
Fastest lap	C. Vincent/K. Scott	BSA		89.11

1969

Class	Winner	Machine	Laps	Speed
Senior 500cc	G. Agostini	MV	6	104.75
Fastest lap	G. Agostini	MV		106.25
Junior 350cc	G. Agostini	MV	6	101.81
Fastest lap	G. Agostini	MV		104.00
Lightweight 250cc	K. Carruthers	Benelli	6	95.95
Fastest lap	K. Carruthers	Benelli		99.01
Lightweight 125cc	D. A. Simmonds	Kawasaki	3	91.08
Fastest lap	D. A. Simmonds	Kawasaki		92.46
Production	A. M. Rogers	250 Ducati	3	83.79
Fastest lap	C. S. Mortimer	250 Ducati		85.13
Production	W. G. Penny	500 Honda	3	88.18
Fastest lap	T. Dunnell	500 Kawasaki		90.84
Production	M. Uphill	750 Triumph	3	99.99
Fastest lap	M. Uphill	750 Triumph		100.37
Sidecar 500cc	K. Enders/ R. Englehardt	BMW	3	92.48
Fastest lap	K. Enders/ R. Englehardt	BMW		92.54
Sidecar 750cc	S. Schauzu/ H. Schneider	BMW	3	89.83
Fastest lap	S. Schauzu/ H. Schneider	BMW		92.06

THE SEVENTIES: 1970–79

Course length: 37.73 miles

Race distance: up to 6 laps; 188 to 226 miles

Lap record: from 108.77mph (S. M. B. Hailwood, 1967) to 114.18mph
  (A. George, 1979)

Main bikes: MV Agusta, Yamaha, Honda, Kawasaki, Ducati

Top riders: Phil Read, Mike Hailwood, Charlie and John Williams,
  Mick Grant, Tom Herron, Chas Mortimer

The Seventies must go down as the races' most fraught decade. In 1970, no less than six riders were killed in practice and racing, including Spain's Santiago Herrero. Then, spurred by Gilberto Parlotti's death in 1972, the movement to remove the TT (and Ulster GP) from the World Championship calendar gathered pace. Agostini, Read and Gould boycotted the 1973 TT, and in 1977, the British GP moved to Silverstone. Although the TT was no longer able to attract all the top stars, prize money soared, factory interest (particularly in the Senior and F1) remained high and the concept of the TT as a motorcycle festival took root. Stimulated further by Hailwood's return in 1978, spectator attendances reached record levels.

Machinery, ironically, became more diverse than ever. In the smaller classes (and even in the Senior), Yamaha's TZ twins were ubiquitous, while Suzuki's RG500 square four proved surprisingly adept over the Mountain Course. The world 750 series promoted a new generation of three and four-cylinder 750cc two-strokes, while from 1977, the new Formula One class had a similar effect for big four-strokes. Chassis development was brisk, with slick tyres, monoshock rear ends, cast wheels and disc brakes all becoming standard. Full-face helmets also became commonplace.

Although the races became conspicuous by the absence of top grand prix riders, a new band of talented Brits was testing the TT waters. Mick Grant, Tom Herron, Alex George, Chas Mortimer, Tony Rutter, Charlie, John and Peter Williams, all cut their TT teeth, but the man of the decade was old Mike Hailwood who, in 1979, posted a record 14th TT win. In 1976, a shy Ulsterman made his debut; his name was William Joseph Dunlop.

1970

Class	Winner	Machine	Laps	Speed
Senior 500cc	G. Agostini	MV	6	101.52
Fastest lap	G. Agostini	MV		105.29
Junior 350cc	G. Agostini	MV	6	101.77
Fastest lap	G. Agostini	MV		104.56
Lightweight 250cc	K. Carruthers	Yamaha	6	96.13
Fastest lap	K. Carruthers	Yamaha		98.04
Lightweight 125cc	D. Braun	Suzuki	3	89.27
Fastest lap	D. A. Simmonds	Kawasaki		90.90
Production	C. S. Mortimer	250 Ducati	5	84.87
Fastest lap	C. S. Mortimer	250 Ducati		86.37
Production	F. Whiteway	500 Suzuki	5	89.94
Fastest lap	F. Whiteway	500 Suzuki		90.75
Production	M. Uphill	750 Triumph	5	97.71
Fastest lap	P. Williams	750 Norton		99.99
Sidecar 500cc	K. Enders/ W. Kalauch	BMW	3	92.93
Fastest lap	K. Enders/ W. Kalauch	BMW		93.79
Sidecar 750cc	S. Schauzu/ H. Schneider	BMW	3	90.20
Fastest lap	K. Enders/ R. Englehardt	BMW		92.37

Class	Winner	Machine	Laps	Speed
Senior 500cc	G. Agostini	MV	6	102.59
Fastest lap	G. Agostini	MV		104.86
Junior 350cc	A. Jefferies	Yamsel	5	89.98
Fastest lap	P. Read	Yamaha		100.37
Lightweight 250cc	P. Read	Yamaha	4	98.02
Fastest lap	P. Read	Yamaha		100.00
Lightweight 125cc	C. Mortimer	Yamaha	3	83.96
Fastest lap	C. Mortimer	Yamaha		87.05
Formula 750	A. Jefferies	Triumph	3	102.85
Fastest lap	A. Jefferies	Triumph		103.21
Production	B. Smith	250 Honda	4	84.14
Fastest lap	C. Williams	250 Yamaha		84.64
Production	J. Williams	500 Honda	4	91.04
Fastest lap	J. Williams	500 Honda		91.45
Production	R. Pickrell	750 Triumph	4	100.07
Fastest lap	P. Williams	750 Norton		101.06
Sidecar 500cc	S. Schauzu/ W. Kalauch	BMW	3	86.21
Fastest lap	G. Auerbacher/ H. Hahn	BMW		87.27
Sidecar 750cc	G. Auerbacher/ H. Hahn	BMW	3	86.86
Fastest lap	S. Schauzu/ W. Kalauch	BMW		93.44

1972

Class	Winner	Machine	Laps	Speed
Senior 500cc	G. Agostini	MV	6	104.02
Fastest lap	G. Agostini	MV		105.39
Junior 350cc	G. Agostini	MV	5	102.03
Fastest lap	G. Agostini	MV		103.34
Lightweight 250cc	P. Read	Yamaha	4	99.68
Fastest lap	P. Read	Yamaha		100.61
Lightweight 125cc	C. Mortimer	Yamaha	3	87.49
Fastest lap	C. Mortimer	Yamaha		90.58
Formula 750	R. Pickrell	Triumph	5	104.23
Fastest lap	R. Pickrell	Triumph		105.68
Production	J. Williams	250 Honda	4	85.32
Fastest lap	J. Williams	250 Honda		85.73
Production	S. Woods	500 Suzuki	4	92.20
Fastest lap	S. Woods	500 Suzuki		93.61
Production	R. Pickrell	750 Triumph	4	100.00
Fastest lap	R. Pickrell	750 Triumph		101.61
Sidecar 500cc	S. Schauzu/W. Kalauch	BMW	3	91.85
Fastest lap	H. Luthringshauser/ J. Cusnik	BMW		92.53
Sidecar 750cc	S. Schauzu/W. Kalauch	BMW	3	90.97
Fastest lap	S. Schauzu/W. Kalauch	BMW		91.33

Class	Winner	Machine	Laps	Speed
Senior 500cc	J. Findlay	Suzuki	6	101.55
Fastest lap	M. Grant	Yamaha		104.41
Junior 350cc	A. T. Rutter	Yamaha	5	101.99
Fastest lap	A. T. Rutter	Yamaha		104.22
Lightweight 250cc	C. Williams	Yamaha	4	100.05
Fastest lap	C. Williams	Yamaha		102.24
Lightweight 125cc	T. H. Robb	Yamaha	3	88.90
Fastest lap	T. H. Robb	Yamaha		89.24
Formula 750	P. Williams	Norton	5	105.47
Fastest lap	P. Williams	Norton		107.27
Production	C. Williams	250 Yamaha	4	81.76
Fastest lap	E. Roberts	250 Yamaha		84.06
Production	W. A. Smith	500 Honda	4	88.10
Fastest lap	S. Woods	500 Suzuki		94.44
Production	A. Jefferies	750 Triumph	4	95.62
Fastest lap	P. Williams	750 Norton		100.52
Sidecar 500cc	K. Enders/R. Englehardt	BMW	3	94.93
Fastest lap	K. Enders/R. Englehardt	BMW		95.22
Sidecar 750cc	K. Enders/R. Englehardt	BMW	3	93.01
Fastest lap	K. Enders/R. Englehardt	BMW		96.86

1974

Class	Winner	Machine	Laps	Speed
Senior 500cc	P. Carpenter	Yamaha	6	96.99
Fastest lap	C. Williams	Yamaha		101.92
Junior 350cc	A. T. Rutter	Yamaha	5	104.44
Fastest lap	A. T. Rutter	Yamaha		106.39
Lightweight 250cc	C. Williams	Yamaha	4	94.16
Fastest lap	M. Grant	Yamaha		97.85
Lightweight 125cc	C. Horton	Yamaha	3	88.44
Fastest lap	= A. Hockley/C. Horton	both Yamaha		88.78
Formula 750	C. Mortimer	Yamaha	6	100.52
Fastest lap	C. Williams	Yamaha		106.61
Production	M. Sharpe	247 Yamaha	4	86.95
Fastest lap	E. Roberts	250 Yamaha		88.48
Production	K. Martin	492 Kawasaki	4	93.85
Fastest lap	K. Martin	492 Kawasaki		95.21
Production	M. Grant	741 Triumph	4	99.72
Fastest lap	M. Grant	741 Triumph		100.74
Sidecar 500cc	H. Luthringshauser/ H. Hahn	BMW	3	92.97
Fastest lap	J. Gawley/K. Birch	Konig		93.36
Sidecar 750cc	S. Schauzu/W. Kalauch	BMW	3	96.59
Fastest lap	R. Steinhausen/ K. Scheurer	Konig		98.18

Class	Winner	Machine	Laps	Speed
Senior 500cc	M. Grant	Kawasaki	6	100.27
Fastest lap	M. Grant	Kawasaki		102.93
Junior 350cc	C. Williams	Yamaha	5	104.38
Fastest lap	A. George	Yamaha		106.29
Lightweight 250cc	C. Mortimer	Yamaha	4	101.78
Fastest lap	D. Chatterton	Yamaha		103.54
Classic 1,000cc	J. Williams	Yamaha	6	105.33
Fastest lap	M. Grant	Kawasaki		109.82
Production	D. Croxford/A. George	748 Triumph	10	99.60
Fastest lap	A. George	748 Triumph		102.82
Sidecar 500cc	R. Steinhausen/J. Huber	Konig	3	95.94
Fastest lap	M. Hobson/G. Russell	Yamaha		96.71
Sidecar 1,000cc	S. Schauzu/W. Kalauch	BMW	3	97.55
Fastest lap	S. Schauzu/W. Kalauch	BMW		99.31

Class	Winner	Machine	Laps	Speed
Senior 500cc	T. Herron	Yamaha	6	105.15
Fastest lap	J. Williams	Suzuki		112.27
Junior 350cc	C. Mortimer	Yamaha	5	106.78
Fastest lap	A. T. Rutter	Yamaha		108.69
Lightweight 250cc	T. Herron	Yamaha	4	103.55
Fastest lap	T. Herron	Yamaha		103.55
Classic 1,000cc	J. Williams	Suzuki	6	108.18
Fastest lap	J. Williams	Suzuki		110.21
Production	B. Simpson/ C. Mortimer	250 Yamaha	10	87.00
Fastest lap	R. Nicholls	900 Ducati		103.13
Sidecar 500cc	R. Steinhausen/ J. Huber	Konig	3	96.42
Fastest lap	S. Schauzu/W. Kalauch	Aro		97.50
Sidecar 1,000cc	M. Hobson/M. Burns	Yamaha	3	97.77
Fastest lap	M. Hobson/M. Burns	Yamaha		99.96

1977

Class	Winner	Machine	Laps	Speed
Senior 500cc	P. Read	Suzuki	5	106.97
Fastest lap	P. Read	Suzuki		110.01
TT Formula 1	P. Read	Honda	4	97.02
Fastest lap	P. Read	Honda		101.74
TT Formula 2	A. Jackson	Honda	4	99.36
Fastest lap	A. Jackson	Honda		101.15
TT Formula 3	J. Kidson	Honda	4	93.28
Fastest lap	J. Kidson	Honda		94.81
Junior 250cc	C. Williams	Yamaha	3	99.62
Fastest lap	I. Richards	Yamaha		101.45
Classic 1,000cc	M. Grant	Kawasaki	6	110.76
Fastest lap	M. Grant	Kawasaki		112.77
Jubilee Race	W. J. Dunlop	Yamaha	4	108.86
Fastest lap	W. J. Dunlop	Yamaha		110.93
Sidecar 1,000cc 'A'	G. O'Dell/K. Arthur	Yamaha	4	100.03
Fastest lap	G. O'Dell/K. Arthur	Yamaha		102.80
Sidecar 1,000cc 'B'	M. Hobson/S. Collins	Yamaha	4	99.74
Fastest lap	M. Hobson/S. Collins	Yamaha		101.74

1978

Class	Winner	Machine	Laps	Speed
Senior 500cc	T. Herron	Suzuki	6	111.74
Fastest lap	P. Hennen	Suzuki		113.83
TT Formula 1	S. M. B. Hailwood	Ducati	6	108.51
Fastest lap	S. M. B. Hailwood	Ducati		110.62
TT Formula 2	A. Jackson	Honda	4	99.35
Fastest lap	A. Jackson	Honda		103.21
TT Formula 3	W. A. Smith	Honda	4	94.47
Fastest lap	W. A. Smith	Honda		96.13
Junior 250cc	C. Mortimer	Yamaha	6	100.70
Fastest lap	C. Mortimer	Yamaha		102.06
Classic 1,000cc	M. Grant	Kawasaki	6	112.40
Fastest lap	M. Grant	Kawasaki		114.33
Sidecar 1,000cc 'A'	D. Greasley/G. Russell	Yamaha	3	101.75
Fastest lap	R. Biland/K. Williams	Yamaha		103.81
Sidecar 1,000cc 'B'	R. Steinhausen/ W. Kalauch	Yamaha	3	93.67
Fastest lap	R. Steinhausen/ W. Kalauch	Yamaha		96.14

1979

Class	Winner	Machine	Laps	Speed
Senior 500cc	S. M. B. Hailwood	Suzuki	6	111.75
Fastest lap	S. M. B. Hailwood	Suzuki		114.02
TT Formula 1	A. George	Honda	6	110.57
Fastest lap	A. George	Honda		112.94
TT Formula 2	A. Jackson	Honda	4	101.55
Fastest lap	A. Jackson	Honda		103.40
TT Formula 3	B. Smith	Yamaha	4	97.82
Fastest lap	B. Smith	Yamaha		99.37
Junior 250cc	C. Williams	Yamaha	6	105.13
Fastest lap	C. Williams	Yamaha		106.83
Classic 1,000cc	A. George	Honda	6	113.08
Fastest lap	A. George	Honda		114.18
Sidecar 1,000cc 'A'	T. Ireson/C. Pollington	Yamaha	3	102.14
Fastest lap	M. Boddice/C. Birks	Yamaha		103.26
Sidecar 1,000cc 'B'	T. Ireson/C. Pollington	Yamaha	3	98.13
Fastest lap	R. Steinhausen/ K. Arthur	MSAI		102.17

THE EIGHTIES: 1980–89

Course length: 37.73 miles

Race distance: up to 6 laps; 226 miles

Lap record: from 115.22mph (W. J. Dunlop 1980) to 122.63mph
  (S. Hislop, 1989)

Main bikes: Honda, Suzuki, Yamaha, Kawasaki, Ducati

Top riders: Joey Dunlop, Mick Grant, Charlie Williams, Rob McElnea,
  Graeme Crosby, Steve Hislop

If the Seventies had been the TT's most troubled decade, the
Eighties dawned to a wave of cautious confidence. The TT might
no longer host the World Championship, but the Formula One
series was beginning to attract wider interest, both from the
(mainly Japanese) factories and from countries keen to have a
round of their own. Prize money was second to no other race
meeting, and entries were massively oversubscribed. Then there
was the growing attraction of, for want of a better expression,
'Bikers' Island'. The race programme, however, was becoming
unwieldy, with as many as 14 TT winners in some years.

On the track, two-strokes still dominated up to 500cc, with big
four-stroke multis and Ducati desmo twins ruling in F1 and F2
respectively. The bike of the decade was Honda's exquisite
RVF750 Vee-four, on which Joey Dunlop was virtually
unbeatable.

1980

Class	Winner	Machine	Laps	Speed
Senior 500cc	G. Crosby	Suzuki	6	109.65
Fastest lap	S. Woods	Suzuki		111.37
TT Formula 1	M. Grant	Honda	6	105.29
Fastest lap	S. McClements	Honda		106.88
TT Formula 2	C. Williams	Yamaha	4	96.24
Fastest lap	C. Williams	Yamaha		98.17
TT Formula 3	B. Smith	Yamaha	4	91.98
Fastest lap	B. Smith	Yamaha		95.82
Junior 250cc	C. Williams	Yamaha	4	102.22
Fastest lap	D. Robinson	Yamaha		104.53
Classic 1,000cc	W. J. Dunlop	Yamaha	6	112.72
Fastest lap	W. J. Dunlop	Yamaha		115.22
Sidecar 1,000cc 'A'	T. Ireson/C. Pollington	Yamaha	3	98.13
Fastest lap	J. Taylor/B. Johannson	Yamaha		100.61
Sidecar 1,000cc 'B'	J. Taylor/B. Johannson	Yamaha	3	103.55
Fastest lap	J. Taylor/B. Johannson	Yamaha		106.08

1981

Class	Winner	Machine	Laps	Speed
Senior 500cc	M. Grant	Suzuki	6	106.14
Fastest lap	M. Grant	Suzuki		112.68
TT Formula 1	G. Crosby	Suzuki	6	111.81
Fastest lap	G. Crosby	Suzuki		113.70
TT Formula 2	A. Rutter	Ducati	4	101.91
Fastest lap	A. Rutter	Ducati		103.51
TT Formula 3	B. Smith	Yamaha	4	99.66
Fastest lap	B. Smith	Yamaha		101.31
Junior 250cc	S. Tonkin	Armstrong CCM	6	106.21
Fastest lap	G. McGregor	Kawasaki		109.22
Classic 1,000cc	G. Crosby	Suzuki	6	113.58
Fastest lap	W. J. Dunlop	Honda		115.40
Sidecar 1,000cc 'A'	J. Taylor/B. Johannson	Yamaha	3	107.02
Fastest lap	J. Taylor/B. Johannson	Yamaha		108.12
Sidecar 1,000cc 'B'	J. Taylor/B. Johannson	Yamaha	3	104.55
Fastest lap	J. Taylor/B. Johannson	Yamaha		107.54

1982

Class	Winner	Machine	Laps	Speed
Senior 500cc	N. Brown	Suzuki	6	110.98
Fastest lap	C. Williams	Yamaha		115.08
TT Formula 1	R. Haslam	Honda	6	113.33
Fastest lap	M. Grant	Suzuki		114.93
TT Formula 2	A. Rutter	Ducati	4	108.05
Fastest lap	A. Rutter	Ducati		109.27
TT Formula 3	G. Padgett	Yamaha	4	96.17
Fastest lap	G. Padgett	Yamaha		97.36
Junior 350cc	A. T. Rutter	Yamaha	6	108.58
Fastest lap	G. McGregor	Yamaha		112.03
Junior 250cc	C. Law	Waddon Ehrlich	6	105.32
Fastest lap	C. Williams	Yamaha		108.00
Classic 1,000cc	D. Ireland	Suzuki	6	109.21
Fastest lap	C. Williams	Yamaha		113.47
Sidecar 1,000cc 'A'	T. Ireson/D. Williams	Yamaha	3	106.29
Fastest lap	M. Boddice/C. Birks	Yamaha		107.52
Sidecar 1,000cc 'B'	J. Taylor/B. Johannson	Yamaha	3	106.09
Fastest lap	J. Taylor/B. Johannson	Yamaha		108.29

1983

Class	Winner	Machine	Laps	Speed
Senior Classic	R. McElnea	Suzuki	6	114.81
Fastest lap	N. Brown	Suzuki		116.19
TT Formula 1	W. J. Dunlop	Honda	6	114.03
Fastest lap	W. J. Dunlop	Honda		115.73
TT Formula 2	A. Rutter	Ducati	4	108.20
Fastest lap	A. Rutter	Ducati		109.44
Junior 350cc	P. Mellor	Spondon Yamaha	6	107.44
Fastest lap	C. Law	Yamaha		109.71
Junior 250cc	C. Law	EMC	6	108.09
Fastest lap	C. Law	EMC		110.03
Sidecar 1,000cc 'A'	D. Greasley/S. Atkinson	Yamaha	3	104.25
Fastest lap	D. Greasley/S. Atkinson	Yamaha		105.01
Sidecar 1,000cc 'B'	M. Boddice/C. Birks	Yamaha	3	105.11
Fastest lap	M. Boddice/C. Birks	Yamaha		106.19

1984

Class	Winner	Machine	Laps	Speed
Senior 500cc	R. McElnea	Suzuki	6	115.66
Fastest lap	W. J. Dunlop	Honda		118.47
TT Formula 1	W. J. Dunlop	Honda	6	111.68
Fastest lap	W. J. Dunlop	Honda		115.8
TT Formula 2	G. McGregor	Yamaha	4	108.78
Fastest lap	G. McGregor	Yamaha		110.0
Junior 250cc	G. McGregor	EMC	6	109.57
Fastest lap	G. McGregor	EMC		111.06
Premier Classic	R. McElnea	Suzuki	6	116.12
Fastest lap	R. McElnea	Suzuki		117.13
Production C	P. Mellor	250 Yamaha	3	92.58
Fastest lap	P. Mellor	250 Yamaha		94.01
Production B	T. Nation	750 Honda	3	102.24
Fastest lap	T. Nation	750 Honda		102.97
Production A	G. Johnson	900 Kawasaki	3	105.28
Fastest lap	G. Johnson	900 Kawasaki		106.13
Historic 500cc	D. Roper	500 Matchless	3	96.11
Fastest lap	D. Roper	500 Matchless		97.21
Historic 350cc	S. Cull	350 Aermacchi	3	94.26
Fastest lap	J. Millar	350 Aermacchi		95.28
Sidecar 1,000cc 'A'	M. Boddice/C. Birks	Yamaha	3	103.97
Fastest lap	M. Boddice/C. Birks	Yamaha		107.45
Sidecar 1,000cc 'B'	S. Abbott/S. Smith	Yamaha	3	105.29
Fastest lap	M. Boddice/C. Birks	Yamaha		106.90
Sidecar F2 'A'	C. Pritchard/K. Morgan	Yamaha	3	83.19
Fastest lap	B. Hodgkins/J. Parkins	Yamaha		92.24
Sidecar F2 'B'	B. Hodgkins/J. Parkins	Yamaha	3	85.24
Fastest lap	D. Saville/D. Hall	Sabre		92.55

Class	Winner	Machine	Laps	Speed
Senior 1,000cc	W. J. Dunlop	750 Honda	6	113.69
Fastest lap	R. Marshall	500 Honda		116.07
TT Formula 1	W. J. Dunlop	Honda	6	113.95
Fastest lap	W. J. Dunlop	Honda		116.42
TT Formula 2	A. Rutter	Ducati	6	107.79
Fastest lap	B. Reid	Yamaha		110.46
Junior 250cc	W. J. Dunlop	Honda	6	109.91
Fastest lap	B. Reid	EMC		112.08
Production A	M. Oxley	250 Honda	3	94.84
Fastest lap	M. Oxley	250 Honda		96.40
Production B	M. Grant	750 Suzuki	3	104.36
Fastest lap	G. Williams	750 Suzuki		105.93
Production C	G. Johnson	998 Honda	3	105.12
Fastest lap	B. Simpson	900 Kawasaki		105.83
Sidecar 1,000cc 'A'	D. Hallam/J. Gibbard	Yamaha	3	104.45
Fastest lap	M. Boddice/C. Birks	Yamaha		107.10
Sidecar 1,000cc 'B'	M. Boddice/C. Birks	Yamaha	3	105.26
Fastest lap	M. Boddice/C. Birks	Yamaha		107.37
Sidecar F2 'A'	D. Saville/D. Hall	Derbyshire	3	93.08
Fastest lap	D. Saville/D. Hall	Derbyshire		94.08
Sidecar F2 'B'	B. Hodgkins/J. Parkins	Yamaha	3	92.08
Fastest lap	D. Saville/D. Hall	Derbyshire		93.37

1986

Class	Winner	Machine	Laps	Speed
Senior 1,000cc	R. Burnett	Honda	6	113.98
Fastest lap	T. Nation	Suzuki		116.55
TT Formula 1	W. J. Dunlop	Honda	6	112.96
Fastest lap	W. J. Dunlop	Honda		113.98
TT Formula 2	B. Reid	Yamaha	4	109.72
Fastest lap	B. Reid	Yamaha		111.75
Junior 350cc	D. Leach	Yamaha	6	110.63
Fastest lap	D. Leach	Yamaha		112.05
Junior 250cc	S. Cull	Honda	6	109.62
Fastest lap	P. Mellor	EMC		111.42
Production D	B. Woodland	400 Suzuki	3	99.82
Fastest lap	M. Oxley	250 Yamaha		100.82
Production C	G. Padgett	400 Suzuki	3	102.98
Fastest lap	G. Padgett	400 Suzuki		104.43
Production B	P. Mellor	750 Suzuki	3	109.23
Fastest lap	P. Mellor	750 Suzuki		110.70
Production A	T. Nation	1100 Suzuki	3	111.99
Fastest lap	T. Nation	1100 Suzuki		113.26
Sidecar 1,000cc 'A'	L. Burton/P. Cushnahan	Yamaha	3	104.53
Fastest lap	L. Burton/P. Cushnahan	Yamaha		105.90
Sidecar 1,000cc 'B'	N. Rollason/D. Williams	Barton	3	103.81
Fastest lap	D. Hallam/J. Gibbard	Yamaha		105.47
Sidecar F2 'A'	D. Saville/D. Hall	Windle	3	95.77
Fastest lap	D. Saville/D. Hall	Windle		96.34
Sidecar F2 'B'	C. Hopper/N. Burgess	Armstrong	3	92.77
Fastest lap	D. Saville/D. Hall	Windle		96.85

Class	Winner	Machine	Laps	Speed
Senior 1,300cc	W. J. Dunlop	Honda	4	99.85
Fastest lap	W. J. Dunlop	Honda		105.08
TT Formula 1	W. J. Dunlop	Honda	6	115.03
Fastest lap	W. J. Dunlop	Honda		117.55
TT Formula 2	S. Hislop	Yamaha	6	110.40
Fastest lap	E. Laycock	Yamaha		112.36
Junior 350cc	E. Laycock	EMC	6	108.52
Fastest lap	S. Hislop	Yamaha		111.51
Production D	B. Woodland	400 Yamaha	3	102.98
Fastest lap	B. Woodland	400 Yamaha		103.36
Production B	G. Johnson	750 Yamaha	3	109.98
Fastest lap	T. Nation	750 Yamaha		103.79
Production Classes A and C cancelled due to adverse weather				
Sidecar 1,000cc 'A'	M. Boddice/D. Williams	Yamaha	3	104.76
Fastest lap	M. Boddice/D. Williams	Yamaha		105.73
Sidecar 1,000cc 'B'	L. Burton/P. Cushnahan	Yamaha	3	105.53
Fastest lap	L. Burton/P. Cushnahan	Yamaha		105.9
Sidecar F2 'A'	D. Saville/D. Hall	Sabre	3	96.49
Fastest lap	D. Saville/D. Hall	Sabre		96.82
Sidecar F2 'B'	D. Saville/D. Hall	Sabre	3	95.07
Fastest lap	D. Saville/D. Hall	Sabre		96.3

1988

Class	Winner	Machine	Laps	Speed
Senior 1,300cc	W. J. Dunlop	Honda	6	117.38
Fastest lap	S. Cull	Honda		119.08
TT Formula 1	W. J. Dunlop	Honda	6	116.25
Fastest lap	W. J. Dunlop	Honda		118.54
TT Formula 2	S. Hislop	Yamaha	6	110.40
Fastest lap	E. Laycock	Yamaha		113.41
Junior 350cc	W. J. Dunlop	Honda	4	111.87
Fastest lap	S. Hislop	Yamaha		112.36
Production D	B. Woodland	400 Yamaha	4	102.21
Fastest lap	B. Woodland	400 Yamaha		103.79
Production C	B. Morrison	600 Honda	4	108.42
Fastest lap	S. Hislop	600 Honda		109.83
Production B	S. Hislop	750 Honda	4	112.29
Fastest lap	G. Johnson	750 Yamaha		112.98
Production A	D. Leach	1000 Yamaha	4	114.32
Fastest lap	G. Johnson	1000 Yamaha		116.55
Sidecar 1,000cc 'A'	M. Boddice/C. Birks	Yamaha	3	106.27
Fastest lap	M. Boddice/C. Birks	Yamaha		107.15
Sidecar 1,000cc 'B'	M. Boddice/C. Birks	Yamaha	3	106.46
Fastest lap	L. Burton/P. Cushnahan	Yamaha		107.66
Sidecar F2 'A'	M. Hamblin/R. Smith	Yamaha	3	94.86
Fastest lap	D. Saville/D. Hall	Sabre		96.70
Sidecar F2 'B'	D. Saville/D. Hall	Sabre	3	96.46
Fastest lap	D. Saville/D. Hall	Sabre		96.82

1989

Class	Winner	Machine	Laps	Speed
Senior 1,300cc	S. Hislop	Honda	6	118.23
Fastest lap	S. Hislop	Honda		120.69
TT Formula 1	S. Hislop	Honda	6	119.36
Fastest lap	S. Hislop	Honda		121.34
Junior 350cc	J. Rea	Yamaha	4	112.12
Fastest lap	E. Laycock	Yamaha		114.04
Lightweight 125cc	R. Dunlop	Honda	2	102.56
Fastest lap	R. Dunlop	Honda		103.02
Supersports 400cc	E. Laycock	Suzuki	4	105.27
Fastest lap	E. Laycock	Suzuki		106.90
Supersports 600cc	S. Hislop	Honda	4	112.58
Fastest lap	D. Leach	Yamaha		113.60
Production B	C. Fogarty	750 Honda	4	114.68
Fastest lap	D. Leach	750 Yamaha		116.91
Production A	D. Leach	1000 Yamaha	4	115.61
Fastest lap	N. Jefferies	1000 Yamaha		117.27
Sidecar 1,000cc 'A'	D. Molyneux/C. Hardman	Yamaha	3	104.56
Fastest lap	K. Howles/S. Pointer	Yamaha		105.65
Sidecar 1,000cc 'B'	M. Boddice/C. Birks	Yamaha	3	107.17
Fastest lap	M. Boddice/C. Birks	Yamaha		108.31
Sidecar F2 'A'	D. Saville/R. Crossley	Sabre	3	98.15
Fastest lap	D. Saville/R. Crossley	Sabre		99.23
Sidecar F2 'B'	D. Saville/R. Crossley	Sabre	3	98.56
Fastest lap	D. Saville/R. Crossley	Sabre		99.11

THE NINETIES: 1990–99

Course length: 37.73 miles
Race distance: up to 6 laps; 226 miles
Lap record: from 123.48mph (S. Hislop, 1991) to 124.45mph
  (J. Moodie, 1999)
Main bikes: Honda, Yamaha
Top riders: Joey Dunlop, Steve Hislop, Robert Dunlop, Phillip McCallen,
  Carl Fogarty, Brian Reid, Ian Simpson, Jim Moodie, Nick and David
  Jefferies

The Nineties was the decade in which the decline feared after 1976 truly took hold. By 1999, only Honda retained any real factory interest in the races, the rest being largely made up of private teams. Two-strokes still filled the fields at 125cc and 250cc, but were on their way out. Four-strokes sprouted microchips and electronic fuel injection, but then by decade's end, so did the typical sports roadster. In the larger classes, with rare exceptions, the TT had become an event for modified production machines. The outright lap record largely stagnated.

If Steve Hislop was the races' most sublime exponent, Joey Dunlop was its most remarkable. In 1993, the great Irishman overhauled Hailwood's record of 14 wins, taking his tally to 23 by decade's end. But few of his main opponents came from outside the British Isles. The TT may rightly claim to be 'the last of the great road races', but by this time it was no longer a major player on the international racing scene.

Class	Winner	Machine	Laps	Speed
Senior 750cc	C. Fogarty	Honda	6	110.95
Fastest lap	D. Leach	Yamaha		116.47
TT Formula 1	C. Fogarty	Honda	6	118.35
Fastest lap	S. Hislop	Honda		122.63
Junior 350cc	I. Lougher	Yamaha	4	115.16
Fastest lap	I. Lougher	Yamaha		117.80
Lightweight 125cc	R. Dunlop	Honda	3	103.41
Fastest lap	R. Dunlop	Honda		104.09
Supersports 400cc	D. Leach	Yamaha	3	107.73
Fastest lap	D. Leach	Yamaha		109.39
Supersports 600cc	B. Reid	Yamaha	4	111.98
Fastest lap	D. Leach	Yamaha		114.21
Sidecar F2 'A'	D. Saville/N. Roche	Sabre	3	100.72
Fastest lap	D. Saville/N. Roche	Yamaha		100.97
Sidecar F2 'B'	D. Saville/N. Roche	Sabre	2	100.17
Fastest lap	D. Saville/N. Roche	Yamaha		100.55

1991

Class	Winner	Machine	Laps	Speed
Senior 750cc	S. Hislop	Honda	6	121.09
Fastest lap	S. Hislop	Honda		123.27
TT Formula 1	S. Hislop	Honda	6	121.00
Fastest lap	S. Hislop	Honda		123.4
Junior 350cc	R. Dunlop	Yamaha	4	114.89
Fastest lap	P. McCallen	Honda		116.75
Lightweight 125cc	R. Dunlop	Honda	4	103.68
Fastest lap	R. Dunlop	Honda		106.71
Supersports 400cc	D. Leach	Yamaha	4	105.49
Fastest lap	D. Leach	Yamaha		109.39
Supersports 600cc	S. Hislop	Honda	4	114.28
Fastest lap	S. Hislop	Honda		115.69
Sidecar F2 'A'	M. Boddice/D. Wells	Honda	3	99.26
Fastest lap	M. Boddice/D. Wells	Honda		99.85
Sidecar F2 'B'	M. Boddice/D. Wells	Honda	3	99.27
Fastest lap	M. Boddice/D. Wells	Honda		100.15

Class	Winner	Machine	Laps	Speed
Senior 750cc	S. Hislop	Norton	6	121.28
Fastest lap	C. Fogarty	Yamaha		123.61
TT Formula 1	P. McCallen	Honda	6	119.80
Fastest lap	S. Hislop	Norton		123.30
Junior 350cc	B. Reid	Yamaha	4	115.13
Fastest lap	S. Hislop	Yamaha		117.51
Lightweight 125cc	W. J. Dunlop	Honda	4	106.49
Fastest lap	W. J. Dunlop	Honda		108.69
Supersports 400cc	B. Reid	Yamaha	4	110.50
Fastest lap	B. Reid	Yamaha		112.27
Supersports 600cc	P. McCallen	Honda	4	115.04
Fastest lap	S. Hislop	Honda		117.01
Sidecar F2 'A'	G. Bell/K. Cornbill	Yamaha	3	101.50
Fastest lap	G. Bell/K. Cornbill	Yamaha		102.54
Sidecar F2 'B'	G. Bell/K. Cornbill	Yamaha	3	101.49
Fastest lap	G. Bell/K. Cornbill	Yamaha		101.66

1993

Class	Winner	Machine	Laps	Speed
Senior 750cc	P. McCallen	Honda	6	118.32
Fastest lap	P. McCallen	Honda		120.65
TT Formula 1	N. Jefferies	Honda	6	118.15
Fastest lap	M. Farmer	Ducati		120.58
Junior 350cc	B. Reid	Yamaha	4	115.14
Fastest lap	R. Dunlop	Yamaha		116.75
Lightweight 125cc	W. J. Dunlop	Honda	4	107.26
Fastest lap	W. J. Dunlop	Honda		108.55
Supersports 400cc	J. Moodie	Yamaha	4	111.43
Fastest lap	J. Moodie	Yamaha		112.40
Supersports 600cc	J. Moodie	Honda	4	115.06
Fastest lap	J. Moodie	Honda		116.77
Sidecar F2 'A'	D. Molyneux/K. Ellison	Yamaha	3	103.33
Fastest lap	D. Molyneux/K. Ellison	Yamaha		104.27
Sidecar F2 'B'	D. Molyneux/K. Ellison	Yamaha	3	103.16
Fastest lap	D. Molyneux/K. Ellison	Yamaha		103.29

1994

Class	Winner	Machine	Laps	Speed
Senior 750cc	S. Hislop	Honda	6	119.25
Fastest lap	S. Hislop	Honda		122.50
TT Formula 1	S. Hislop	Honda	6	119.54
Fastest lap	P. McCallen	Honda		122.08
Junior 350cc	W. J. Dunlop	Honda	4	114.67
Fastest lap	B. Reid	Yamaha		115.97
Lightweight 125cc	W. J. Dunlop	Honda	4	105.74
Fastest lap	W. J. Dunlop	Honda		107.40
Supersports 400cc	J. Moodie	Yamaha	4	108.20
Fastest lap	J. Moodie	Yamaha		110.77
Supersports 600cc	I. Duffus	Yamaha	4	115.30
Fastest lap	J. Moodie	Yamaha		116.71
Singles TT	J. Moodie	Yamaha	4	111.29
Fastest lap	J. Moodie	Yamaha		112.66
Sidecar F2 'A'	R. Fisher/M. Wynn	Yamaha	3	105.71
Fastest lap	R. Fisher/M. Wynn	Yamaha		106.49
Sidecar F2 'B'	R. Fisher/M. Wynn	Yamaha	3	103.39
Fastest lap	R. Fisher/M. Wynn	Yamaha		105.45

1995

Class	Winner	Machine	Laps	Speed
Senior 750cc	W. J. Dunlop	Honda	6	119.11
Fastest lap	S. Ward	Honda		121.73
TT Formula 1	P. McCallen	Honda	6	117.84
Fastest lap	P. McCallen	Honda		120.85
Junior 600cc	I. Duffus	Honda	4	116.58
Fastest lap	I. Duffus	Honda		117.87
Lightweight 250cc	W. J. Dunlop	Honda	4	115.68
Fastest lap	W. J. Dunlop	Honda		117.57
Lightweight 125cc	M. Baldwin	Honda	4	107.14
Fastest lap	M. Baldwin	Honda		109.01
Supersports 400cc	D. Leach	Yamaha	4	107.98
Fastest lap	D. Leach	Yamaha		109.13
Singles TT	R. Holden	Ducati	4	110.78
Fastest lap	R. Holden	Ducati		111.66
Sidecar F2 'A'	R. Fisher/B. Hutchinson	Yamaha	3	106.47
Fastest lap	R. Fisher/B. Hutchinson	Yamaha		107.16
Sidecar F2 'B'	R. Fisher/B. Hutchinson	Yamaha	3	107.58
Fastest lap	R. Fisher/B. Hutchinson	Yamaha		107.67

1996

Class	Winner	Machine	Laps	Speed
Senior 750cc	P. McCallen	Honda	6	119.76
Fastest lap	P. McCallen	Honda		122.14
TT Formula 1	P. McCallen	Honda	6	116.18
Fastest lap	P. McCallen	Honda		120.84
Junior 600cc	P. McCallen	Honda	3	117.65
Fastest lap	P. McCallen	Honda		118.94
Lightweight 250cc	W. J. Dunlop	Honda	4	115.31
Fastest lap	P. McCallen	Honda		116.94
Lightweight 125cc	W. J. Dunlop	Honda	2	106.33
Fastest lap	W. J. Dunlop	Honda		107.62
Supersports 400cc	N. Piercy	Yamaha	4	106.29
Fastest lap	N. Piercy	Yamaha		107.03
Production	P. McCallen	900 Honda	3	117.32
Fastest lap	P. McCallen	Honda		118.93
Singles TT	J. Moodie	Yamaha	2	108.19
Fastest lap	D. Morris	BMW		109.08
Sidecar F2 'A'	D. Molyneux/P. Hill	DMR	3	109.81
Fastest lap	D. Molyneux/P. Hill	DMR		110.63
Sidecar F2 'B'	D. Molyneux/P. Hill	DMR	3	110.28
Fastest lap	D. Molyneux/P. Hill	DMR		111.02

1997

Class	Winner	Machine	Laps	Speed
Senior 750cc	P. McCallen	Honda	6	119.55
Fastest lap	P. McCallen	Honda		122.22
TT Formula 1	P. McCallen	Honda	6	119.90
Fastest lap	P. McCallen	Honda		122.98
Junior 600cc	I. Simpson	Honda	4	118.41
Fastest lap	I. Simpson	Honda		119.86
Lightweight 250cc	W. J. Dunlop	Honda	4	115.59
Fastest lap	J. McGuinness	Aprilia		116.83
Lightweight 125cc	I. Lougher	Honda	4	107.89
Fastest lap	I. Lougher	Honda		109.25
Supersports 400cc	N. Piercy	Yamaha	4	105.70
Fastest lap	N. Piercy	Yamaha		107.39
Production	P. McCallen	900 Honda	2	117.12
Fastest lap	P. McCallen	Honda		117.53
Singles TT	D. Morris	BMW	4	110.46
Fastest lap	D. Morris	BMW		112.07
Sidecar F2 'A'	R. Hanks/P. Biggs	NRH Ireson	3	106.95
Fastest lap	R. Fisher/R. Long	Yamaha		109.23
Sidecar F2 'B'	R. Fisher/R. Long	Yamaha	3	109.89
Fastest lap	R. Fisher/R. Long	Yamaha		110.45

1998

Class	Winner	Machine	Laps	Speed
Senior 750cc	I. Simpson	Honda	6	119.79
Fastest lap	M. Rutter	Honda		123.04
TT Formula 1	I. Simpson	Honda	4	118.74
Fastest lap	I. Simpson	Honda		122.28
Junior 600cc	M. Rutter	Honda	3	114.37
Fastest lap	J. Moodie	Honda		118.49
Lightweight 250cc	W. J. Dunlop	Honda	2	96.61
Fastest lap	W. J. Dunlop	Honda		100.50
Lightweight 125cc	R. Dunlop	Honda	3	106.38
Fastest lap	I. Lougher	Honda		107.53
Supersports 400cc	P. Williams	Honda	2	89.71
Fastest lap	P. Williams	Yamaha		90.11
Production	J. Moodie	900 Honda	3	119.19
Fastest lap	J. Moodie	Honda		120.70
Singles TT	D. Morris	BMW	3	107.48
Fastest lap	D. Morris	BMW		109.68
Sidecar F2 'A'	Race cancelled			
Sidecar F2 'B'	D. Molyneux/D. Jewell	Honda	3	106.52
Fastest lap	D. Molyneux/D. Jewell	Honda		108.22

Class	Winner	Machine	Laps	Speed
Senior 750cc	D. Jefferies	Yamaha	6	121.27
Fastest lap	J. Moodie	Honda		124.45
TT Formula 1	D. Jefferies	Yamaha	4	121.35
Fastest lap	D. Jefferies	Yamaha		121.35
Junior 600cc	J. Moodie	Honda	4	118.11
Fastest lap	J. Moodie	Honda		118.11
Lightweight 250cc	J. McGuinness	Honda	2	116.79
Fastest lap	J. McGuinness	Honda		116.79
Lightweight 125cc	I. Lougher	Honda	4	107.43
Fastest lap	I. Lougher	Honda		107.43
Lightweight 400cc	P. Williams	Honda	4	109.01
Fastest lap	P. Williams	Honda		110.79
Production	D. Jefferies	1000 Yamaha	2	119.50
Fastest lap	D. Jefferies	Yamaha		119.50
Singles TT	D. Morris	BMW	4	110.56
Fastest lap	D. Morris	BMW		110.56
Sidecar F2 'A'	D. Molyneux/C Hallam	Honda	3	111.90
Fastest lap	D. Molyneux/C. Hallam	Honda		111.90
Sidecar F2 'B'	R. Fisher/R. Long	Honda	3	108.76
Fastest lap	R. Fisher/R. Long	Honda		108.76

THE 2000s: 2000–06

Course length: **37.73 miles**
Race distance: 6 laps; 226 miles
Lap record: 125.69mph (D. Jefferies, 2000) to 129.451mph
(J. McGuinness, 2006)
Main bikes: Honda, Suzuki, Yamaha
Top riders: David Jefferies, Bruce Anstey, Ian Lougher, Adrian Archibald,
John McGuinness, Dave Molyneux

The decade began with the emotional high of Joey's unforgettable final triple, but within weeks the great man was dead, killed racing in Estonia. This and other tragedies put a cloud over road racing, nowhere more so than in its Irish redoubt. All too briefly, David Jefferies's remarkable sequence of triple wins and lap records lit a fire under the races, but his tragic death in practice during 2003 left the TT reeling once more.

Jefferies's mantle was assumed by his close friend John McGuinness who, from 2004, dominated the premier classes just as the Yorkshireman had done, taking the lap record close to 130mph in 2006. As the races' centenary approached, a new breed of young tyro – men like Guy Martin, Ian Hutchinson, Martin Finnegan and Cameron Donald – began to emerge as the men most likely to take his place.

On the machine front, the review of 2004/5 saw the end of two-stroke engines as the event became entirely production-based, adopting the Superbike/Supersports/Superstock classes common elsewhere. In its tenth decade, the TT had come full circle. The races began as a test of basic street technology – such as it was 95 years before – and that is essentially what they have evolved to become today. The difference is that 2007 production technology is far from basic, and horsepower has soared from a handful to over 200. The TT is again the ultimate test of great road bikes.

2000

Class	Winner	Machine	Laps	Speed
Senior 1,000cc	D. Jefferies	Yamaha	6	121.95
Fastest lap	D. Jefferies	Yamaha		125.69
TT Formula 1	W. J. Dunlop	Honda	6	120.99
Fastest lap	D. Jefferies	Yamaha		123.18
Junior 600cc	D. Jefferies	Yamaha	4	119.33
Fastest lap	A. Archibald	Honda		121.15
Lightweight 250cc	W. J. Dunlop	Honda	3	116.01
Fastest lap	W. J. Dunlop	Honda		116.55
Lightweight 125cc	W. J. Dunlop	Honda	4	107.14
Fastest lap	W. J. Dunlop	Honda		108.56
Lightweight 400cc	B. Richmond	Honda	3	104.13
Fastest lap	D. Marsten-Mygdal	Honda		105.94
Production	D. Jefferies	1000 Yamaha	2	98.58
Fastest lap	D. Jefferies	Yamaha		99.34
Singles TT	J. McGuinness	AMDM Chrysalis	4	109.63
Fastest lap	J. McGuinness	AMDM Chrysalis		111.43
Sidecar F2 'A'	R. Fisher/R. Long	Honda	3	109.94
Fastest lap	R. Fisher/R. Long	Honda		109.94
Sidecar F2 'B'	R. Fisher/R. Long	Honda	3	108.02
Fastest lap	I. Bell/N. Carpenter	Yamaha		109.02

2001

No racing due to UK Foot and Mouth disease.

2002

Class	Winner	Machine	Laps	Speed
Senior 1,000cc	D. Jefferies	Suzuki	6	124.74
Fastest lap	D. Jefferies	Suzuki		127.29
TT Formula 1	D. Jefferies	Suzuki	6	123.38
Fastest lap	D. Jefferies	Suzuki		126.68
Junior 600cc	J. Moodie	Yamaha	4	119.92
Fastest lap	J. Moodie	Yamaha		120.63
Lightweight 250cc	B. Anstey	Yamaha	4	115.32
Fastest lap	B. Anstey	Yamaha		118.03
Lightweight 125cc	I. Lougher	Honda	4	108.65
Fastest lap	I. Lougher	Honda		110.21
Lightweight 400cc	R. Quayle	Honda	4	109.27
Fastest lap	R. Quayle	Honda		110.57
Production 1000cc	D. Jefferies	1000 Suzuki	3	122.64
Fastest lap	D. Jefferies	1000 Suzuki		124.31
Production 600cc	I. Lougher	600 Suzuki	3	118.85
Fastest lap	I. Lougher	600 Suzuki		120.25
Sidecar F2 'A'	R. Fisher/R. Long	Yamaha	3	110.55
Fastest lap	R. Fisher/R. Long	Yamaha		109.94
Sidecar F2 'B'	R. Fisher/R. Long	Yamaha	3	110.75
Fastest lap	R. Fisher/R. Long	Yamaha		111.58

2003

Class	Winner	Machine	Laps	Speed
Senior 1,000cc	A. Archibald	Suzuki	4	124.53
Fastest lap	A. Archibald	Suzuki		126.82
TT Formula 1	A. Archibald	Suzuki	6	123.18
Fastest lap	A. Archibald	Suzuki		125.43
Junior 600cc	B. Anstey	Triumph	4	120.36
Fastest lap	R. Farquhar	Kawasaki		122.30
Lightweight 125cc	C. Palmer	Honda	4	108.65
Fastest lap	C. Palmer	Honda		110.41
Lightweight 400cc	J. McGuinness	Honda	4	109.52
Fastest lap	J. McGuinness	Honda		111.36
Production 1000cc	S. Harris	1000 Suzuki	3	123.55
Fastest lap	S. Harris	1000 Suzuki		123.55
Production 600cc	S. Harris	600 Suzuki	2	119.75
Fastest lap	S. Harris	600 Suzuki		119.75
Sidecar F2 'A'	I. Bell/N. Carpenter	DMR Yamaha	3	110.16
Fastest lap	I. Bell/N. Carpenter	DMR Yamaha		110.81
Sidecar F2 'B'	D. Molyneux/C. Hallam	DMR Honda	3	105.42
Fastest lap	D. Molyneux/C. Hallam	DMR Honda		108.99

Class	Winner	Machine	Laps	Speed
Senior	A. Archibald	Suzuki	4	123.81
Fastest lap	J. McGuinness	Yamaha		127.19
TT Formula 1	J. McGuinness	Yamaha	4	125.38
Fastest lap	J. McGuinness	Yamaha		127.68
Junior 600cc	J. McGuinness	Yamaha	4	120.57
Fastest lap	J. McGuinness	Yamaha		122.87
Lightweight 125cc	C. Palmer	Honda	4	108.93
Fastest lap	C. Palmer	Honda		110.52
Lightweight 400cc	J. McGuinness	Honda	4	110.28
Fastest lap	J. McGuinness	Honda		112.04
Production 1000cc	B. Anstey	Suzuki	3	123.72
Fastest lap	B. Anstey	Suzuki		125.10
Production 600cc	R. Farquhar	Kawasaki	3	117.54
Fastest lap	R. Farquhar	Kawasaki		118.94
Sidecar 'A'	D. Molyneux/D. Sayle	DMR Honda	3	111.33
Fastest lap	D. Molyneux/D. Sayle	DMR Honda		112.61
Sidecar 'B'	D. Molyneux/D. Sayle	DMR Honda	3	111.20
Fastest lap	D. Molyneux/D. Sayle	DMR Honda		113.17

2005

Class	Winner	Machine	Laps	Speed
Senior	J. McGuinness	Yamaha	6	124.324
Fastest lap	J. McGuinness	Yamaha		127.326
Superbike	J. McGuinness	Yamaha	6	124.124
Fastest lap	J. McGuinness	Yamaha		126.879
Supersport Junior 'A'	I. Lougher	Honda	4	120.928
Fastest lap	R. Farquhar	Kawasaki		122.639
Supersport Junior 'B'	R. Farquhar	Kawasaki	4	120.697
Fastest lap	J. Griffiths	Kawasaki		122.540
Superstock	B. Anstey	Suzuki	3	124.242
Fastest lap	A. Archibald	Suzuki		126.641
Sidecar 'A'	N. Crowe/D. Hope	DMR Honda	3	109.85
Fastest lap	D. Molyneux/D. Sayle	DMR Honda		111.99
Sidecar 'B'	D. Molyneux/D. Sayle	DMR Honda	3	114.901
Fastest lap	D. Molyneux/D. Sayle	DMR Honda		116.044

2006

Class	Winner	Machine	Laps	Speed
Senior	J. McGuinness	Honda	6	126.178
Fastest lap	J. McGuinness	Honda		129.451
Superbike	J. McGuinness	Honda	6	124.764
Fastest lap	J. McGuinness	Honda		127.933
Supersport Junior	J. McGuinness	Honda	6	122.264
Fastest lap	J. McGuinness	Honda		123.975
Superstock	B. Anstey	Suzuki	4	124.147
Fastest lap	B. Anstey	Suzuki		126.204
Sidecar 'A'	N. Crowe/D. Hope	DMR Honda	3	112.342
Fastest lap	N. Crowe/D. Hope	DMR Honda		113.571
Sidecar 'B'	N. Crowe/D. Hope	DMR Honda	3	111.467
Fastest lap	N. Crowe/D. Hope	DMR Honda		112.315

Isle of Man race winners

Total 26

Joey Dunlop   4 Senior, 3 Junior, 1 Classic, 7 TT F1, 1 Junior Classic, 5 Ultra-Lightweight, 5 Lightweight

Total 14

Mike Hailwood   7 Senior, 2 Junior, 1 125cc, 1 TT F1, 3 Lightweight

Total 11

Steve Hislop   4 Senior, 3 TT F1, 1 Production, 2 Supersport 600, TT F2

Phillip McCallen   4 TT F1, 1 Supersport 600, 3 Senior, 1 Junior, 2 Production

John McGuinness   2 Senior, 2 Superbike, 1 TTF1, 2 Junior, 1 Lightweight, 1 Singles, 2 Lightweight 400

Dave Molyneux   11 sidecar F2

Total 10

Giacomo Agostini   5 Senior, 5 Junior

Rob Fisher   10 sidecar

Stanley Woods   4 Senior, 5 Junior, 1 Lightweight

Total 9

Mick Boddice   9 Sidecar

David Jefferies   1 Junior, 2 TT F1, 2 Senior, 3 Production

Dave Saville   9 Sidecar

Siegfried Schauzu   9 Sidecar

Charlie Williams   1 Junior, 5 Lightweight, 1 TT F2, 2 Production

Total 8

Jim Moodie   1 Supersport 600, 2 Supersport 400, 2 Singles, 1 Production, 2 Junior

Chas Mortimer   1 Junior, 2 Lightweight, 2 125cc, 1 Formula
                   750, 2 Production
Phil Read   1 Senior, 1 Junior, 2 Lightweight, 3 125cc,
                   1 TTF1
Tony Rutter   4 Junior, 4 TTF2

Total 7
Mick Grant   2 Senior, 2 Classic, 1 TT F1, 2 Production
Ian Lougher   3 Ultra-Lightweight, 1 Lightweight, 1
                   Production 750, 1 Production 600, 1 Junior

Total 6
Geoff Duke   3 Senior, 2 Junior, 1 Clubman
Jimmy Guthrie   2 Senior, 3 Junior, 1 Lightweight
Jim Redman   3 Junior, 3 Lightweight
John Surtees   4 Senior, 2 Junior

Total 5
Bruce Anstey   1 Junior 250, 1 Junior 600, 1 Production
                   1000, 2 Superstock
Alec Bennett   3 Senior, 2 Junior
Robert Dunlop   4 Ultra-Lightweight, 1 Junior.
Brian Reid   1 TT F2, 1 Supersport 600, 2 Junior,
                   1 Supersport 400
Carlo Ubbiali   1 Lightweight, 4 125cc.

Total 4
Klaus Enders   4 sidecar
Freddie Frith   1 Senior, 3 Junior
Wal Handley   1 Senior, 1 Junior, 1 Lightweight,
                   1 Ultra-Lightweight
Trevor Ireson   4 Sidecar
Dave Leach   2 Production, 2 Supersport 400
Ray Pickrell   1 Formula 750, 3 Production

Tarquinio Provini	2 Lightweight, 2 125cc
Barry Smith	1 50cc, 3 TT F2
Bill Smith	1 TTF3, 3 Production
Rolf Steinhausen	4 Sidecar
Jock Taylor	4 Sidecar
John Williams	2 Classic, 2 Production

Total 3

Ray Amm	2 Senior, 1 Junior
Adrian Archibald	1 F1, 2 Senior
Graeme Crosby	1 Senior, 1 Classic, 1 TT F1
Nick Crowe	3 Sidecar
Harold Daniell	3 Senior
Max Deubel	3 Sidecar
Carl Fogarty	1 Production, 1 Senior, 1 TT F1
Alex George	1 Classic, 1 TT F1, 1 Production
Tom Herron	2 Senior, 1 Lightweight
Alan Jackson	3 TT F2
Tony Jefferies	1 Junior, 1 Formula 750, 1 Production
Geoff Johnson	3 Production
Phil Mellor	1 Junior, 2 Production
Rob McElnea	1 Senior, 2 Classic
Bob McIntyre	1 Senior, 1 Junior, 1 Formula 500
David Morris	3 Singles
Walter Schneider	3 Sidecar
Ian Simpson	2 Junior, 1 TT F1
Luigi Taveri	2 125cc, 1 50cc
Barry Woodland	3 Production

Total 2

Fergus Anderson	2 Lightweight
Hugh Anderson	1 125cc, 1 50cc
Manliff Barrington	2 Lightweight
Artie Bell	1 Senior, 1 Junior

Geoff Bell	2 Sidecar
Lowry Burton	2 Sidecar
Kel Carruthers	2 Lightweight
Bernard Codd	2 Clubman's
Charlie Collier	2 Short Course
Steve Cull	1 Lightweight, 1 Historic
Howard Davies	2 Senior
Freddie Dixon	1 Junior, 1 Sidecar
Charles Dodson	2 Senior
Iain Duffus	1 Supersport 600, 1 Junior
Ryan Farquhar	1 Junior, 1 Production 600
Marc Flynn	2 Production 750
Bob Foster	1 Lightweight, 1 Junior
Dick Greasley	2 Sidecar
Shaun Harris	1 Production 1000, 1 Production 600
John Hartle	1 Junior, 1 Production
Fritz Hillebrand	2 Sidecar
Mac Hobson	2 Sidecar
Gary Hocking	1 Senior, 1 Lightweight
Tim Hunt	1 Senior, 1 Junior
Bill Ivy	1 Lightweight, 1 125cc
Alistair King	1 Clubman's, 1 Formula 350
Con Law	2 Lightweight
Eddie Laycock	1 Junior, 1 Supersport 400
Bill Lomas	1 Junior, 1 Lightweight
Graeme McGregor	1 Lightweight, 1 TT F2
Brian Morrison	1 TT F2, 1 Production
Trevor Nation	2 Production
Gary Padgett	1 TT F3, 1 Production
Chris Palmer	2 125cc
Nigel Piercy	2 Supersports 400
Jock Porter	1 Lightweight, 1 Ultra-Lightweight
Cecil Sandford	1 Lightweight, 1 125cc
Tom Sheard	1 Senior, 1 Junior

Eddie Twemlow	2 Lightweight
Malcolm Uphill	2 Production
Eric Williams	2 Junior
Paul Williams	2 Lightweight 400

Total 1

Steve Abbott	1 Sidecar
Dario Ambrosini	1 Lightweight
F. A. Applebee	1 Senior
Ivor Arber	1 Clubman's
Reg Armstrong	1 Senior
Georg Auerbacher	1 Sidecar
Mark Baldwin	1 125cc
Harry Bashall	1 Junior
Ian Bell	1 Sidecar
Dieter Braun	1 125cc
Eric Briggs	1 Clubman's
Norman Brown	1 Senior
Ralph Bryans	1 50cc
Jimmy Buchan	1 Clubman's
Trevor Burgess	1 Production
Roger Burnett	1 Senior
Florian Camathias	1 Sidecar
Maurice Cann	1 Lightweight
Phil Carpenter	1 Senior
Phil Carter	1 Clubman's
Harold Clark	1 Clubman's
Rod Coleman	1 Junior
Harry Collier	1 Short Course
Syd Crabtree	1 Lightweight
Dave Croxford	1 Production
J. D. Daniels	1 Clubman's
Leo Davenport	1 Lightweight
Geoff Davison	1 Lightweight

Tommy de la Hay	1	Senior
Ernst Degner	1	50cc
Steve Dey	1	Production 750
Eddie Dow	1	Clubman's
Percy Evans	1	Junior
Helmut Fath	1	Sidecar
Jack Findlay	1	Senior
Frank Fletcher	1	Clubman's
Rem Fowler	1	Short Course
Syd Gleave	1	Lightweight
Oliver Godfrey	1	Senior
Les Graham	1	125cc
Stuart Graham	1	50cc
Werner Haas	1	Lightweight
Roy Hanks	1	sidecar
Dave Hallam	1	Sidecar
Michael Hamblin	1	Sidecar
Bryan Hargreaves	1	Clubman's
Ron Haslam	1	TT F1
R. J. Hazlehurst	1	Clubman's
Freddie Hicks	1	Junior
Bill Hodgkins	1	Sidecar
Robert Holden	1	Singles
Rupert Hollaus	1	125cc
Colin Hopper	1	Sidecar
Clive Horton	1	125cc
Eric Housley	1	Clubman's
Dennis Ireland	1	Classic
Mitsuo Itoh	1	50cc
Brian Jackson	1	Clubman's
Nick Jefferies	1	TT F1
Paddy Johnston	1	Lightweight
Ken Kavanagh	1	Junior
Bob Keeler	1	Clubman's

Neil Kelly	1 Production
John Kidson	1 TT F3
Ewald Kluge	1 Lightweight
Ray Knight	1 Production
Doug Lashmar	1 Clubman's
M. V. Lockwood	1 Clubman's
Frank Longman	1 Lightweight
H. Luthringshauser	1 Sidecar
C. McCandless	1 125cc
Bill McVeigh	1 Clubman's
Jack Marshall	1 Short Course
Keith Martin	1 Production
Hugh Mason	1 Junior
Georg Meier	1 Senior
Ted Mellors	1 Lightweight
Derek Minter	1 Lightweight
George O'Dell	1 Sidecar
Eric Oliver	1 Sidecar
Mat Oxley	1 Production
Gary Padgett	1 Production
Peter Palmer	1 Clubman's
Len Parker	1 Sidecar
Denis Parkinson	1 Clubman's
Bill Penny	1 Production
A. Phillips	1 Clubman's
Derek Powell	1 Clubman's
Cliff Pritchard	1 Sidecar
Cyril Pullen	1 Senior
Brian Purslow	1 Clubman's
Richard Quayle	1 Lightweight 400
Johnny Rea	1 Junior
Harry Reed	1 Short Course
Brett Richmond	1 Lightweight 400
Tommy Robb	1 125cc

Tony Rogers	1	Production
Nigel Rollason	1	Sidecar
Dave Roper	1	Historic
Michael Rutter	1	Junior
Fritz Scheidegger	1	Sidecar
Martin Sharpe	1	Production
Dave Simmonds	1	125cc
Bill Simpson	1	Production
Jimmy Simpson	1	Lightweight
Cyril Taft	1	Clubman's
Omobono Tenni	1	Lightweight
Steve Tonkin	1	Lightweight
Kenneth Twemlow	1	Junior
H. G. Tyrell Smith	1	Junior
George Tucker	1	Sidecar
Chris Vincent	1	Sidecar
Terry Vinicombe	1	Sidecar
Graham Walker	1	Lightweight
Frank Whiteway	1	Production
Cyril Williams	1	Junior
Peter Williams	1	Formula 750
Tim Wood	1	Senior
Tommy Wood	1	Lightweight
Stan Woods	1	Production

Isle of Man TT lap and race records (to 2006)

	Record holder	Machine	Year	hr min sec	mph
Senior					
Lap	John McGuinness	1000 Honda	2006	17.29.6	129.451
Race	John McGuinness	1000 Honda	2006	1.47.38.84	126.178
Superbike					
Lap	John McGuinness	1000 Honda	2006	17.41.71	127.933
Race	John McGuinness	1000 Honda	2006	1.48.52.06	124.764
Supersport Junior					
Lap	John McGuinness	600 Honda	2006	18.15.61	123.975
Race	John McGuinness	600 Honda	2006	1.14.03.73	122.264
Superstock					
Lap	Adrian Archibald	1000 Suzuki	2005	17.52.54	126.641
Race	Bruce Anstey	1000 Suzuki	2005	54.39.74	124.242
Sidecar Formula Two					
Lap	Dave Molyneux/ Dan Sayle	DMR Honda	2005	19.30.49	116.044
Race	Dave Molyneux/ Dan Sayle	DMR Honda	2005	59.06.39	114.901

Obsolete classes

Formula One

Lap	John McGuinness	1000 Yamaha R1	2004	17.43.8	127.68
Race	John McGuinness	1000 Yamaha R1	2004	1.12.13.2	125.38

TT Formula Two

Lap	Eddie Laycock	350 Yamaha	1987	19.57.6	112.36
Race	Steve Hislop	350 Yamaha	1987	2.03.01.4	110.40

Lightweight 250

Lap	John McGuinness	250 Honda	1999	19.08.2	118.29
Race	John McGuinness	250 Honda	1999	1.17.31.7	116.79

Lightweight 400

Lap	Jim Moodie	400 Yamaha	1993	20.08.4	112.40
Race	Jim Moodie	400 Yamaha	1993	1.21.15.4	111.43

Ultra Lightweight 125cc

Lap	Chris Palmer	125 Honda	2004	20.28.9	110.52
Race	Chris Palmer	125 Honda	2004	1.23.07.6	108.93

Production 1000

Lap	Bruce Anstey	1000 Suzuki	2004	18.05.7	125.10
Race	Bruce Anstey	1000 Suzuki	2004	54.53.5	123.72

Production 750

Lap	Ronnie Smith	750 Suzuki	2002	19.02.1	118.93
Race	Ronnie Smith	750 Suzuki	2002	58.00.0	117.09

Production 600

Lap	Ian Lougher	600 Suzuki	2002	18.49.5	120.25
Race	Shaun Harris	600 Suzuki	2003	37.49.79	119.75*

*Shortened race. Best for 3 lap race, Lougher, Suzuki, 2002: 57.08.4, 118.85

Junior 350cc

Lap	Dave Leach	350 Yamaha	1986	20.12.2	112.05
Race	Dave Leach	350 Yamaha	1986	2.02.46.2	110.63

Singles TT

Lap	Jim Moodie	660 Yamaha	1994	20.05.6	112.66
Race	Jim Moodie	660 Yamaha	1994	1.21.21.6	111.29

Sidecar 1,000cc

Lap	Mick Boddice	700 Yamaha	1989	20.54.0	108.31
Race	Mick Boddice	700 Yamaha	1989	1.03.22.0	107.17

Mountain Course fastest laps*

50mph	1911	Frank Philipp, Scott, 50.11mph
55mph	1920	George Dance, Sunbeam, 55.62mph
60mph	1924	Jimmy Simpson, AJS, 64.65mph
65mph	1925	Jimmy Simpson, AJS, 68.97mph
70mph	1926	Jimmy Simpson, AJS, 70.43mph
75mph	1930	Wal Handley, Rudge, 76.28mph
80mph	1931	Jimmy Simpson, Norton, 80.82mph
85mph	1935	Stanley Woods, Moto Guzzi, 86.53mph
90mph	1937	Freddie Frith, Norton, 90.27mph
95mph	1951	Geoff Duke, Norton, 95.22mph
100mph	1957	Bob McIntyre, Gilera, 101.12mph
105mph	1962	Gary Hocking, MV, 105.75mph
110mph	1976	John Williams, Suzuki, 110.21mph
		(112.27 later same week in Senior)
115mph	1980	Joey Dunlop, Yamaha, 115.22mph
120mph	1989	Steve Hislop, Honda, 121.34mph
125mph	2000	David Jefferies, Yamaha, 125.69mph

*5mph increments

Wins by marque*

Honda	130	Matchless	4	Armstrong CCM	1
Yamaha	130	Sabre	4	(Barton) Phoenix	1
Norton	43	Sunbeam	4	Bultaco	1
Suzuki	40	Vincent	4	Derbi	1
MV Agusta	34	Benelli	3	Derbyshire	1
BMW	30	EMC	3	DKW	1
Triumph	15	Gilera	3	DOT	1
BSA	13	Mondial	3	Humber	1
Moto Guzzi	11	Rex-Acme	3	Indian	1
Velocette	11	Cotton	2	Levis	1
AJS	8	HRD	2	NUT	1
Ducati	8	Konig	2	OK-Supreme	1
Excelsior	5	New Gerrard	2	Ossa	1
Kawasaki	5	NSU	2	Spondon (Yamaha)	1
(New) Imperial	5	Scott	2	Waddon	1
Rudge	5	Aermacchi	1	Yamsel	1
Douglas	4	Armstrong	1		

*Excludes pre-TT Classic races

Note: unfortunately there is no consistent convention for determining wins by marque when considering hybrid machines. On the whole the make of engine has generally been considered to be the deciding factor, but then three of Matchless' wins were JAP-powered and Norton's first win came courtesy of a Peugeot twin. The table above, in common with every other the author has encountered, takes no account of this. Both JAP and Blackburne also powered other victorious TT machines, yet are absent from most listings of TT winners. Equally, a different convention might add both Spondon and Yamsel's wins to Yamaha's tally, giving them 132 wins overall.

INDEX